A PRACTICAL GUIDE TO PHOTO

Basic Techniques for Beginners and

Contents

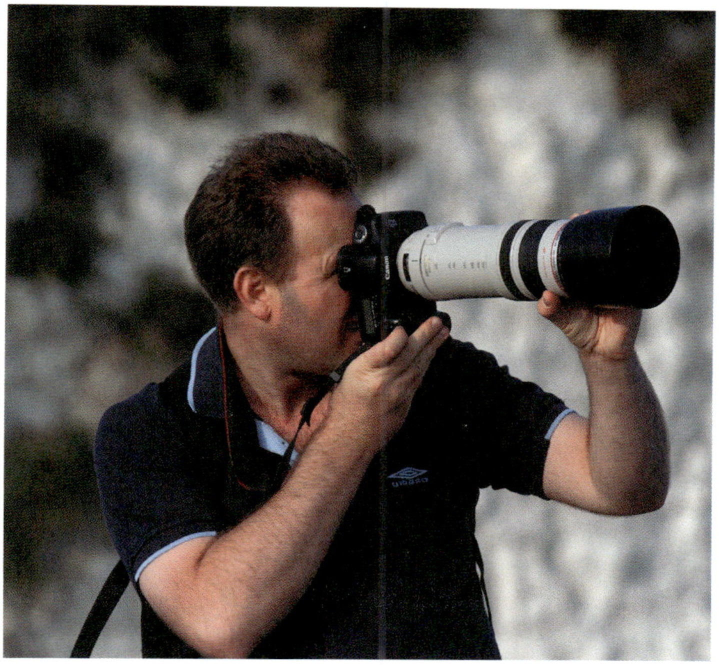

First published in 2016 as an ebook.
Print edition published in 2018

www.ianmiddleton.co.uk

All photos by Ian Middleton, unless otherwise indicated.
Photos of me taken by Ray Gilbert.

www.ianmiddletonphotography.com

Illustrations by
Rebecca Svetina
David Selwood

Published by Schmetterling Productions
ISBN 10: 0-9540779-7-0
ISBN 13: 978-0-9540779-7-6
Email: sales@schmetterlingproductions.co.uk
Website: www.schmetterlingproductions.co.uk

Foreword:

In the chill of the night, way back in the 80s, I was standing in the square outside my house with my brother's tripod and SLR, and a hastily scribbled set of times, shutter speeds and apertures taken down from the Sky at Night television program the evening before. Patrick Moore had been interviewing a photographer who gave out these settings for budding photographers to capture the lunar eclipse, so in a fit of spontaneity I had grabbed my brother's camera and tripod and decided to have a go. The lunar eclipse was just beginning. I had already loaded my roll of 36-film and as the first shadow was cast across the moon, I began shooting. This was my first attempt at doing some serious photography. Until this point I had always taken snapshots using a trusty old compact.

As the dawn light crept in I got closer to the end of my film. Or so I thought! Once the indicator reached 36, I was surprised to find the camera wind on to one more exposure after another until pleasure at the thought of getting a few extra pictures turned to suspicion as the reel never seemed to end. Eventually I had to pack up and head, bleary-eyed through lack of sleep, to work.

After work that day I took the film along to the photography shop and told the guy what had happened. He put the film inside a sealed box and looked through a camera. All exposures were blank. It seemed that I had neglected to load the film properly. So my sleepless night was in vain!

After that instance I decided that I wasn't cut out for photography and a decade passed before I picked up another SLR. What inspired me to take photography seriously again was a four-month journey around Mexico in 1997. This voyage of discovery filled my eyes with enchanting scenes and for the first time I began to see the beauty of nature and the world into which I was born. Upon my return I couldn't help feeling that my little compact camera hadn't truly captured that magic, so I decided to invest in my first SLR and have another go.

Somewhat fortuitously, someone had left an old book on photography for beginners on the canteen table where I was working at the time. I spent the next few weeks with my head buried inside this book and it was here that I learned all about the basic principles of photography; including how to load film correctly. I found this essential to understanding how the camera works. It's these basic principles that have been the foundation for my work and have helped me to develop my skills and work over the years.

I certainly had lots of practice loading film as I went through reels and reels learning and practicing my craft. This time I didn't let my mistakes faze me and instead learned from them. I transferred to digital in 2005, which certainly lowers the cost of making mistakes and allows you the flexibility to experiment and learn.

Today, with high tech digital cameras, most people may feel more comfortable switching to auto and mistakenly believing that the camera can do it all for them. Well, that's true if all you want is a basic good shot. The camera cannot read your mind. All it can do is read a scene and give you an average shot based on what it captures. So in order to take control and get the shots that you want, you have to go beyond the auto settings. Also, although technology has moved on, the basic principles of photography are still the same and apply to all types of camera. Compacts and smartphone cameras all use the same principles, and many of these allow some control over the settings. So you might be surprised what you can do with a little more understanding. Alternatively, with a little extra knowledge you will know what your camera can and can't do.

In this book, I have put together a lot of this information so that you can learn first-hand the essential knowledge that you will need as a photographer. I have tried to put make it as simple, and practical as possible. I hope that you find it as useful as I did while learning it.

Part 1
Introduction to Light & Direction of Light

Photography

From the Greek word which literally means:
"Drawing with light"

Light travels in straight lines and without it we cannot see.

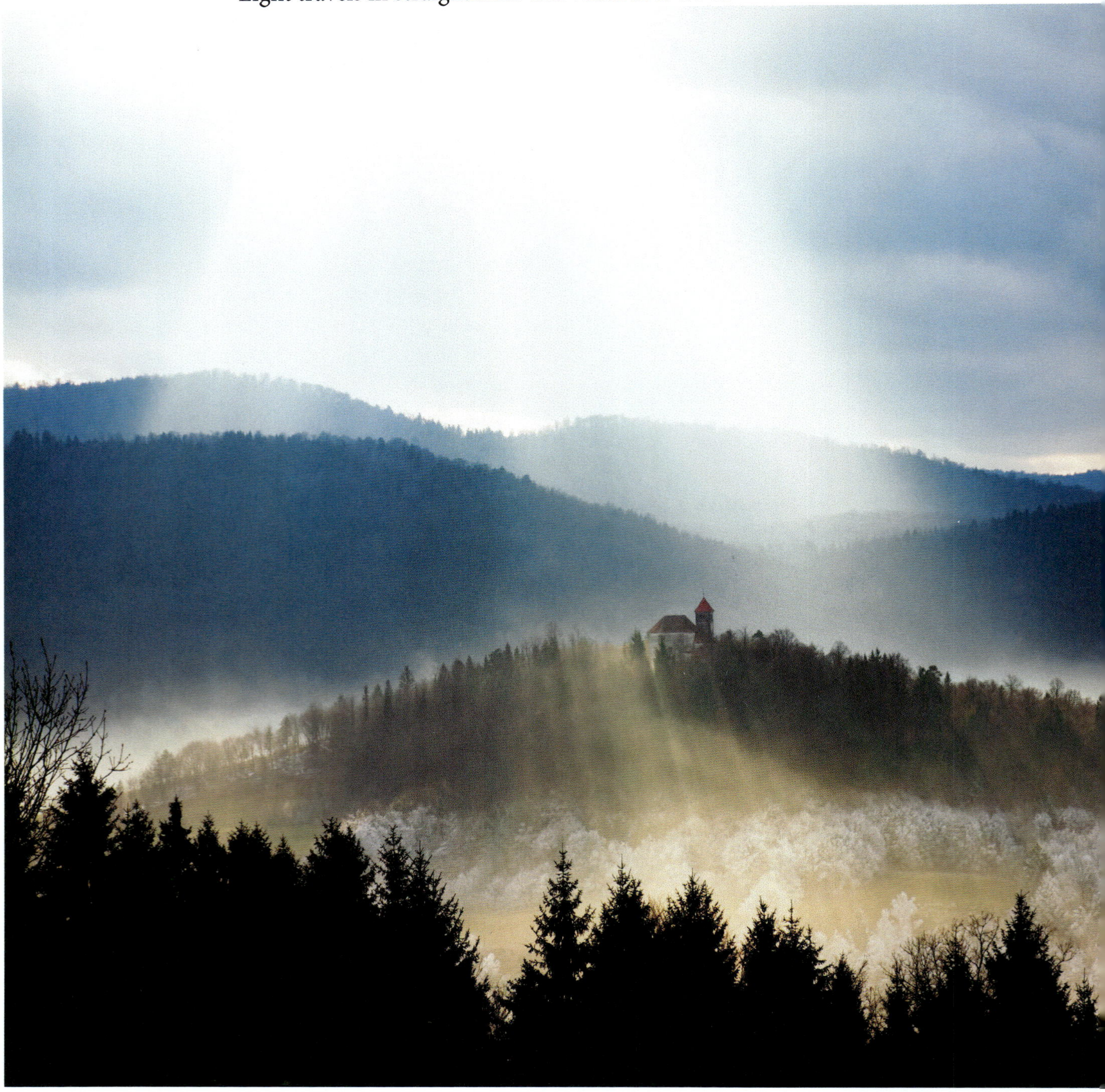

Most objects do not give off their own light, so what we see is the light that is reflected off the subject into our eyes, and this in turn determines how the object or scene appears to us.

When light is low we don't see things so clearly. When there is zero light we see absolutely nothing, even if objects are right there in front of our eyes. So, in the same way that our eyes need light to see, the camera needs light to capture a picture.

Light is everything when it comes to photography, and it not only determines what we see, but also how we see it. All of us are aware that the world around us appears differently depending on the day, the weather, and time of day or year.

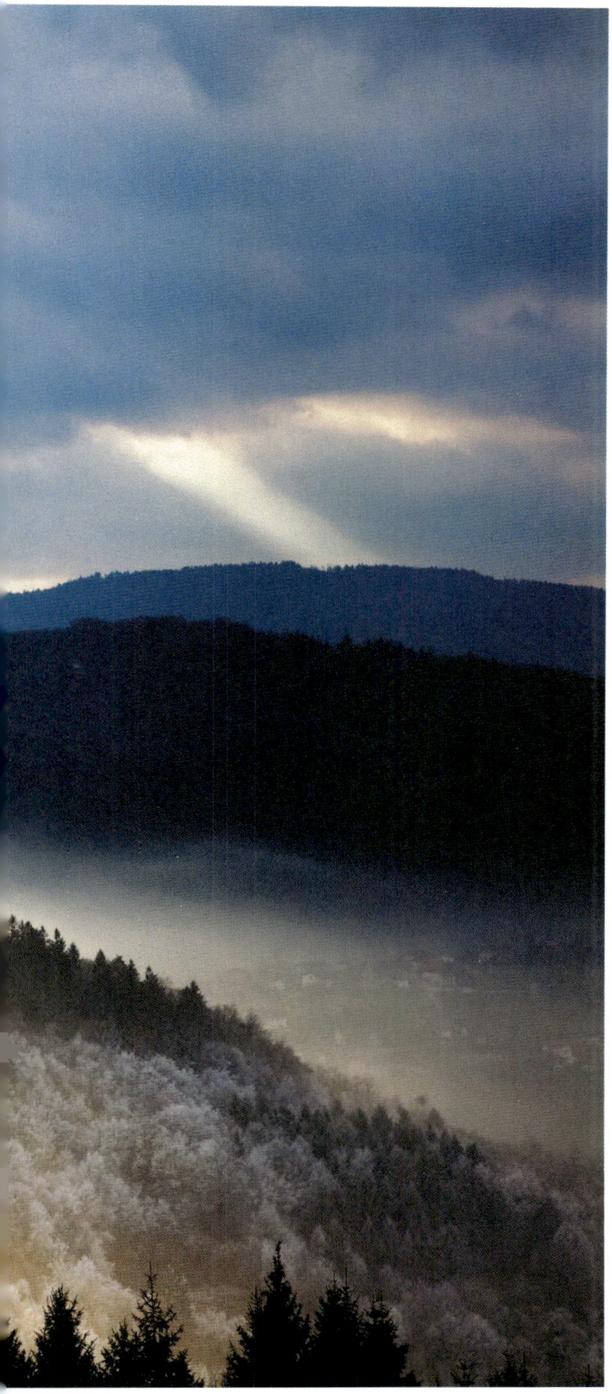

Whatever camera you use, whether a high end DSLR or a cheap compact, you can dramatically improve your photos by simply understanding how to work the light.

So, just as the light determines how we see things, it also dictates, to some degree, how our photo will look. Therefore, not only do we have to consider how much light is available, but also:

- The quality of the light
- The colour of the light
- The direction of the light
- The source of the light
- How the light is falling upon our subject and what effect it has

Light can come from a variety of sources:

- Natural light from the sun (best)
- Artificial light (bulbs etc.)
- Camera flash
- Candles

There are various types of light

1. Direct light (hard light from a small source) (sun, flash, street lights, candles) This produces high contrast images with lots of shadows and definition, along with bright, vivid colours
2. Diffused light (soft light from a large source) (cloudy day, big windows, large studio softboxes) This gives soft, low contrast images with little or no shadow, along with softer more subtle colours
3. Indirect light (Reflected light) (water, bounced flash, large surfaces). Softens and diffuses light. Can also help to fill in unwanted shadows.

Search for the light

It's all about the light and not about photoshop... While many believe that photoshop is some kind of magic tool for photographers, it isn't. The light is our magic tool. It determines from the very start how our image will look. You could never turn the image on the left into the image on the right using software and make it look natural.

On the left image cloud has thrown the tree and foreground into shade, so both are devoid of colour and texture. However, light is still falling on the mountains and the two people in the lower right corner. The patch of white brightly lit cloud behind has also helped make the people stand out.

On the right photo, the cloud cleared and sunlight fell on the foreground and tree, bringing out the colour and texture of the tree.

The different type of light here has created two entirely different scenes. On the next pages we will see just how the different types of light affect our scene.

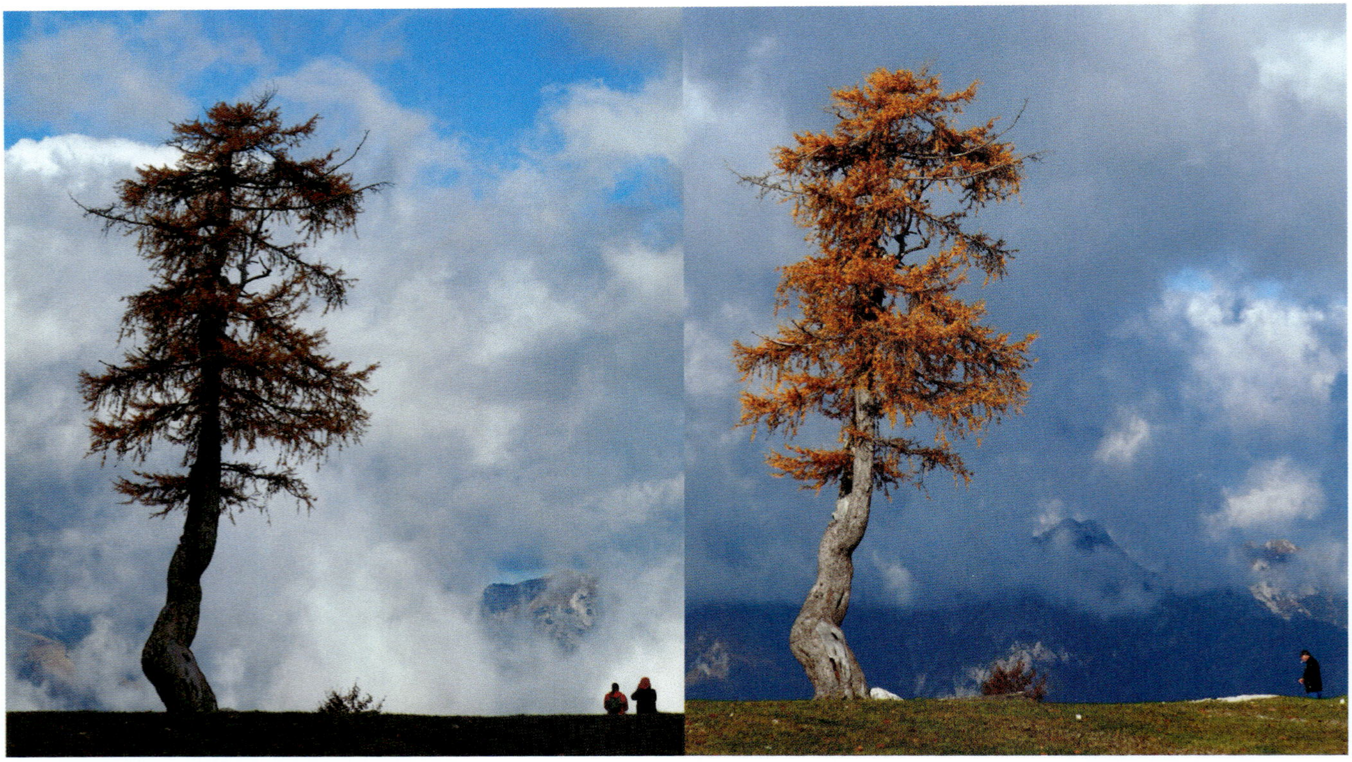

Direct light effects

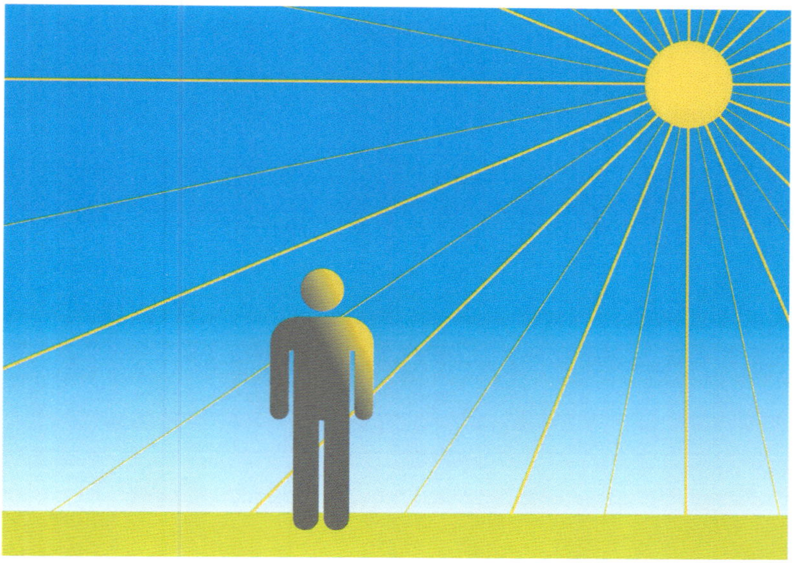

Direct light comes from one direction and therefore produces bright and dark sides to the subject it illuminates. The result, as you can see by the illustration to the right, is a high contrast scene with hard light, hard shadows and hard edges with lots of definition.

The picture of the snowboarder was taken on a bright, clear sunny day, so here direct light from the sun was illuminating the subject. Notice how bright the colours are, and how much detail, definition and sharpness there is on the subject. As the subject was in the air with nothing but the sky behind, then shadows were avoided. This was also taken in winter, when the air was clear and free of moisture. So take note of light quality. It's not enough that it's sunny. While the sun may be out, there could still be a lot of haze and moisture in the air, which affects the clarity of a scene. This is especially true in the summer months when it's hot. Time of year and the time of day are also important. When the sun is higher in the sky, around midday or during the summer months, then the light is harsh and hazy. As this was taken on a mountaintop ski resort in winter, the air was crystal clear which has also resulted in a crystal clear image. During winter the sun is lower in the sky so the light is less harsh. And finally, snow is reflective, so the underside of the boarder and snowboard is also lit. So not only does this image have direct light, but also reflected light.

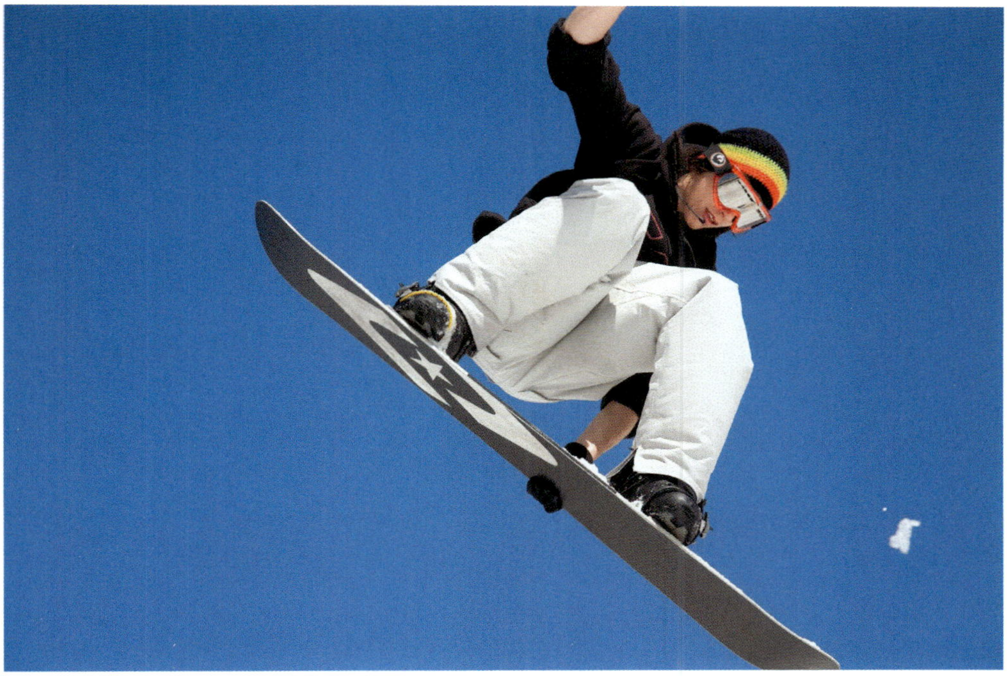

Unwanted shadow

When photographing in direct light, shadows can be a major problem. So you must look carefully when photographing under these conditions.

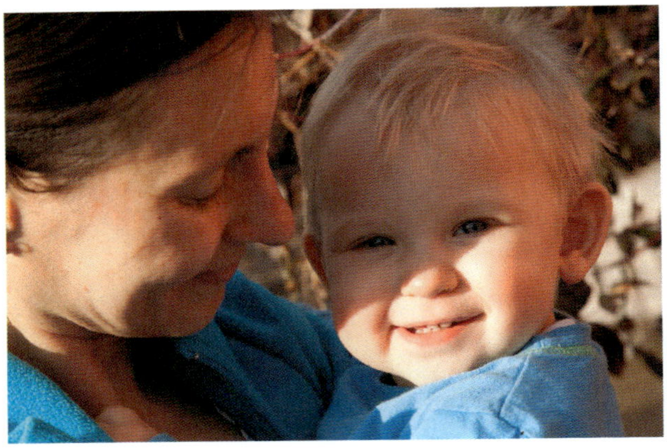

As you can see on the photo above the woman has cast a shadow over the child. You can also use a fill in flash to help reduce these shadows, but the best way is to avoid it completely.

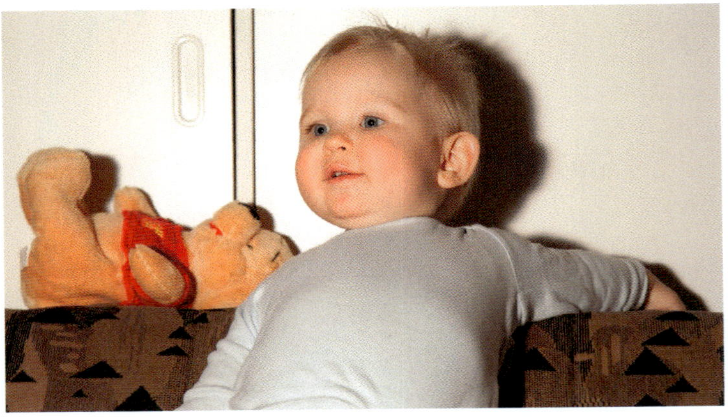

On this photo you can see that the off camera flash has also cast a shadow behind the child and the Winnie the Pooh bear. The shadow has also been enhanced by the bright white background. So take care when using flash. Try to position your subject away from walls or other background surfaces.

Wanted shadow

Not all shadows are unwanted. When used correctly they can enhance, give shape, texture, depth and contrast to an image. A classic example of this is the moon. Study the following two photos:

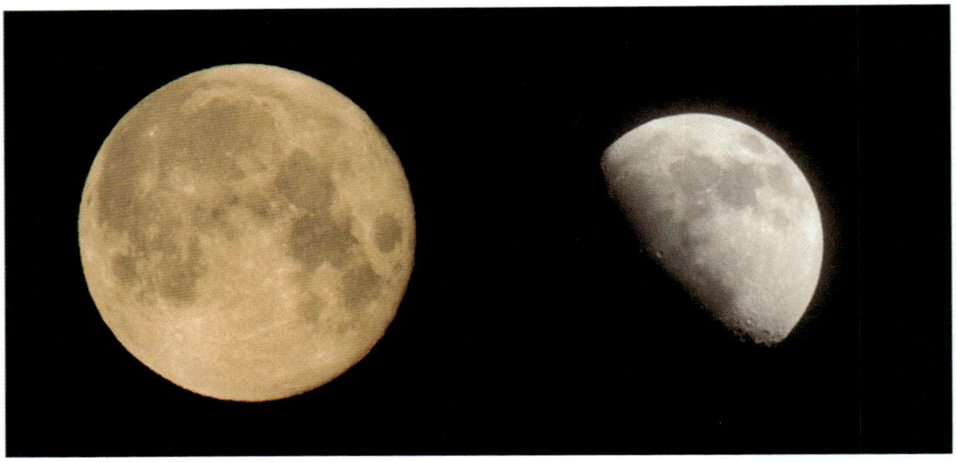

When the moon is full, light is shining directly upon it from the front. In this state there is zero shadow, so the moon looks very flat and two dimensional

When the moon is not full, light is shining from the side. Notice how we can now see some of the craters near to the shadow area and also the moon looks more three dimensional.

Direction of light

As you have just seen, when the subject is lit from the front it appears flat and 2 dimensional, whereas side lighting has produced shadows which has given the subject a more rounded 3 dimensional look. When working with any form of direct light, the angle that the light is coming from is also very important and can determine just how your subject appears. The following illustration helps to give you an idea of the effects the different angles create.

Angle of lighting

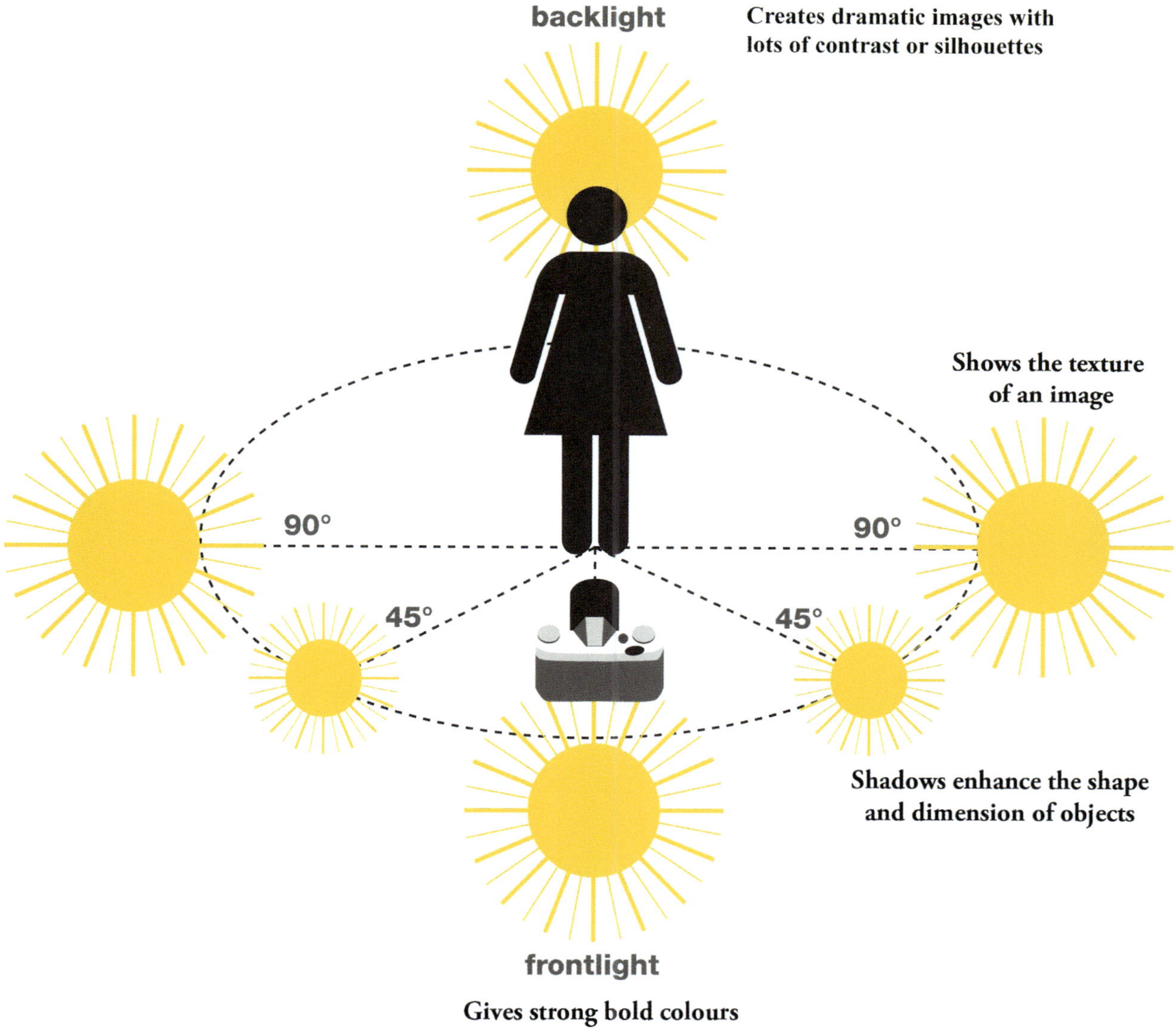

Direct light for landscapes

Much the same can be said for landscapes. We want some direct light to give shape, texture and colour to our landscape photos.

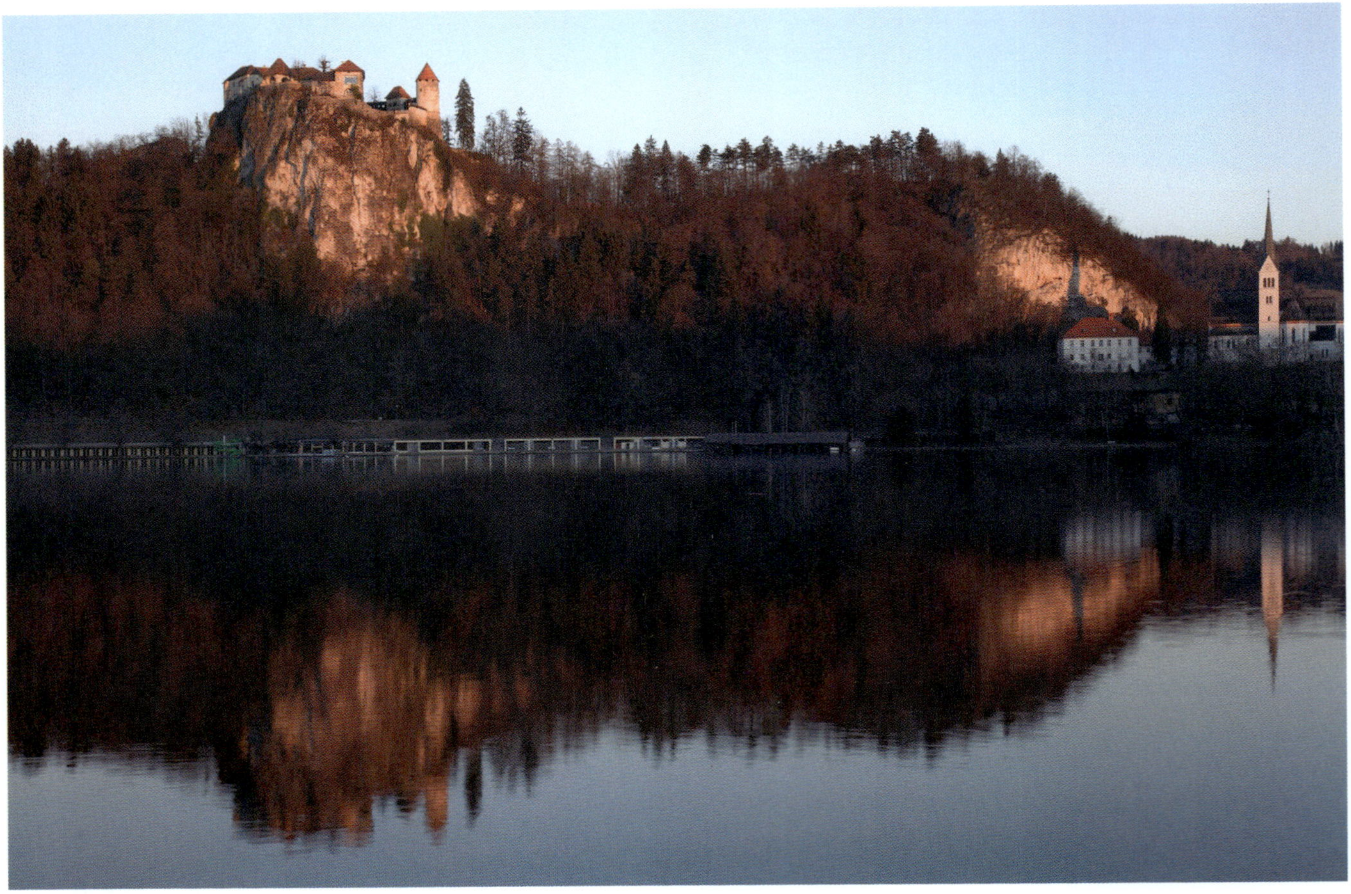

In this photo of Lake Bled in Slovenia, shot at sunrise, the sun coming up from the side has cast soft, warm light over the scene, but the shadows have also added shape, form and contrast to the land. It has also emphasised important areas of the photo. The shadow under the castle and cliff-face have made the castle stand out. Same as with the church bell tower.

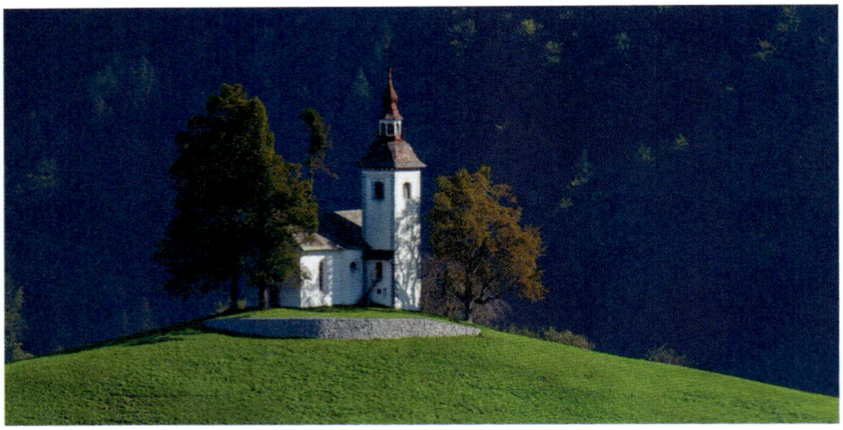

In this photo here, see how the side lighting has cast a soft shadow on the left side of the church bell tower, helping to give it dimension and shape.

Creating shape, texture and colour

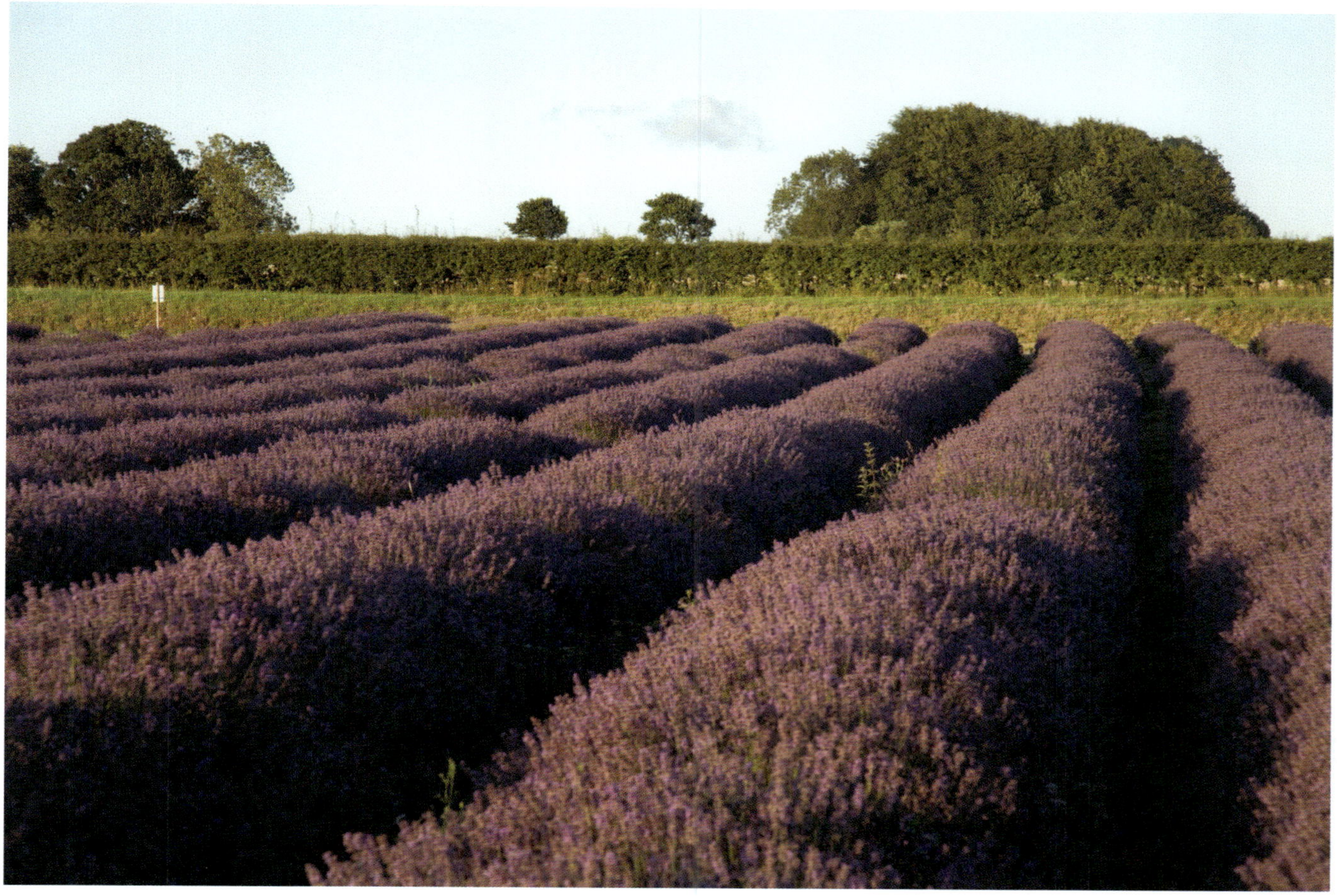

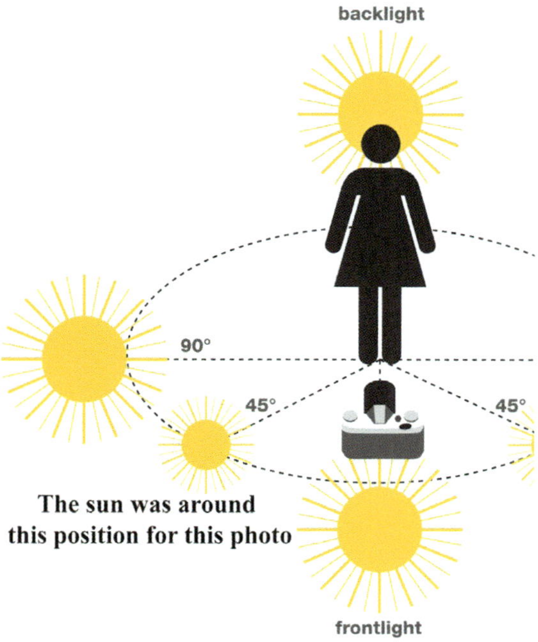

The sun was around this position for this photo

In this photo of a lavender field in Hampshire, the sun was at a 45 degree angle behind me and off to the left. As you can see the side lighting has created shadows between the rows, which helps to emphasise their rounded shape.

This was shot in the evening, so the sun was low in the sky; hence the colour temperature was lower. Also the sun was behind me. So this has all helped to add warmth and depth to the colour.

Creating shape, texture and colour

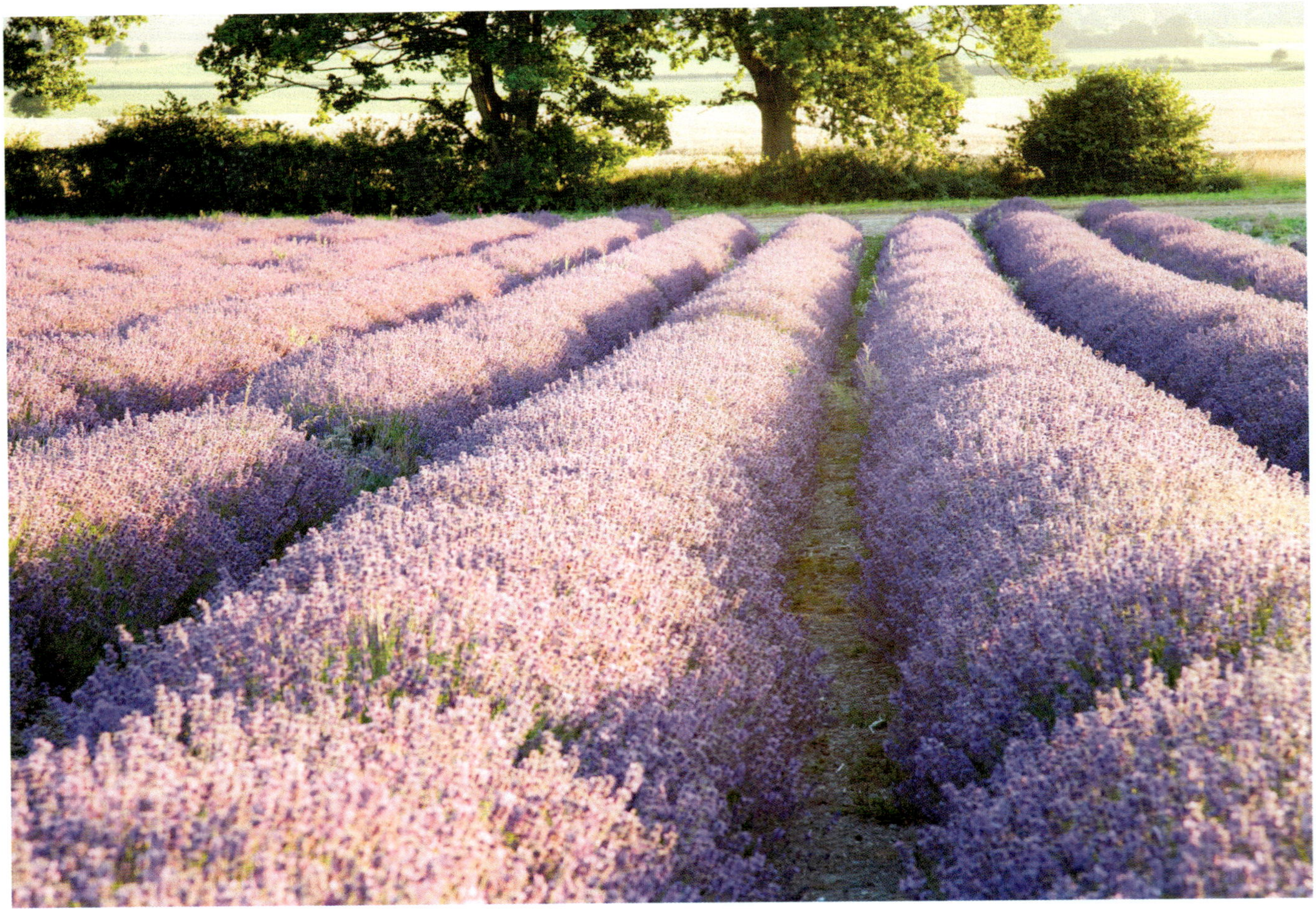

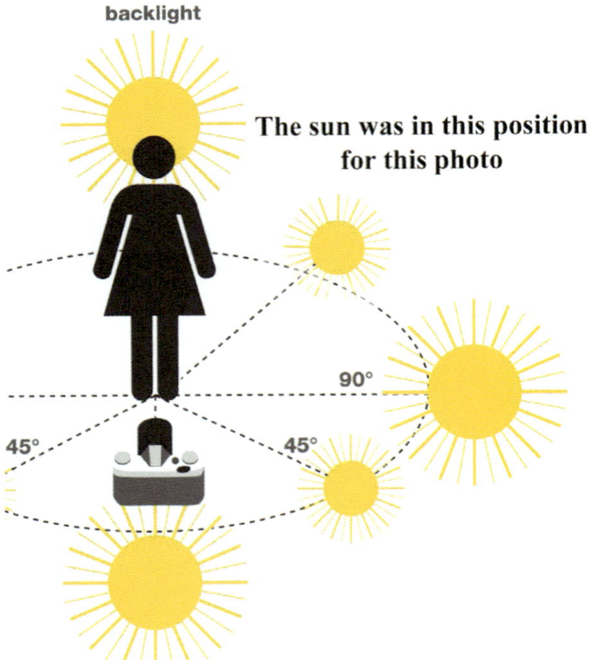

In this photo, taken on the same evening just a short while after, I moved to the opposite side of the field and positioned the sun at a 45 degree in front of me and off to the right. So I was partially shooting into the light.

Notice again how the side lighting has created shape and texture to the rows.

Also here the purple colour is softer and lighter. A classic example of how the angle of light and how you choose to expose your photo can affect how your colours look.

The shadows are softer here because I wasn't shooting directly into the hard light, and also because of how I exposed the photo. More about exposure later.

Creative use of direct light and shadow:

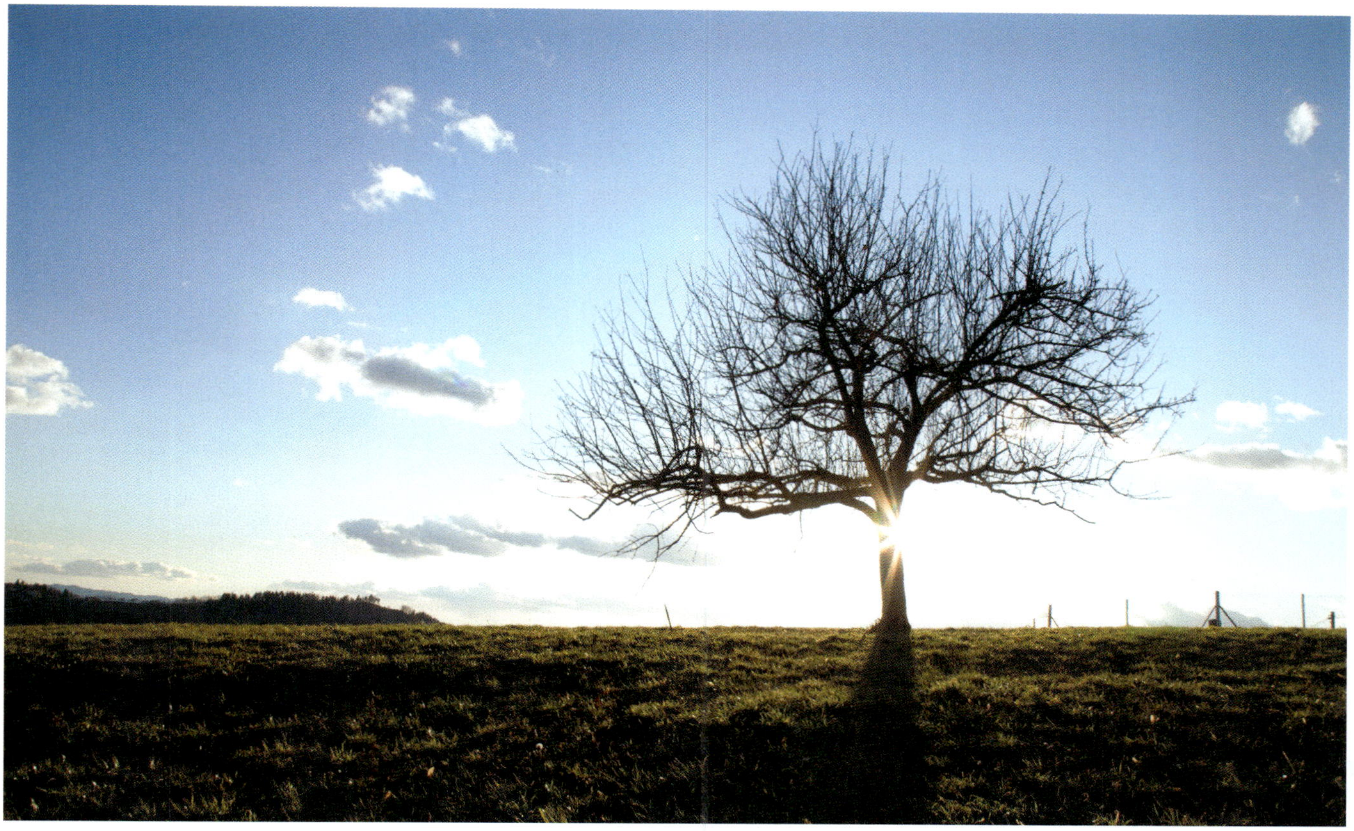

Direct light and shadow can be used for creative effect. In the backlit image above the sunlight, carefully positioned behind the tree to reduce its intensity somewhat, has produced a dramatic image with lots of shadow and contrast.

A classic example of direct backlight. Because the mountains are lit from behind and no direct light is falling on the front of them, the difference in brightness is extreme. Because of the high contrast, you need to expose for the highlights (bright parts) and then the mountains become silhouetted.

Diffused light effects

Diffused light comes from a large source rather than a single small source.

Technically, light is diffused when it passes through a transparent object such as a large white sheet, or a window. The result is that the light is scattered and spread and the diffuser becomes the light source rather than the original light source.

Therefore, the larger the diffuser, the softer the light. The figure above shows how the light is repeatedly scattered through increasingly larger surfaces.

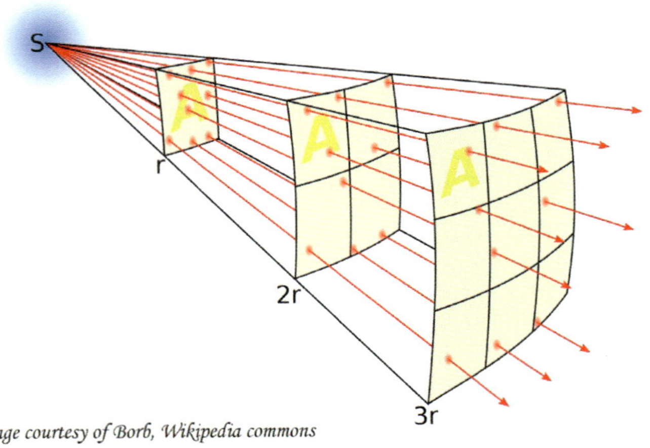

Image courtesy of Borb, Wikipedia commons

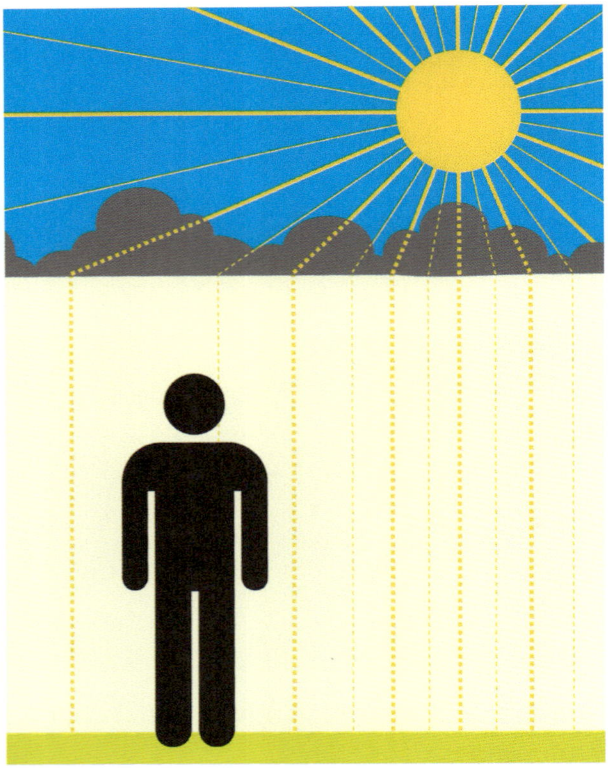

The biggest example of this is the sky on an overcast day. Go outside on a sunny day and look at the sky. You'll be blinded by a single hard beam of light from the sun. But go out on an overcast day and you'll see that there is no single hard beam of light, but the whole sky is evenly lit.

Now look around and you'll see there is little or no shadow. This is because the light is scattered, as you can see in the diagram to the left, and lighting the land evenly, rather than directly.

Diffused light on landscapes

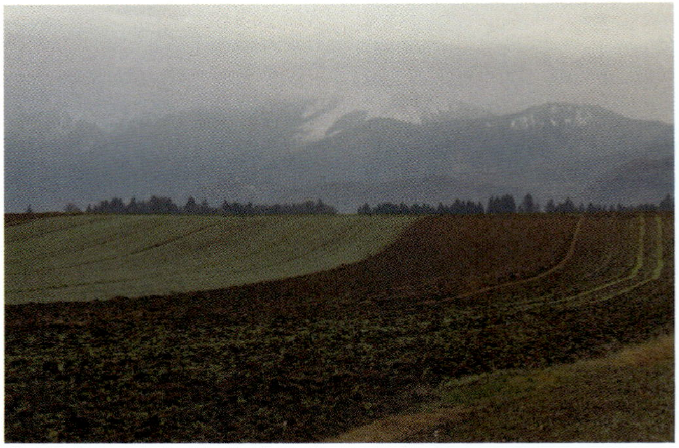

As you can see by the photo to the right, the light of a thick overcast day produces a scene with low contrast and less vibrant colours. Notice the almost complete absence of shadow here.

Diffused light is perfect for people

Diffused light is often the best light when photographing people portraits. As we learned earlier, hard direct light gives lots of definition and therefore also shows up the flaws and lines in our faces. Diffused light eliminates the problem of shadows, and also gives softer, smoother and more flattering results. Also under these conditions you don't have to worry about unwanted shadow.

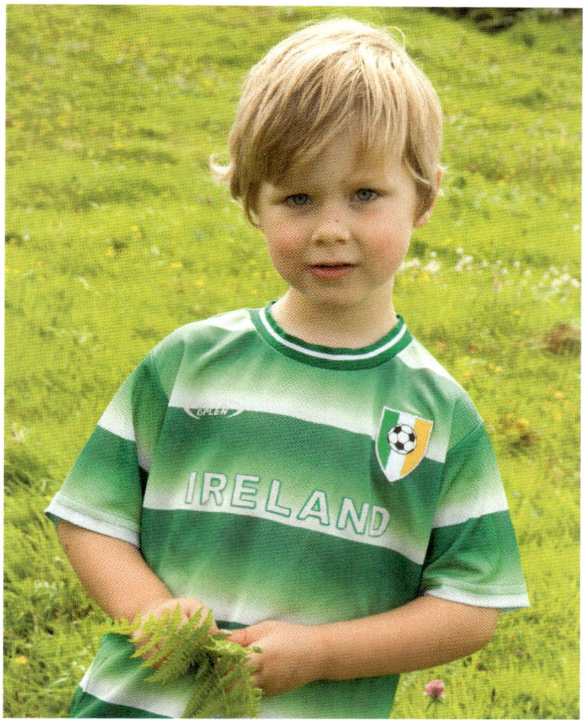

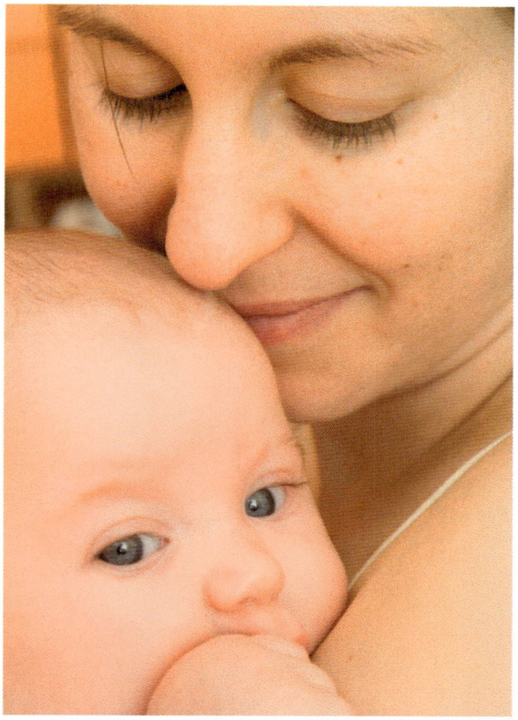

Use overcast days
The picture of the boy above was shot on a lightly overcast day.

Use the window as a diffuser
The photo top right was shot using a large window as a diffuser. By getting them to stand directly in front and facing the window, I've got lovely soft light over both their faces.

Using a tree
On a sunny day the best way to photograph people is to put them in the shade. In the photo to the right a tree has provided bright shade to eliminate any shadows or harsh light.

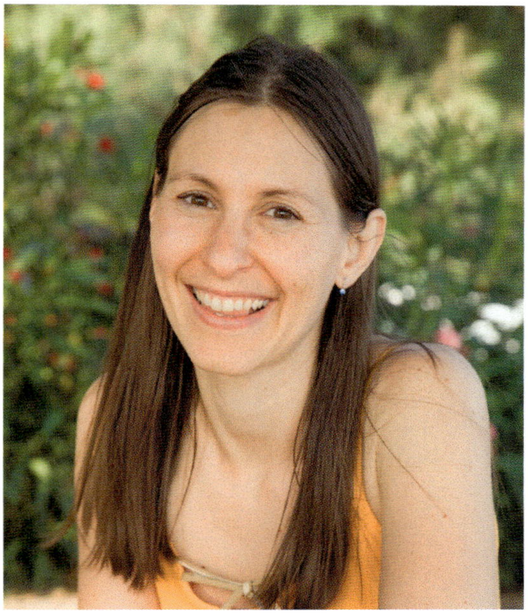

Be careful of the background though. If it's too bright the difference could be too big for the camera to handle, and the background will be overexposed.

Diffused light for landscapes

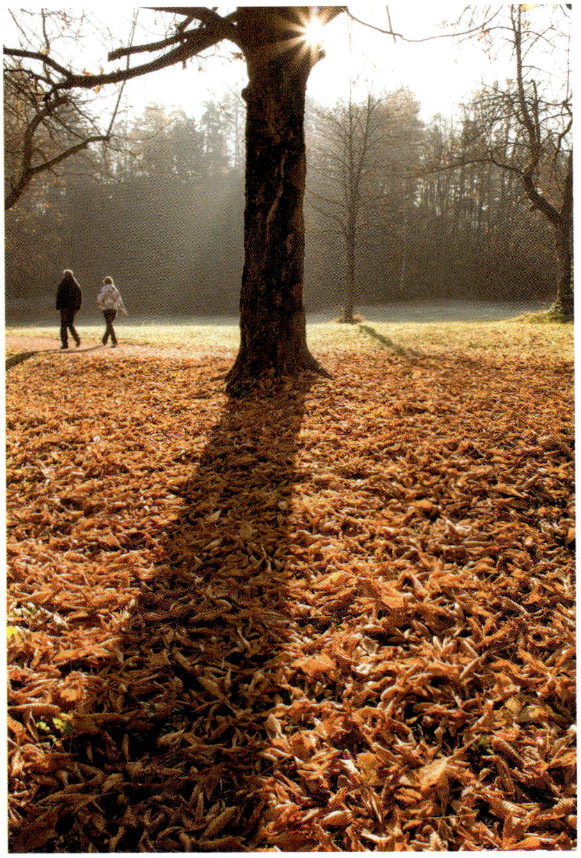

The backlight in the photo on the left has been used to cast a long shadow from the tree trunk, leading our eyes into the image and giving it depth. Additionally, the early morning mist has diffused the light, so unlike the previous backlit images that were high in contrast, this image has lighter shadows, more subtle colours and an overall softer look to it.

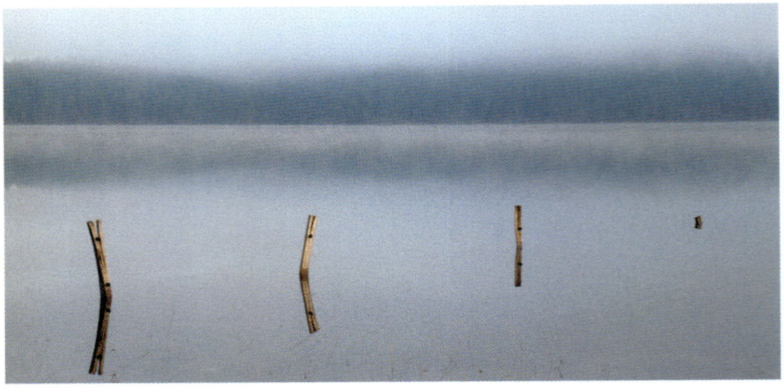

Misty mornings: are also great for diffusing light. Soft, etheral images can be made, like the one above They can help balance the contrast. The photo below would have been more difficult if not for the mist diffusing the light over the lake. Because the leaves are in the shade, the difference in brightness would have been too great.

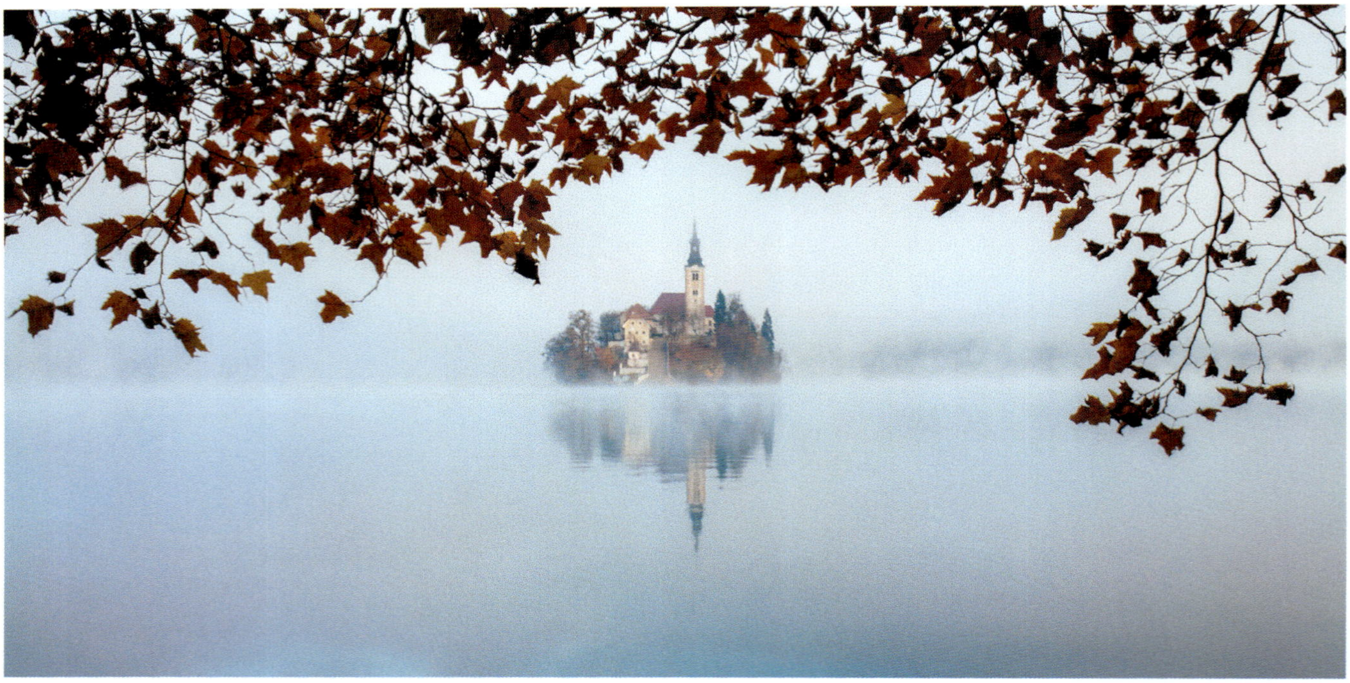

Overcast days for black and white photos

In many cases overcast days are not really desirable for landscapes. A bland white or grey sky is not particularly photogenic. However, they are not a total washout. On these days you can often look for good black and white images. The key is to look for contrasting colours and light that will convert to light and dark tones in black and white.

This image doesn't look terribly exciting in colour.

But looks a bit better in black and white.

Diffused light on water

Direct light is terrible when photographing white water, such as flowing rivers and waterfalls, because the light is too harsh and the white becomes far too bright. See the two examples below:

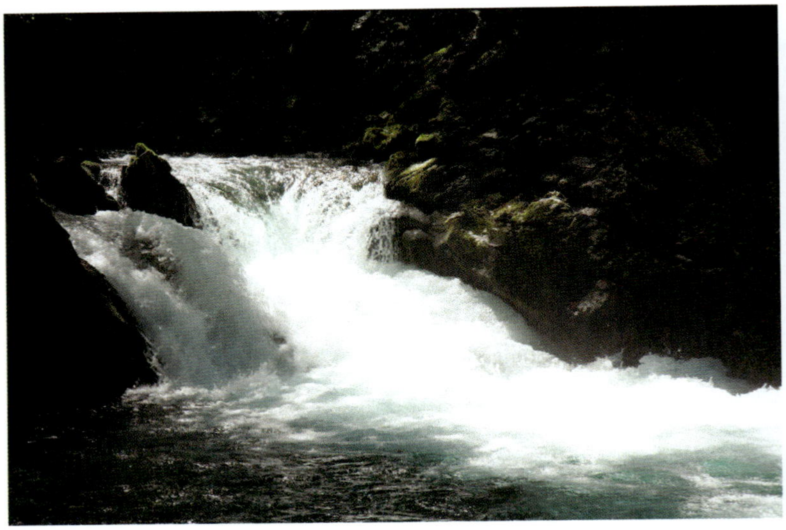

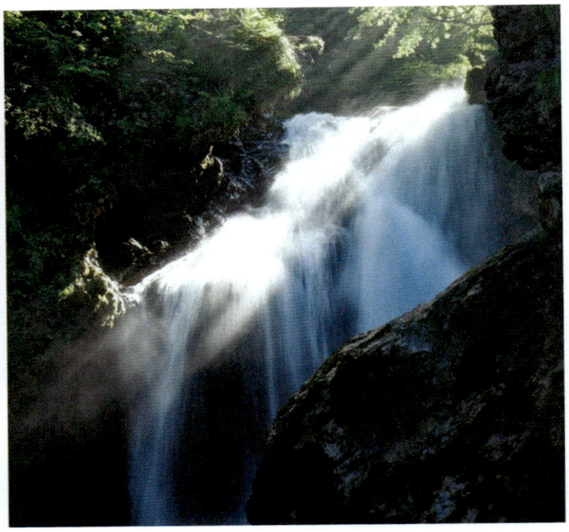

Where direct light is hitting the water it is too bright, and the rest of the photo is also too dark as a result. Much of the water is burned out with zero detail. This is known as being overexposed. Because white water is reflective, it's very difficult to photograph in hard direct light. So you need to photograph these places in overcast conditions, when it's in the shade, or on rainy days. The photo below was shot on a rainy day. See how the white is much softer, and the rest of the scene is also nice and bright.

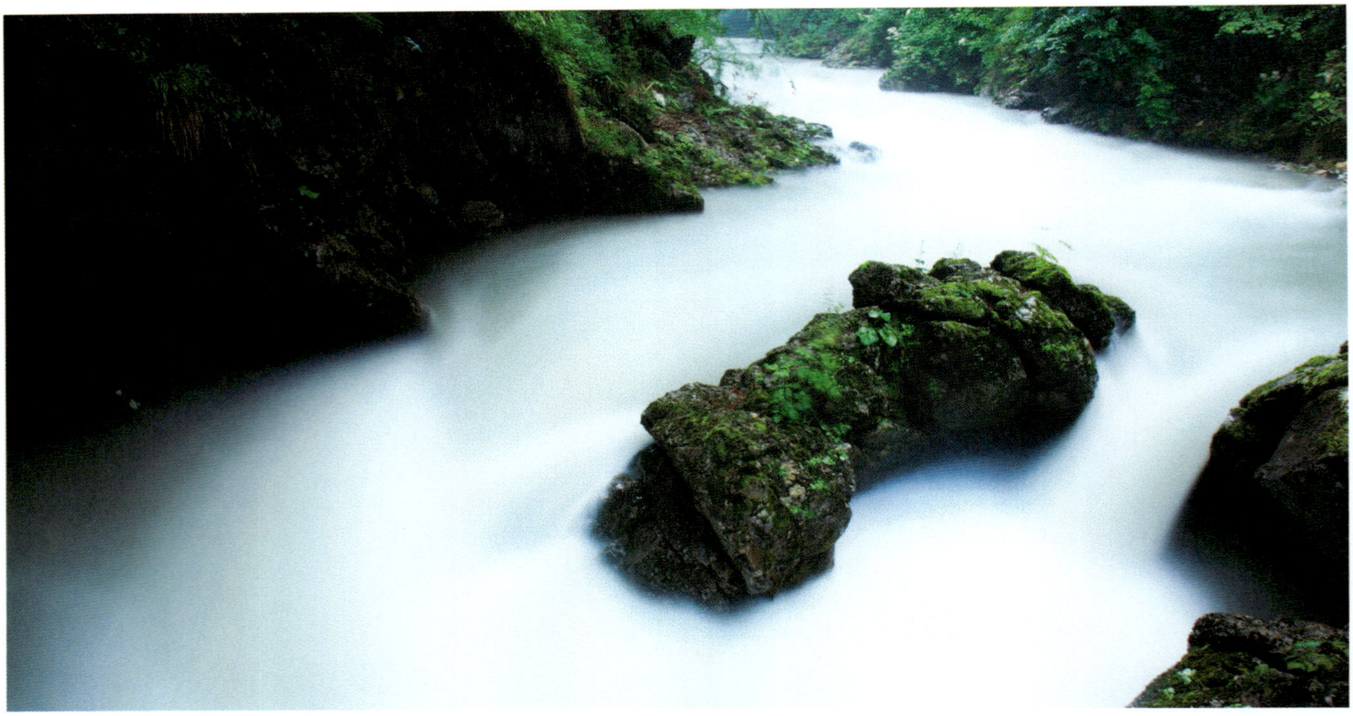

Mixed direct light and diffused light for landscapes

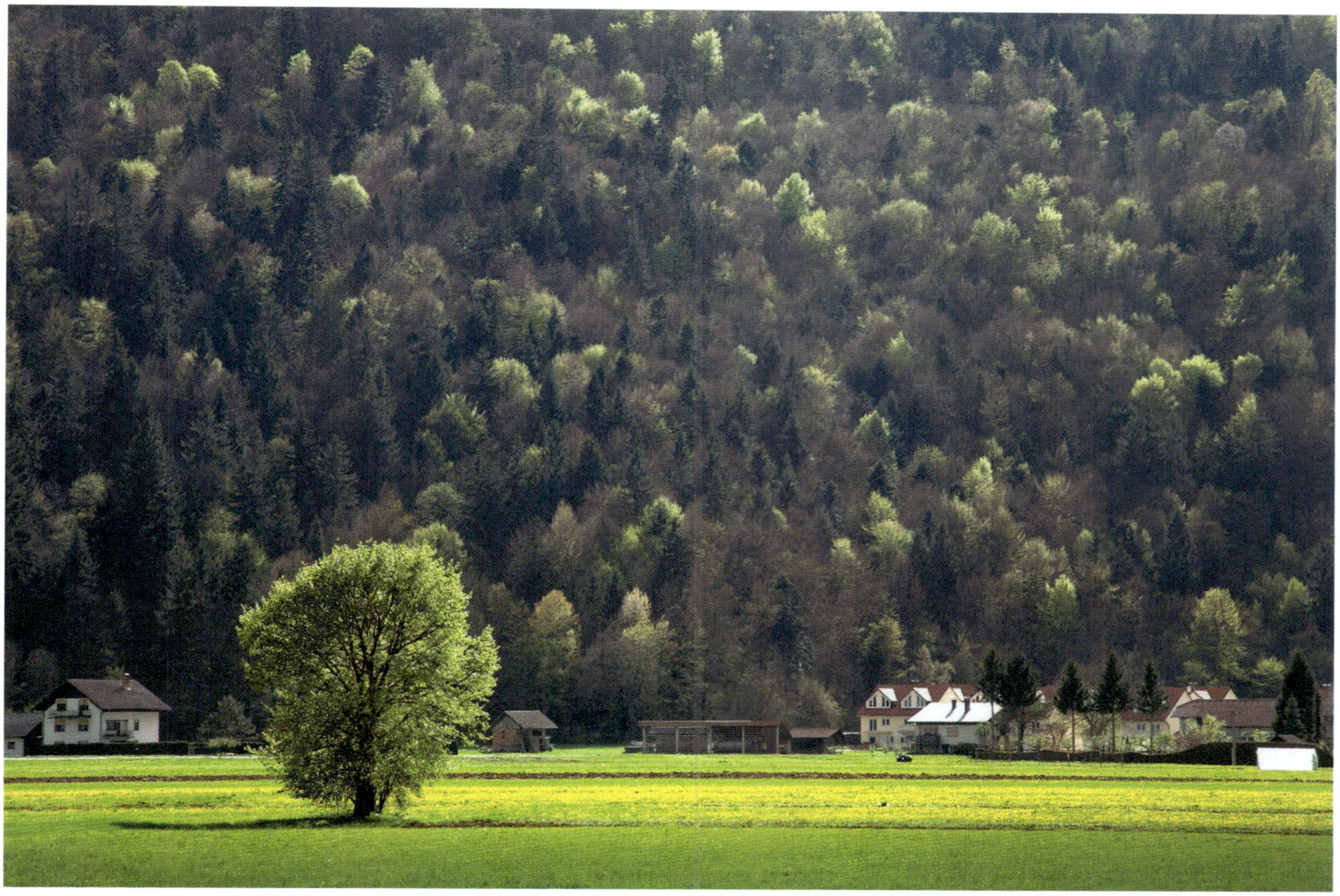

Like many things in life, to get the best results you sometimes have to mix things a bit. So on cloudy days don't sit at home cleaning your camera, because you might be missing some of the best moments. When the cloud is scattered or moving fast due to passing storms or high winds, it can produce a great mix of direct and diffused light; resulting in dramatic lighting effects.

In this photo of the Ljubljana Moors in Slovenia, breaks in the cloud caused rays of light to burst through and illuminate different parts of the land at different levels of brightness. Hard direct light has nicely illuminated the lone tree, grass and vivid yellow of the dandelions. Notice how the trees in the background are more softly lit with diffused light and the area behind the lone tree is in shadow, thus making the lone tree stand out more in the scene.

On days such as this always watch the weather and try to anticipate where and when the breaks will occur. It was raining when I spotted this scene, but I saw that it was a passing shower, so I set up my camera on the tripod, and under an umbrella, used the opportunity to setup my composition and focus on the tree. Then I waited there as passing drivers gaped at the madman getting wet while holding the umbrella over his camera. But when the shower passed and clouds broke, I got this shot.

Shooting into the light for creative effect.

Many will tell you not to shoot into the light. Well, in most cases this is true. But shooting into the light, when done correctly, can produce some very creative effects. But what's important here is that the light is diffused somehow. The less diffused the light, the harder the shadows will be. When the sun is setting its strength is diminished somewhat. But add some light cloud, and its strength is diminished even more. The stronger the light, the higher the contrast and the harder the shadows will be.

As you can see here the strong light has turned the hayrack and forest into a completely blacked out silhouette. It's important here to ensure that your foreground objects can produce a nice, clear shape. A messy foreground produces a messy looking silhouette. Your silhouette must have a clearly defined shape; otherwise it's just a big black mess.

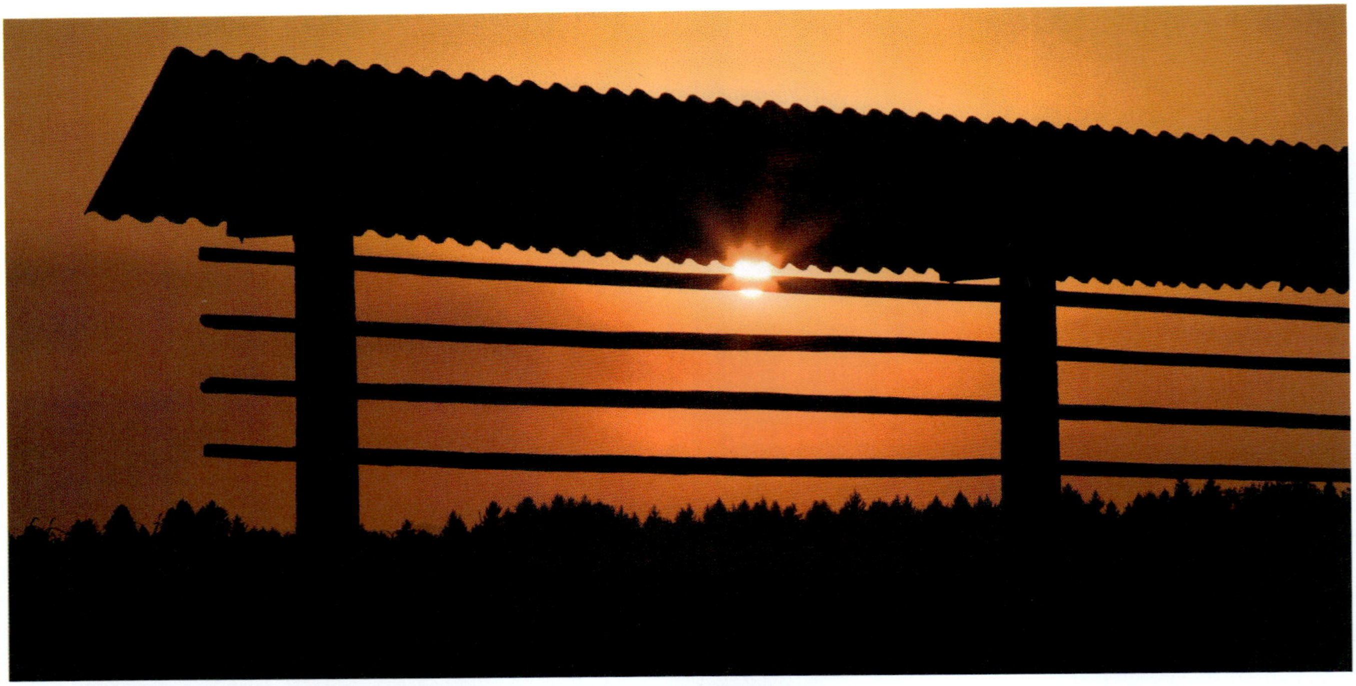

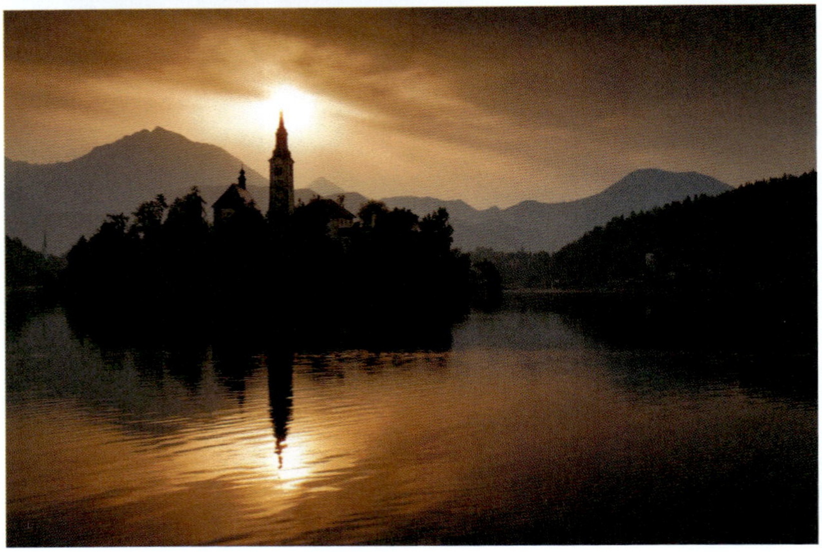

In this photo of Lake Bled in Slovenia, the sun was rising and already quite high when it reached the church spire. Without the cloud the sun would have been much brighter and this shot virtually impossible. However, the cloud diffused the sun and therefore I was able to capture this image.

The cloud has also diffused the light falling across the mountains, and without it the mountains would have been a completely black silhouette.

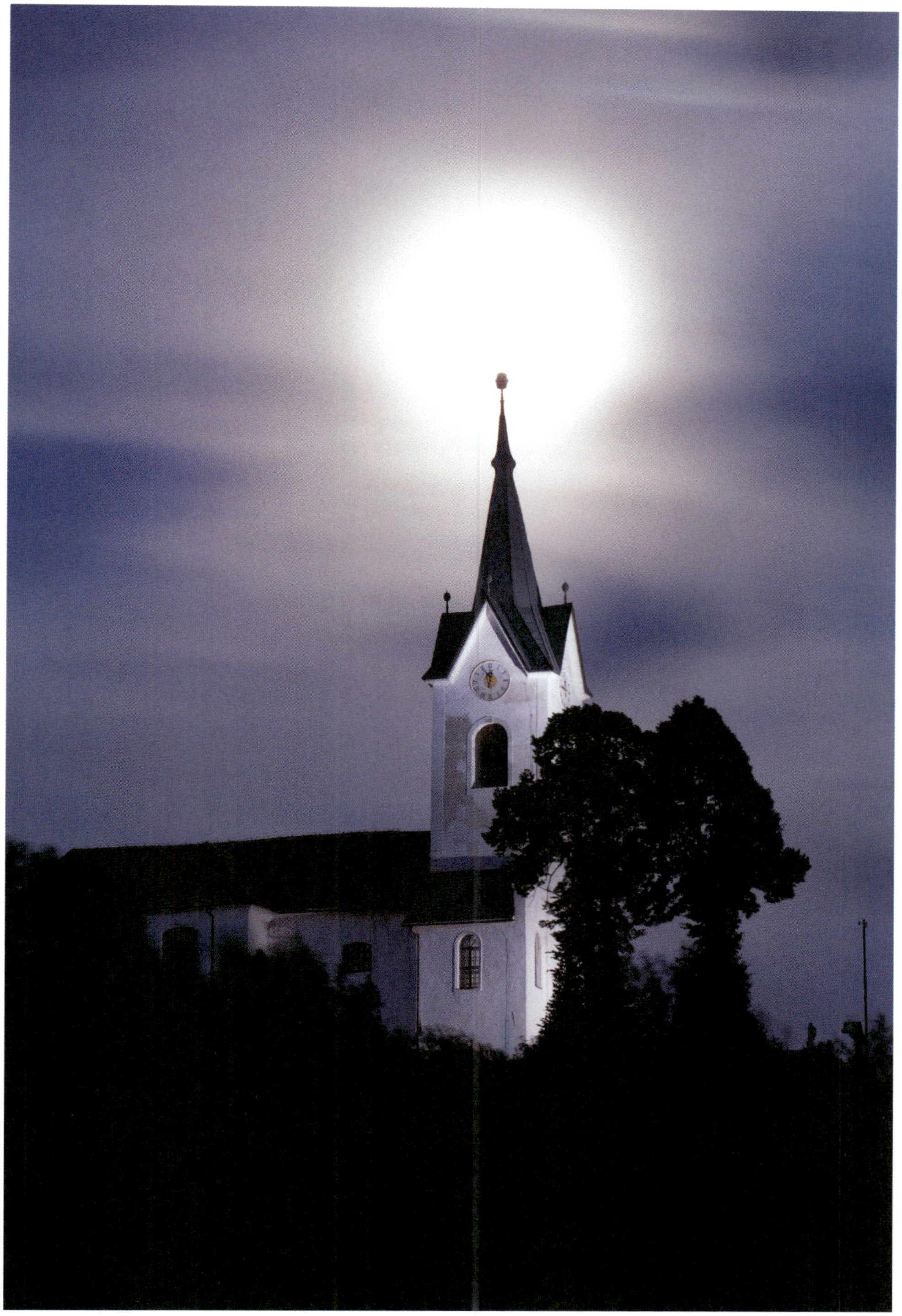

This photo of the Supermoon rising over the church was also made possible by the passing cloud, which diffused the intensity of the moonlight. It was also shot at dusk, so there was still some ambient light in the sky from the setting sun.

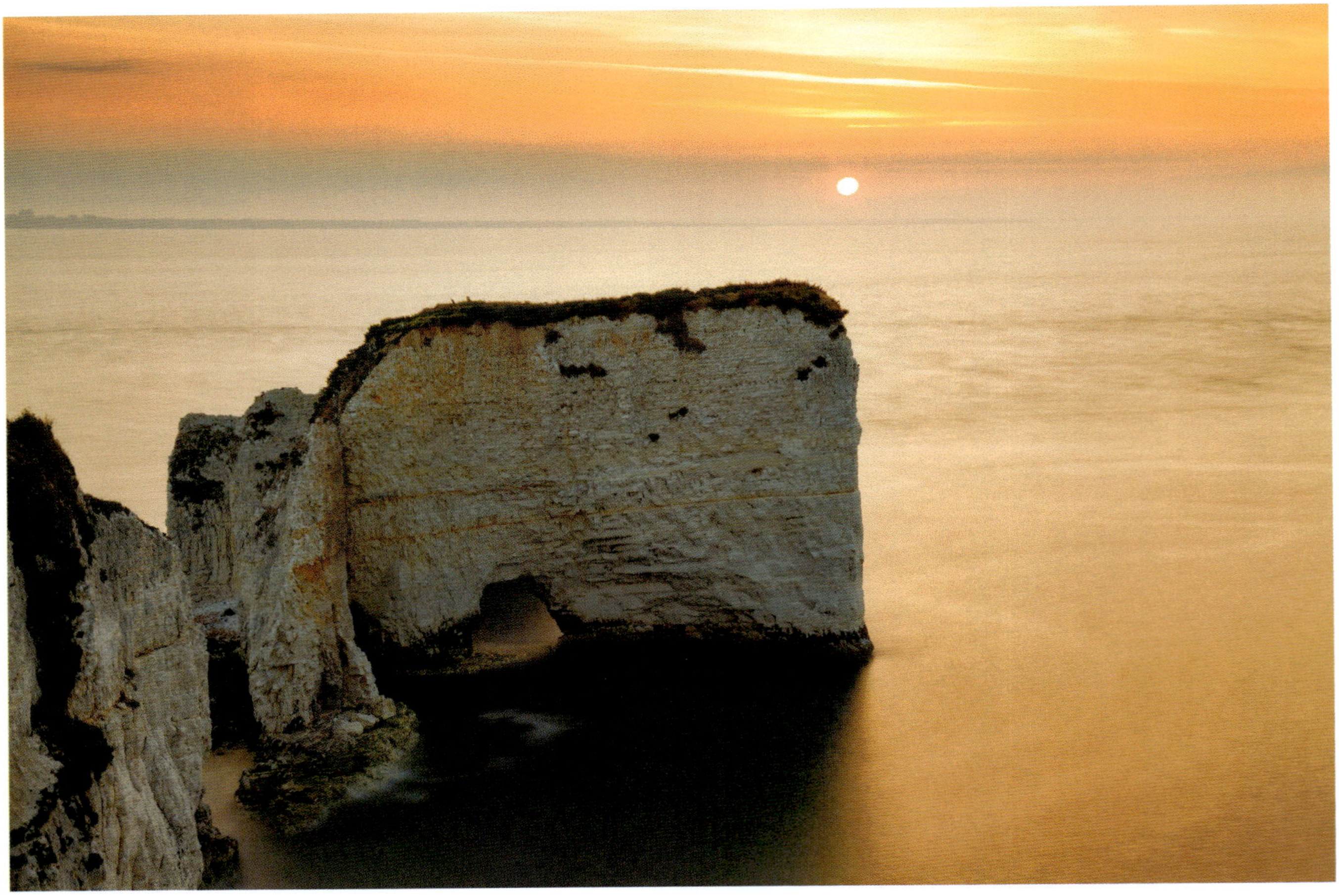

The lower the sun, and the more diffused it is, will also determine how much detail you will get in the foreground. In this photo of Old Harry Rocks in Dorset, England, the thick layer of fog on the horizon and the low angle of the sun has produced very soft morning light and allowed me to capture the detail on the front of the cliff.

Conclusion:

So as we have seen, light has complete control over how we see things. A landscape, or your subject's appearance, is totally determined by the quality, colour, direction and hardness or softness of the light available. As you take your photographs, take some time to study how the light is illuminating your subject and the effect it has. Go out on sunny and overcast days and see how different everything looks. Look at how shadows shape the landscape. Even when you don't have your camera, watch and learn as you are going about whatever it is that you are doing. Study your favourite photos by other photographers and see how the light has affected each picture.

Part 2
How the camera sees and captures images

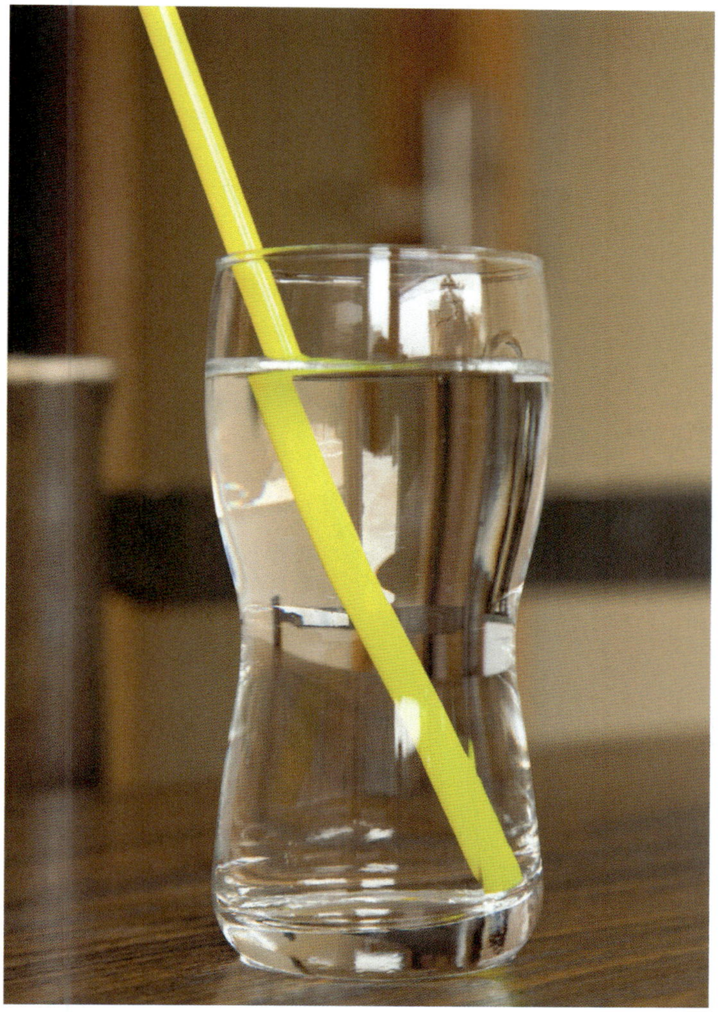

In order to understand photography, it's good to have some basic knowledge about how the camera works. So here we go:

Refraction

When light travels through air its speed is constant, but when it passes through glass or water it slows down. This causes the light rays to be bent, or refracted.

As you can see by the photo to the right, the water has refracted, or bent, the light giving this classic optical illusion with the straw.

Our eyes and the camera use a convex lens to refract incoming light and direct it to a single focal plane, such as the film or digital sensor. The distance between the lens and focal point is called the focal length.

Convex Lens

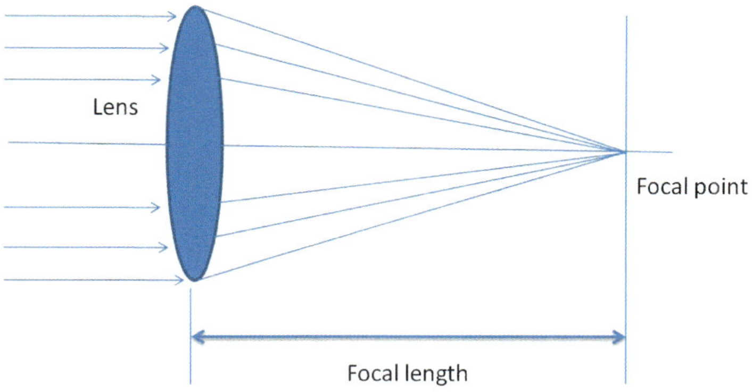

Summary of terms:

Focal point

- The refracted rays converge at a single point of focus, known as the focal plane.

Focal length

- The distance between the lens and the focal point is known as the focal length.

How we see images

Light passes through the lens after first passing through the pupil, and then converges at the focal point: the retina, which then sends the image to our brain via the optical nerve. As you can see the image is upside down, because the light rays are inverted, but our brain flips the image back upright. Our eye is permanently exposed to light, hence we see moving images.

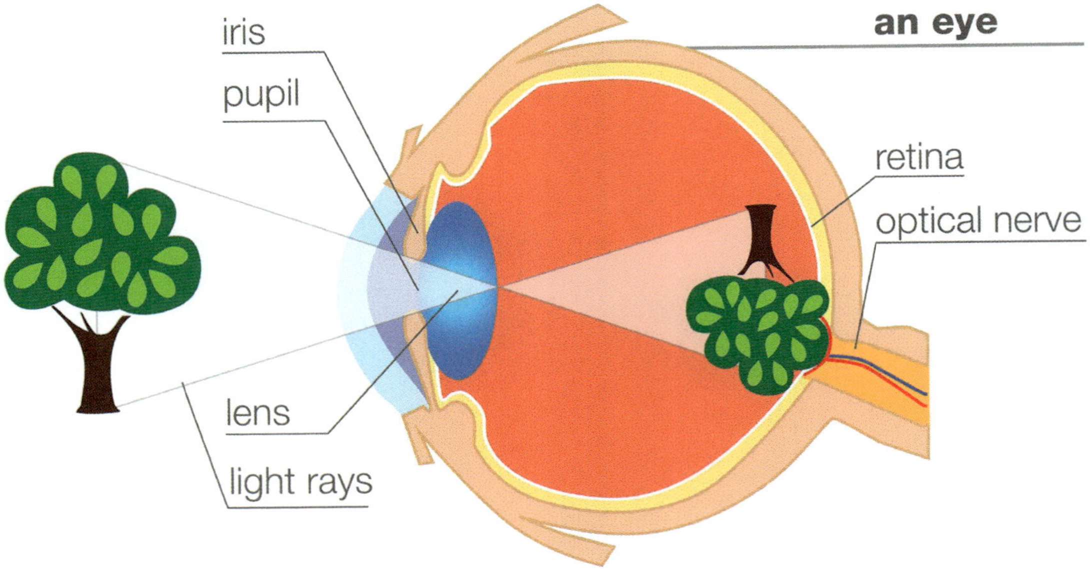

How the camera sees images

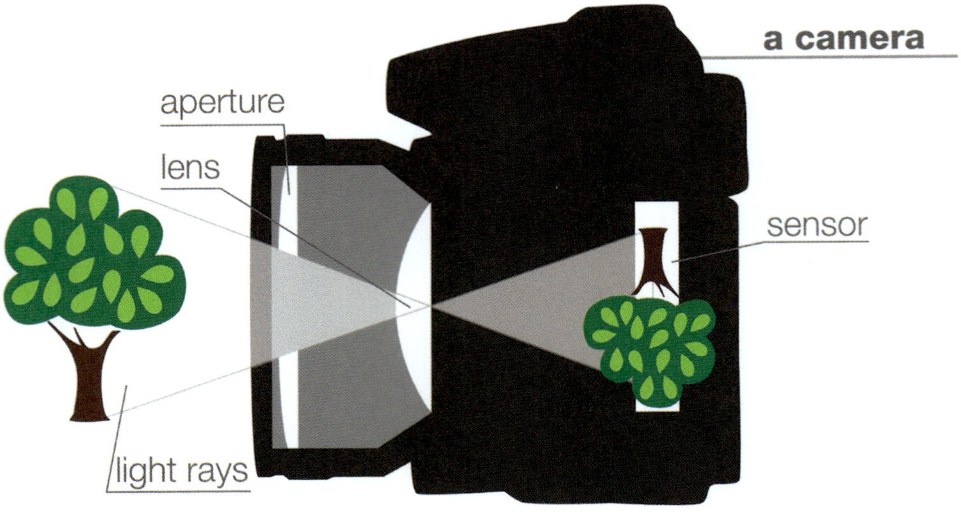

Just like our eye, the camera adopts a similar principle. Only instead of a pupil, it has an aperture. Light passes through the aperture, then the lens (or a series of lenses in most modern lenses), converges at the focal point: the sensor (digital) or film. The image is then sent to the camera's brain (microprocessor). Just as with our eye, the image on the sensor or film is flipped back upright by the camera's software. The camera is only exposed to light for a period of time, known as exposure time. Hence it captures a still image.

PART 3
LENSES AND HOW THEY WORK

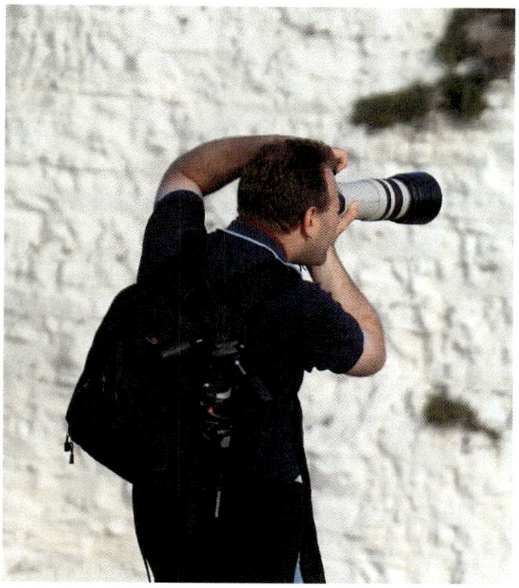

The lens

This is the first point of entry and most important part of the camera. You can have the best camera body in the world, but put a cheap lens on and you may as well have a budget camera.

Imagine owning a top of the range BMW, and then putting a Lada engine inside. Or having 20/20 vision and putting on a pair of badly scratched or low quality glasses. Now I'm not trying to say that any lens other than a top of the range one is rubbish. But the lens is an important factor, and understanding it helps. So look after your lens, keep it clean and free from scratches, even if it's a phone or compact camera. Also, when upgrading, think of the lens first. If money is an issue, spend it on a better lens rather than a better body. The following theory applies to all lenses on all cameras.

Optical zooms and Focal length

As you saw earlier, light passes through the lens and falls upon the focal plane. In an optical zoom the distance between the lens and the focal plane is known as the focal length.

- 50mm – standard field of view equal to what we see with our eyes.
- Below 50mm = wide angle.
- Above 50mm = telephoto.

Some lenses are fixed at a certain focal length (non zoom) and others are variable (zoom function).

Crop factor

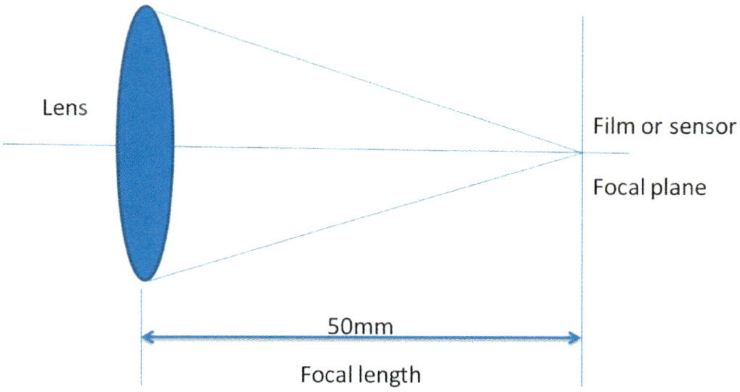

The above is based on using a standard 35mm film or full frame digital sensor. Many cameras contain smaller size sensors. Other sensor sizes, on crop sensor SLRs, compacts and phone cameras will vary. This is called the crop factor. Canon SLRs, for example, have a crop factor of 1.6. This means that you use the following equation to work out your actual focal length.

- Focal length x crop factor- so a sensor with a crop factor of 1.6 at 50mm, will actually be 50 x 1.6 = 80mm.

So the standard field of view of 50mm on a crop sensor will be different. To work it out, use the following:

- Focal length divided by crop factor (50mm / 1.6 = 31.25mm) 31.25 is equivalent to 50mm.

How wide angle and telephoto work

As I explained before, 50mm is the optimal focal length for full frame or 35mm film.

The diagram to the right helps to illustrate this. As you can see, the shortest focal length (fisheye) has the widest angle of view. What falls upon the sensor is what is seen between those two outer points. Therefore:

***Increase* the focal length:** the angle of light narrows, and thus the narrower the field of view. So essentially you are compressing the scene and reducing how much of it falls upon the sensor, effectively isolating a part of it. Think of it as cropping part of the photo away.

***Decrease* the focal length**: the angle of light widens, and thus the wider the field of view. So you are increasing how much of the scene falls upon the sensor.

The photos on the next page illustrate this.

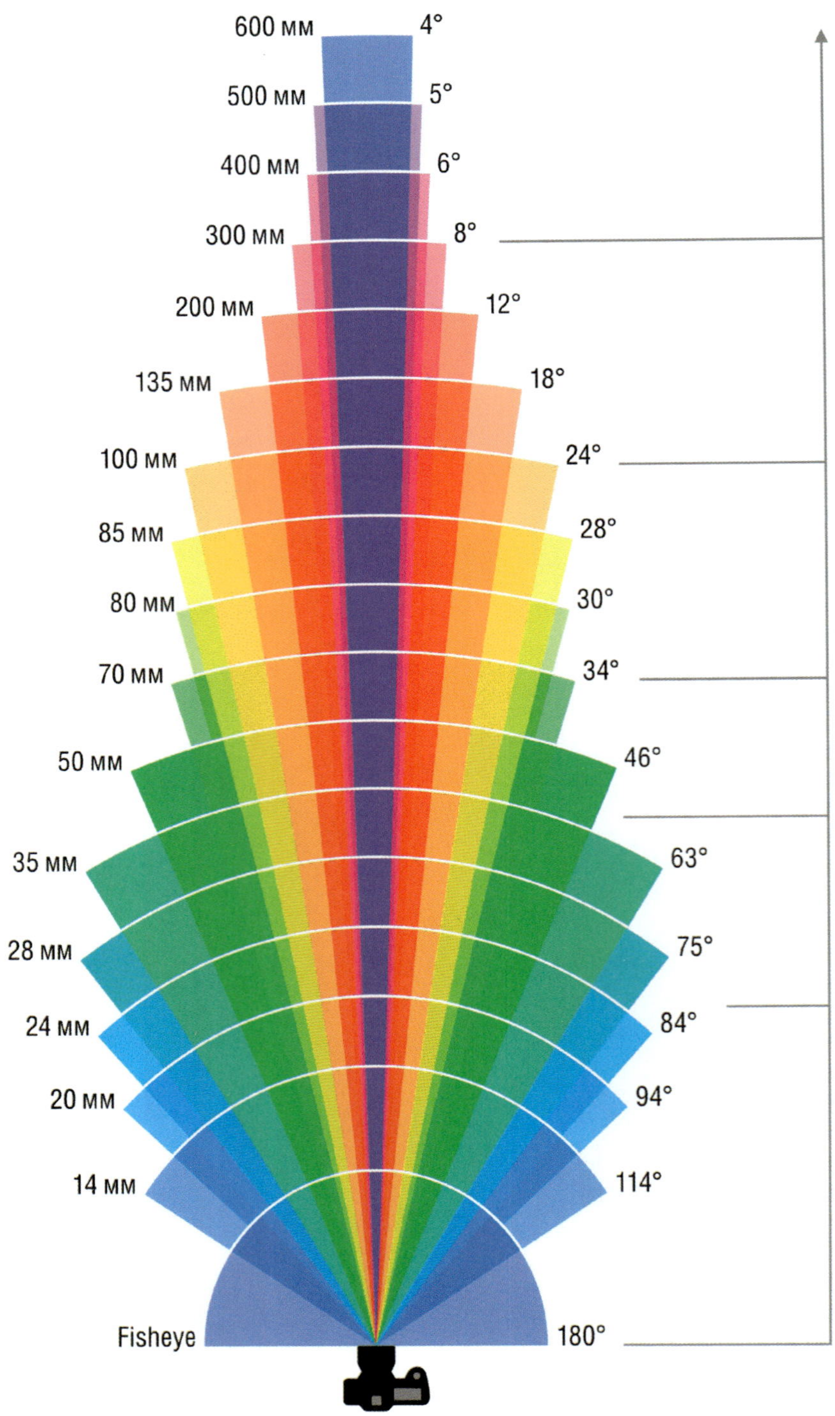

Photo at wide angle

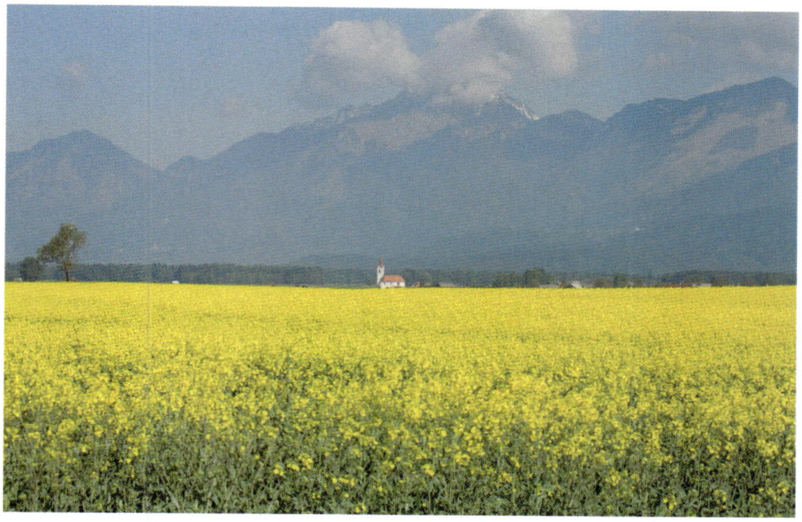

When the focal length is increased the angle of light will be reduced and only this much of the scene will fall upon the sensor

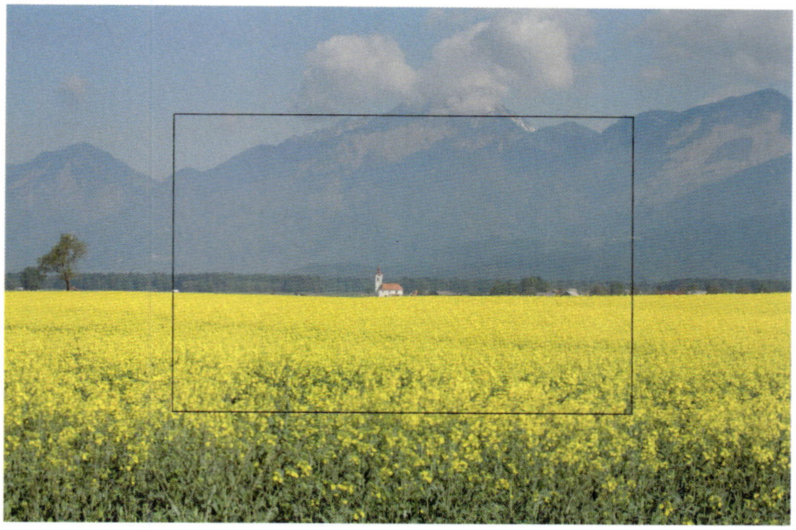

So the zoomed image will then look like this on the sensor

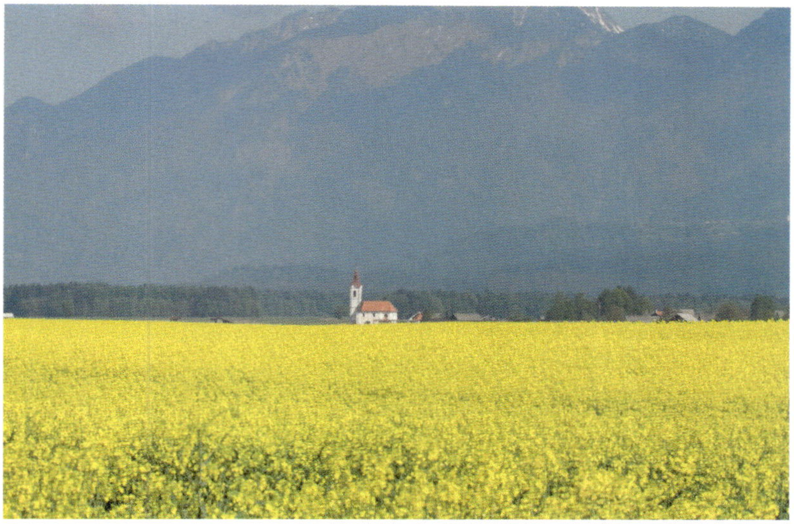

Wide angle lenses and their effect

A wide angle effectively stretches the image and allows a wider view than the normal 50mm will allow. Just like a telephoto allows you to get closer without actually moving further forward, a wide angle allows you get further away without actually moving further back. This can be useful when you don't have room to move back. But again, this comes at a price: *distortion*

The scene is actually bent or warped. If you look at those roadside mirrors that are placed at sharp bends or awkward junctions to enable you to see round the corners, it's a bit like that. The wider the angle, the more straight lines in your scene are bent and distorted. How much your lines are distorted very much depends on the angle at which you are viewing your object. This can be corrected using software, or it can be used for creative effect. Sometimes it is manageable:

Shoot level and straight: When you do this you will minimise the warping effect on objects in your image with straight lines.

Get low and shoot upwards: This accentuates the warping and when done properly can add drama to a landscape image.

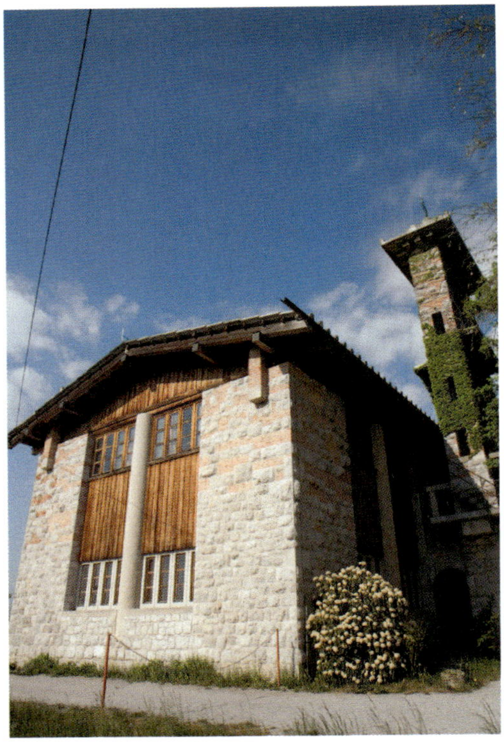

Shooting upwards at 24mm
See how the chimney appears to be leaning and the building's sides are converging.

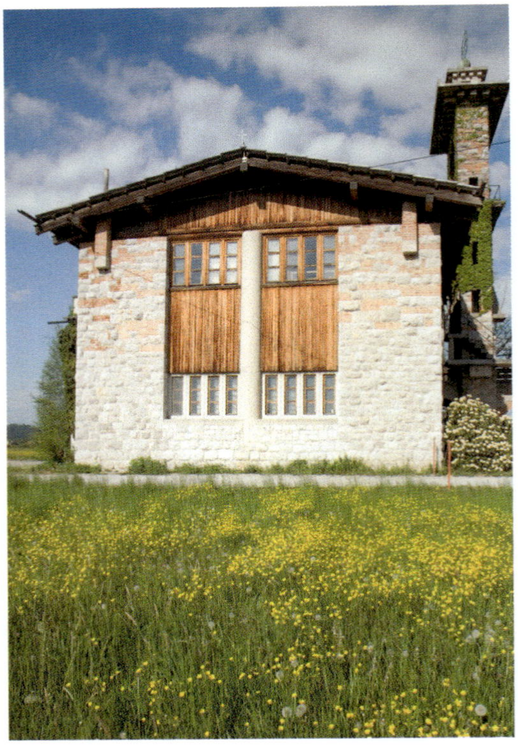

Straight on angle at 24mm
Here I stood upright and moved back a bit. See how the warping here is minimal.

Creative use of wide angle

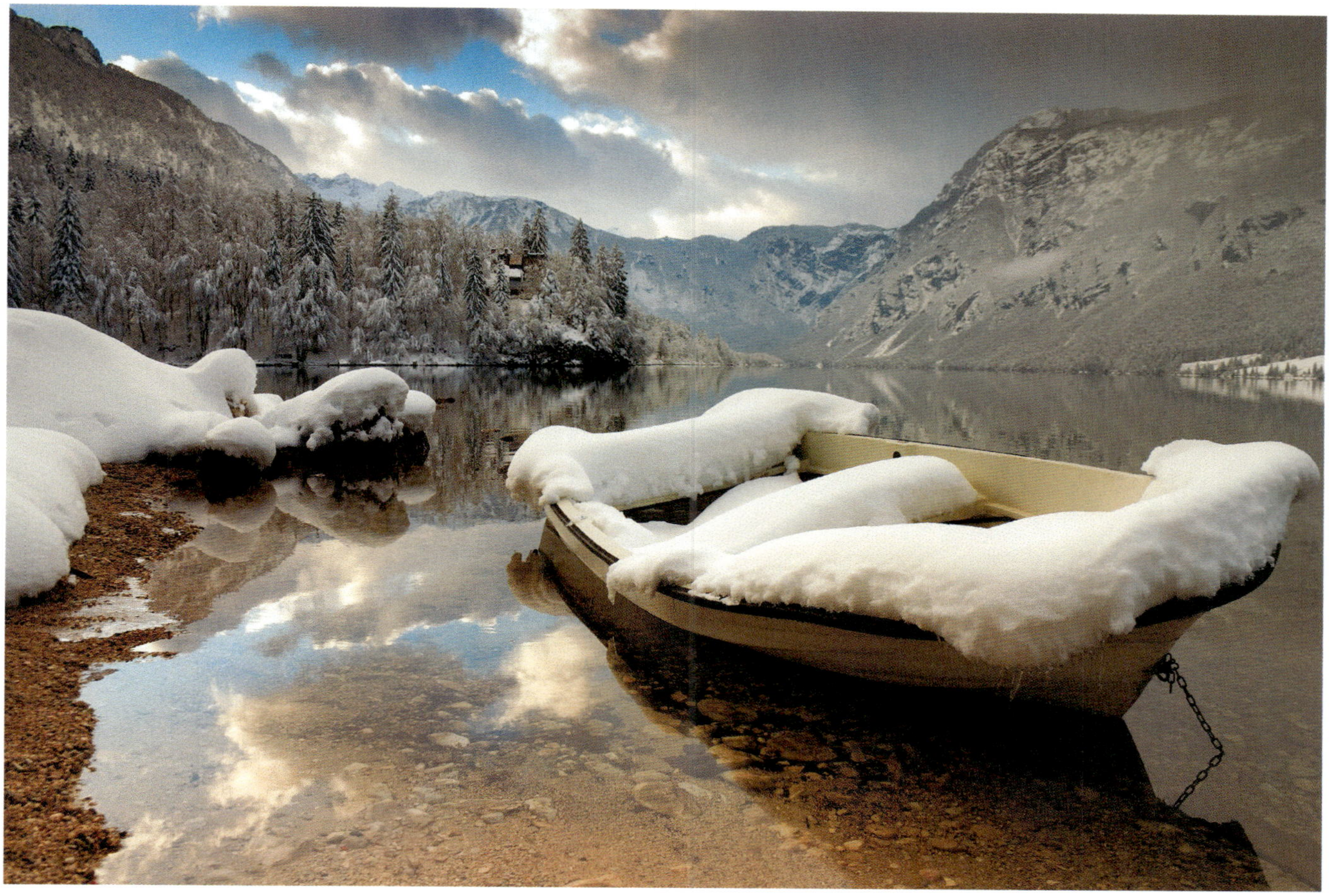

18mm (28.8mm effective focal length – APS 1.6x sensor)

Like most things, we can also put this warping effect to creative use and to add drama to our photos.

In this photo, taken at Lake Bohinj, Slovenia, I moved in low and close using a wide angle. Here the subtle warping has accentuated the curve on the mountains. The close, low angle has also drawn the boat closer to give it a dominant place in the image and made it appear larger in the frame.

Using wide angle to exaggerate scale

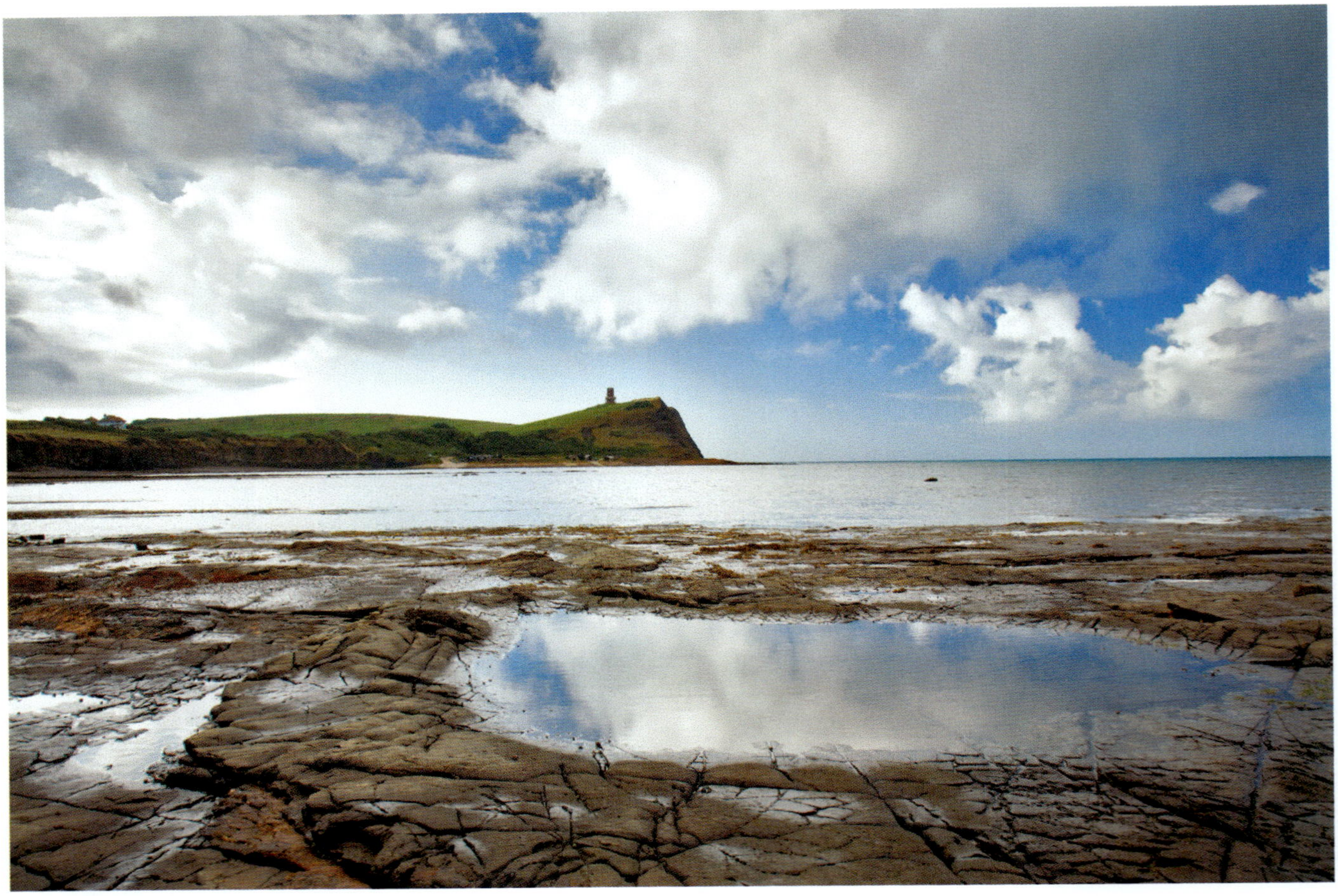

When using wide angle, it has the effect of enlarging objects in the forefront of the frame, while making distant objects much smaller.

This photo, taken at Kimmeridge Bay in Dorset, was shot at 24mm. As you can see, by getting close to the rockpool it appears much larger and has become a dominant feature of the foreground. The hill and Clavell Tower, have been shrunk in size to exaggerate the distance. The distortion has also accentuated the clouds, which adds drama to the sky.

Using wide angle to exaggerate lead in lines

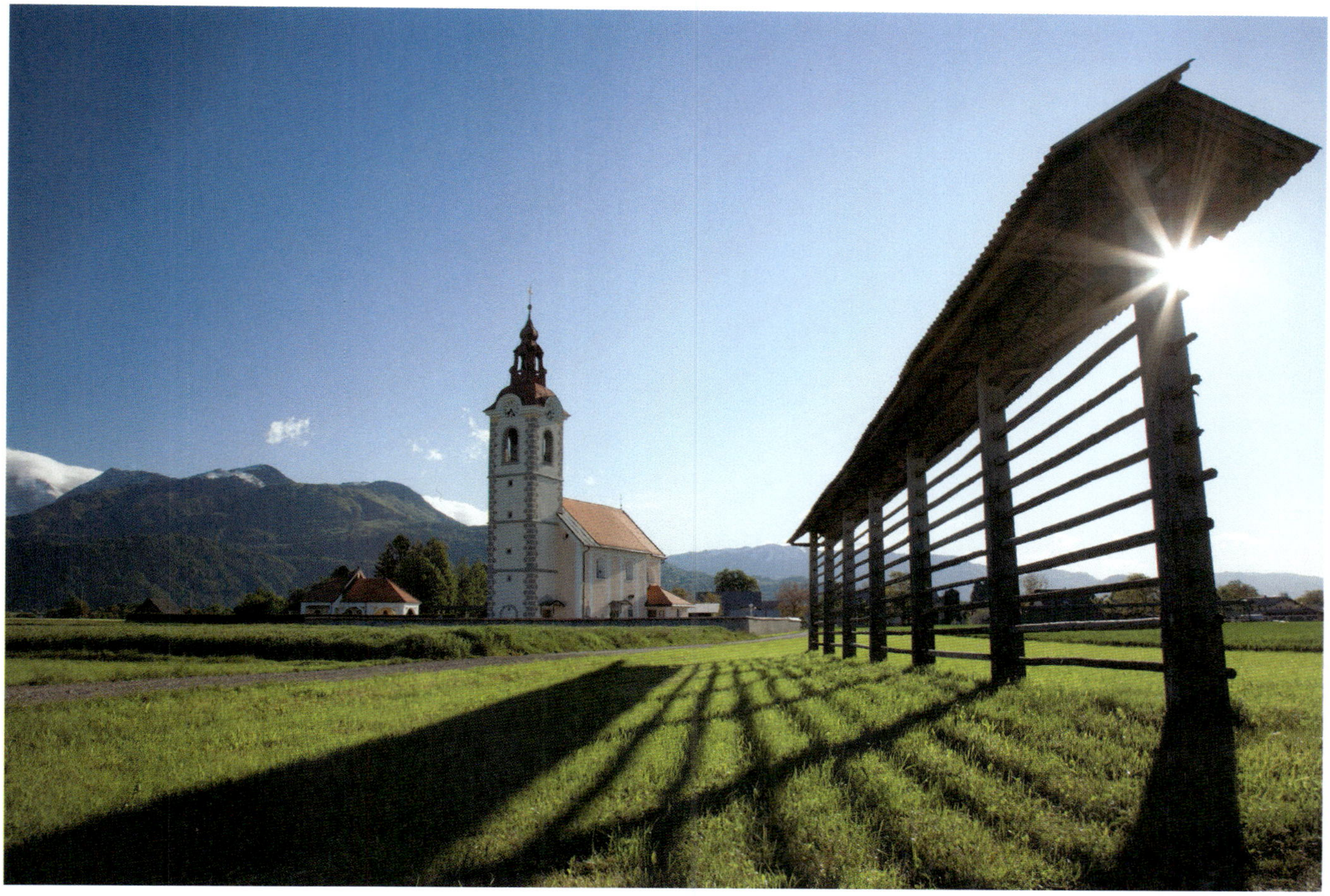

In the photo above, taken in Slovenia, the angle at which the photo was taken would naturally have caused the horizontal lines of the hayrack to converge as they move from front to back. But, using a wide angle, getting low and close, and placing it at the edge of the frame, has pulled the front of the hayrack closer and the distortion has made it larger.

Conversely, the end of the hayrack now appears smaller in comparison to the front, and so the converging lines have been accentuated. The wide angle has also exaggerated the size of the sunburst.

Telephoto effects for landscapes

While a wide angle makes foreground objects larger and distant objects smaller, telephoto has almost the opposite effect. When you zoom in you make *everything* larger.

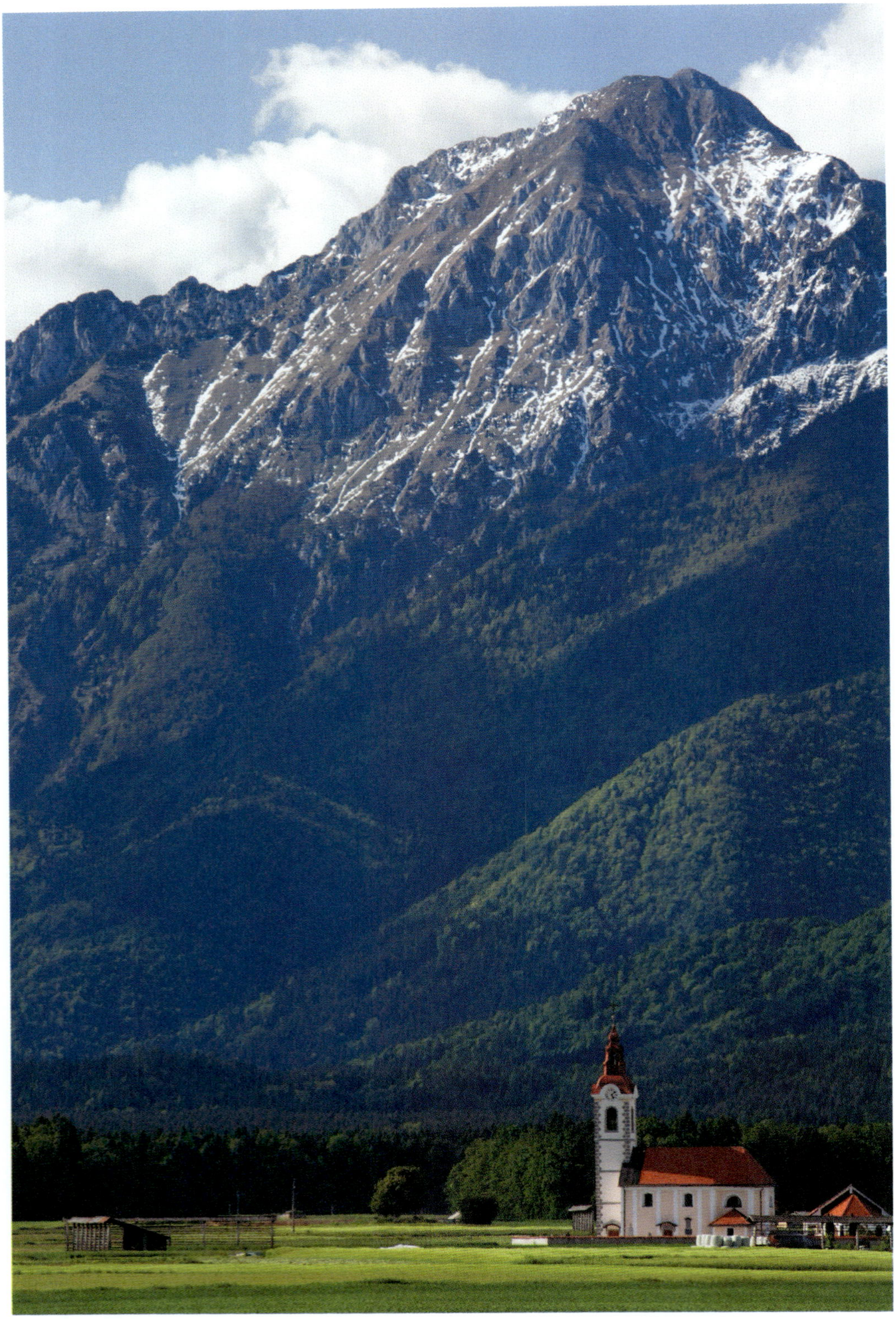

The photo below, also taken in Slovenia, was shot from a distance using a 400mm focal length.

By moving back to a distance and zooming in, I have made the background mountain a dominant feature of the scene, and the church now pales in comparison.

Again I have exaggerated the scale, only this time to make the background object appear larger in comparison to the foreground object.

Had I moved closer to the church and used a shorter focal length, the church would appear larger in the frame, and the mountain, by comparison, wouldn't be so large.

It also gives the illusion of the mountain being right behind the church, when in fact it's many miles away.

Never underestimate the power of a telephoto lens for landscapes

Telephoto lenses play a more predominant role in portrait photography (for reasons you will see later in the aperture section) and wildlife photography: the latter also for obvious reasons, (You don't really want to get close to a grizzly bear, now do you?). Shorter focal lengths and wide angles are often preferred for landscapes, but telephotos are often overlooked as a lens for landscape photography. But, as we have just seen and will see now, they can play a great role:

This dramatic sunset over the western mountains in Slovenia was taken from a church on a hill in the northeast, about 50kms away, using a 400mm focal length.

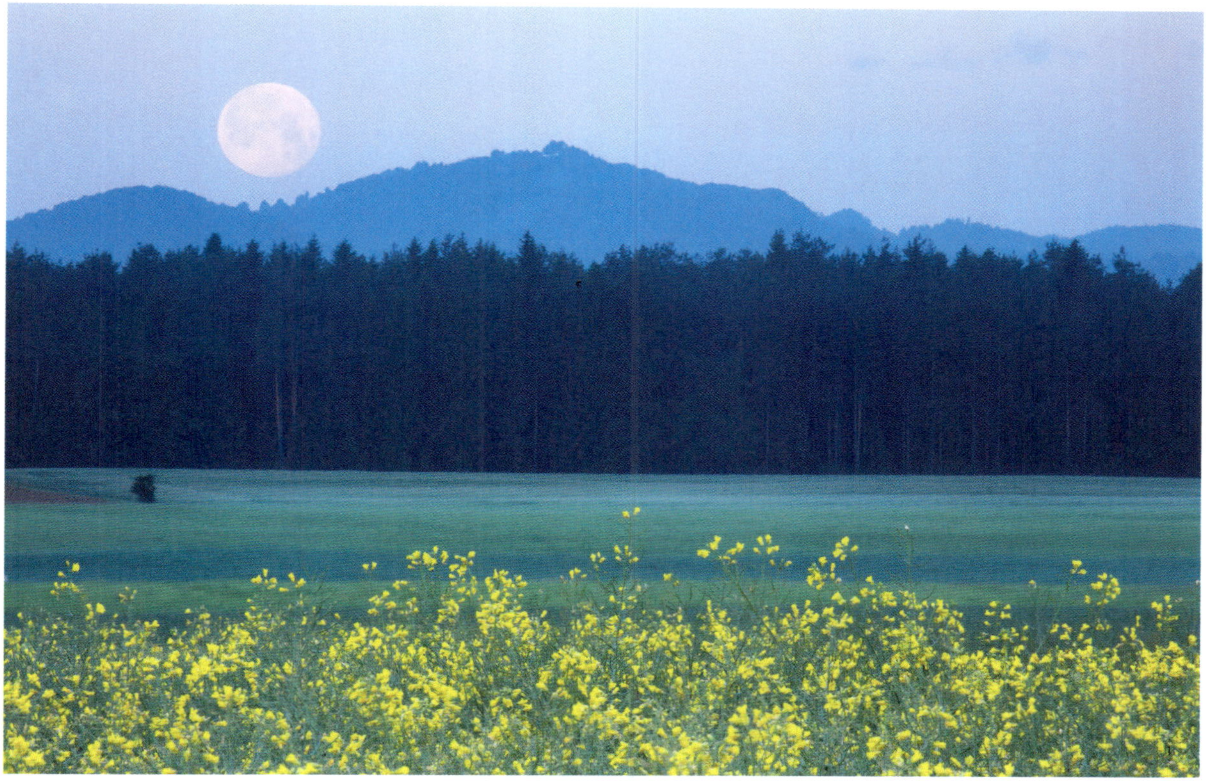

Here I have used a 320mm focal length to exaggerate the size of the setting full moon. The rapeseed was close to me, so unlike the previous photo, where the church was further away, it appears larger in the frame. Once again it gives the illusion that the moon is much closer to the rapeseed.

A telephoto is great for sunsets and sunrises

A telephoto not only makes the sun much bigger in the frame, but can also isolate the area around the setting sun which is the most intense part of the sunset; as you can see by this photo taken from an apartment balcony in Ljubljana using a 400mm focal length.

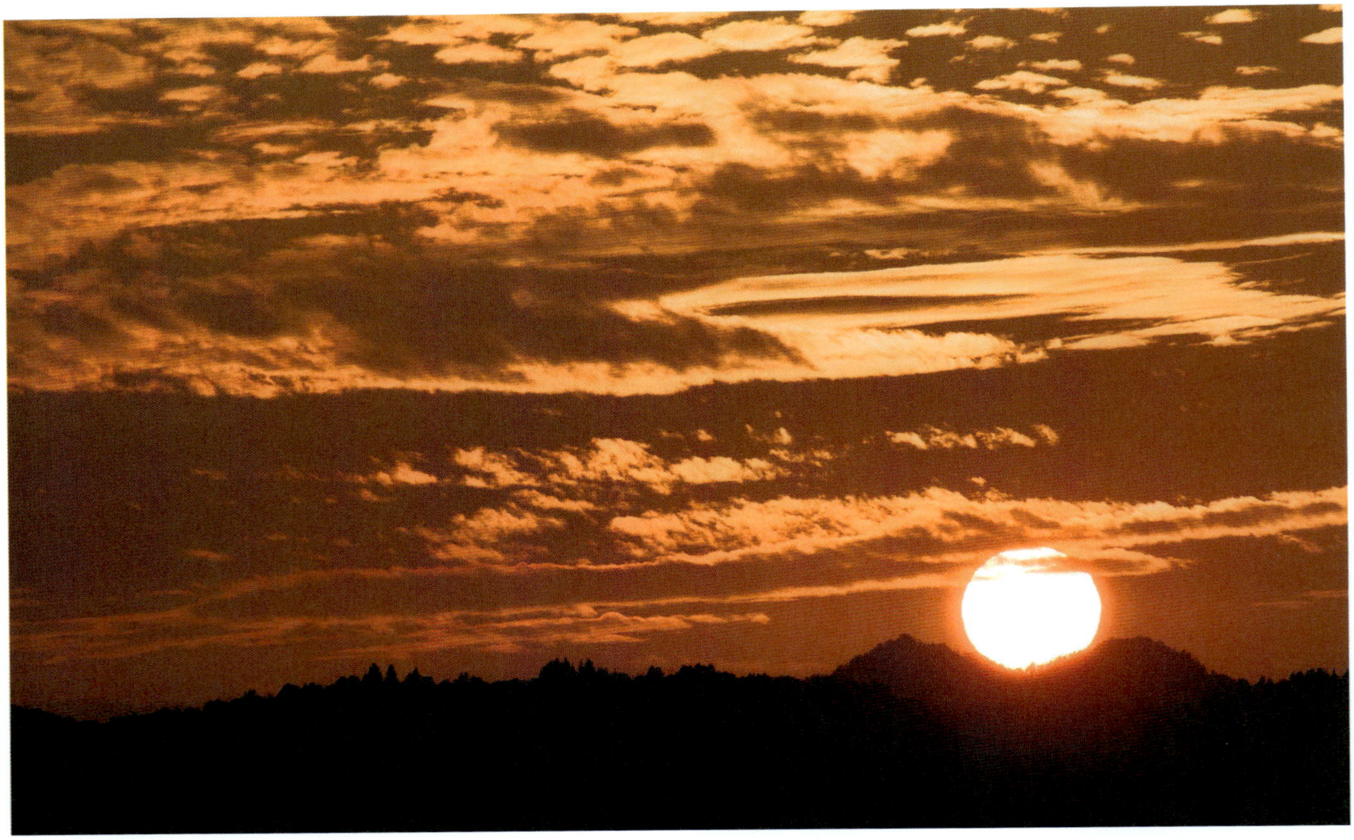

As sunrises go, this was not exactly the most exciting. But by zooming in and isolating a part of the scene where the sun was rising, I have captured the best of the colour, and got a nice church in the shot too.

Incidentally, this is the same church from where I took the sunset photo on the previous page. This photo was taken about halfway between the church and those mountains.

Digital zooms

A digital zoom works on a similar principle of cropping and enlarging the image, but at the expense of image quality.

You will notice that if you use your digital zoom compared to your optical zoom, the optical zoom will produce better results. This is because the optical zoom captures the cropped image at full resolution, whereas the digital zoom crops into the full res image and the resulting image is at a lower resolution, and is then increased in size by the camera's software.

The following images illustrate this:

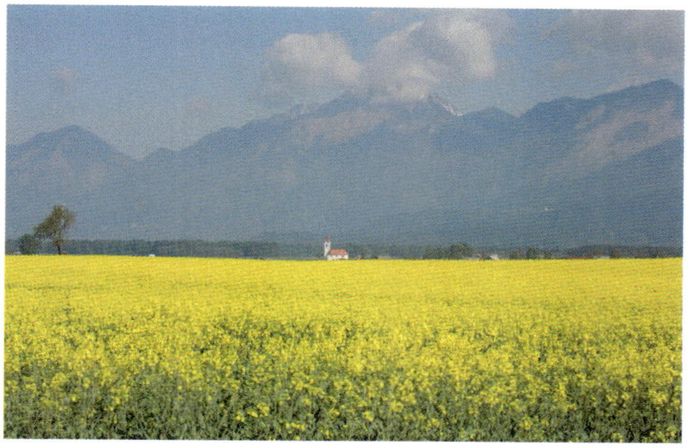

Original 12mp image

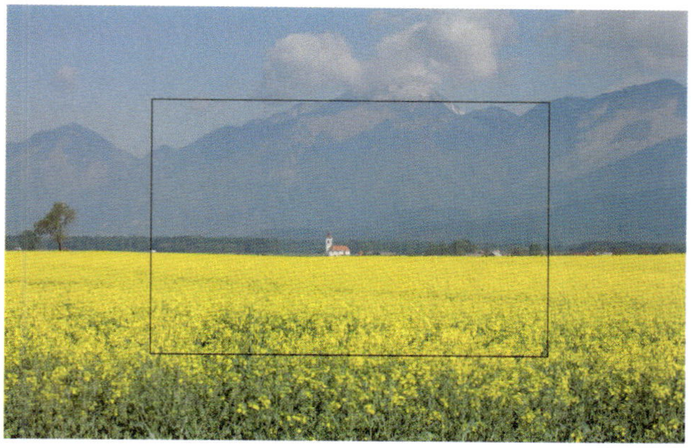

12mp image gets cropped in half

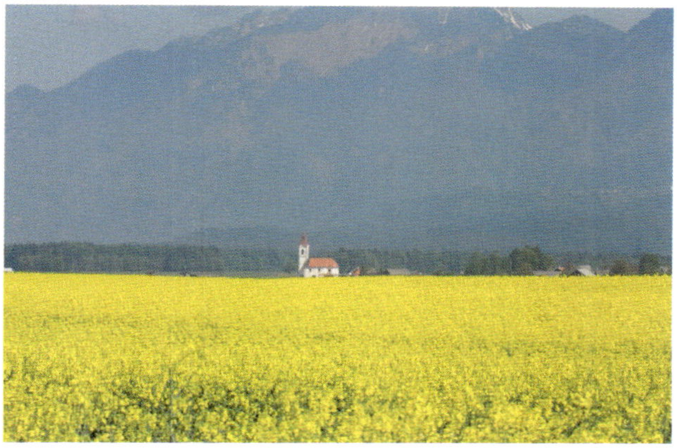

Image is then re-sized back to 12mp
(with loss of quality)

Unlike the optical zoom, there is no change in the angle of light. The focal length is not altered and essentially the original image is just cropped and re-sized using software within the camera. You can achieve the same effect with much more control by doing it yourself on the computer and using better software to obtain a higher quality end image.

If you have the capability, it's best to shoot in RAW and then crop your image to get closer. (See part 9)

Part 4
Focusing (Auto and Manual)

Every photo has a point of focus, and you nearly always choose this yourself; rarely should you let the camera decide for you, unless your camera doesn't allow it. Even then you can move your camera around and lock the focus by half pressing the button you use to take photos, then recomposing and pressing the button down fully to take the shot. The focal point of a scene can be in a variety of places, therefore selection of different focal points is made by adjusting the lens.

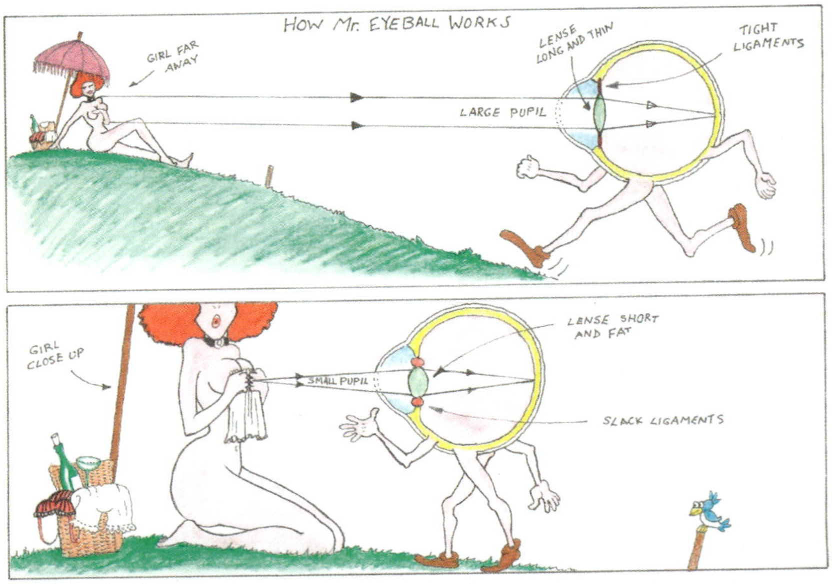

Illustration by David Selwood

Lens is thin or flat: the eye is focused on distant objects.
Lens is fat or squashed: the eye is focused on close objects

Eyes:
Just as our eyes can focus on different objects at different distances, so can the camera. They just do it differently. The eye can change the shape of its lens by using ciliary muscles to squash or relax the lens, which alters the refraction of the light.

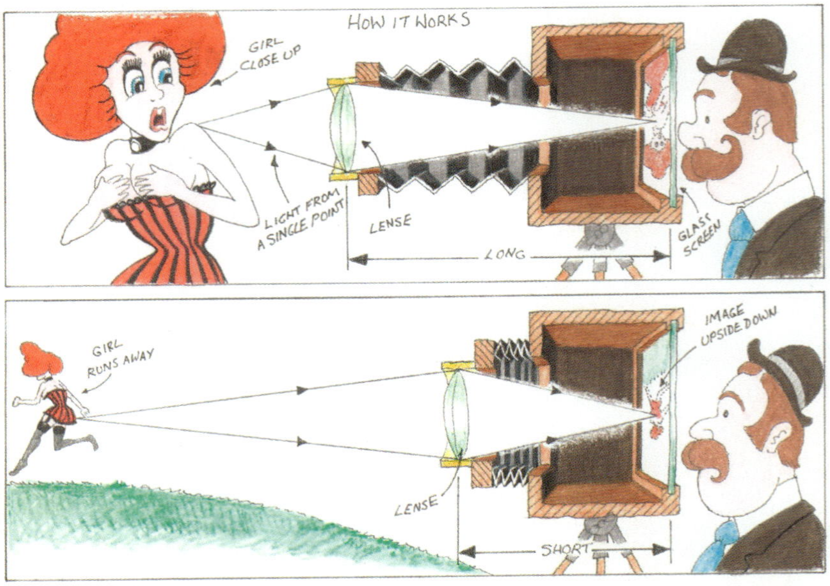

Illustration by David Selwood

Camera:
Of course the camera lens is made of glass and cannot be altered in this way; therefore the lens itself is moved back and forth instead. By varying the distance between the lens and the focal plane we can change the focal point. Essentially the camera is making small adjustments to the focal length in order to focus on a given subject within the scene. This can be done manually or automatically. When the gap measures the lens's given focal length, ie 50mm, then the focus is at infinity. This means that the focal point is far in the distance, such as the horizon. As the focal length increases, the point of focus is closer to the camera. So with an object close to the camera, the focal length is slightly more than 50mm.

Multi-segment focal points and how we can select our focus point.

Always think about your focal point; your point of focus is rarely in the middle of the frame.

Automatic focusing (AF)

Focus points selection options:

- Single point
- Multipoint

Tip: The focus is set according to the distance between you and your subject. Any movement backwards or forwards, either of you or your subject, after the focus has been locked, will throw your subject out of focus. You will need to refocus.

All digital cameras have multi-segment focusing which allows you to use several focus points as well as the main one in the centre. How many they have depends on the camera. It's important to note that the central focus point will always be the most accurate. That being said, the outer points are still very reliable and should be used when composing and choosing your point of focus.

Single point: As the name suggests, this allows you to individually choose one of the points. This is very precise and can help you to focus more exactly on a very small area of the scene. As you can see in each picture, a different focus point has been selected.

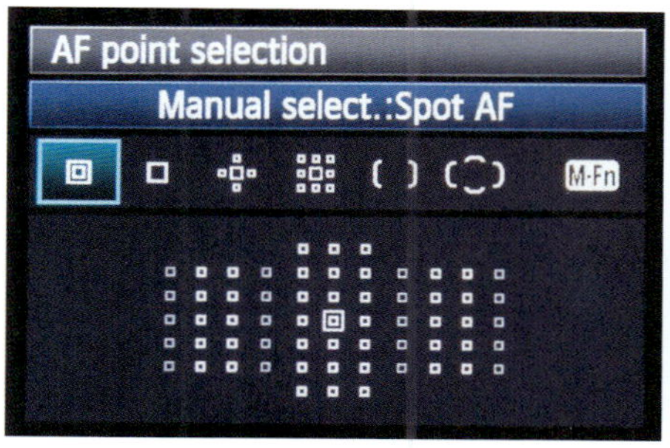

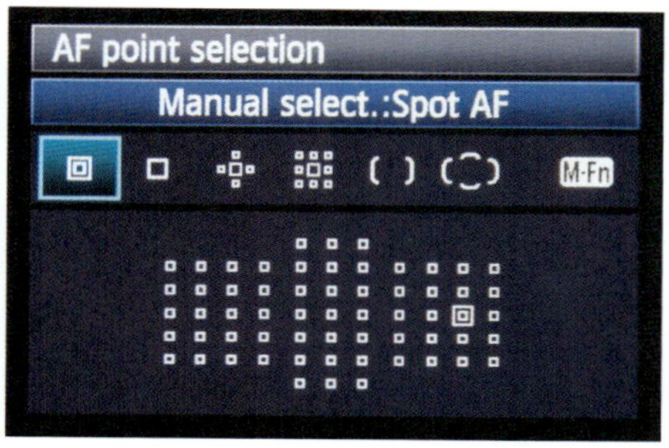

Multipoint selection: This option selects either all the points or multiple points and the camera will then automatically select a point, or an average of several points according to the scene it's seeing. This is useful when your subject is large, for tricky scenes where the light is low and for moving subjects such as people or fireworks. The images above show an expanded AF, where several segments are selected and you can move them about the scene. This still gives you some control over the area you wish to focus on, but also makes it a little easier.

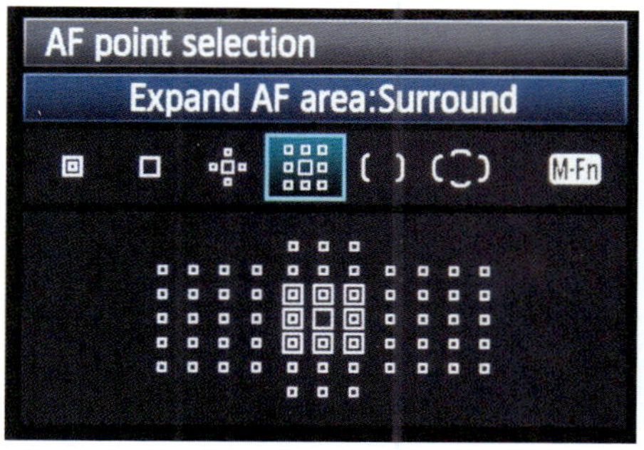

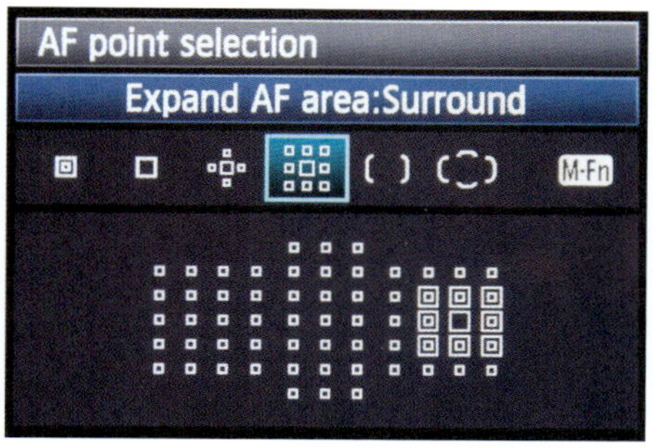

In the image to the left you can see that the whole 61 points have been selected. This is the full auto mode and the camera will choose the focus point from somewhere within that scene.

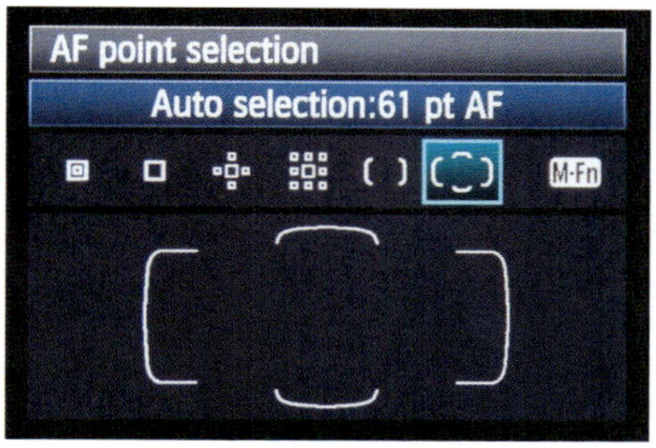

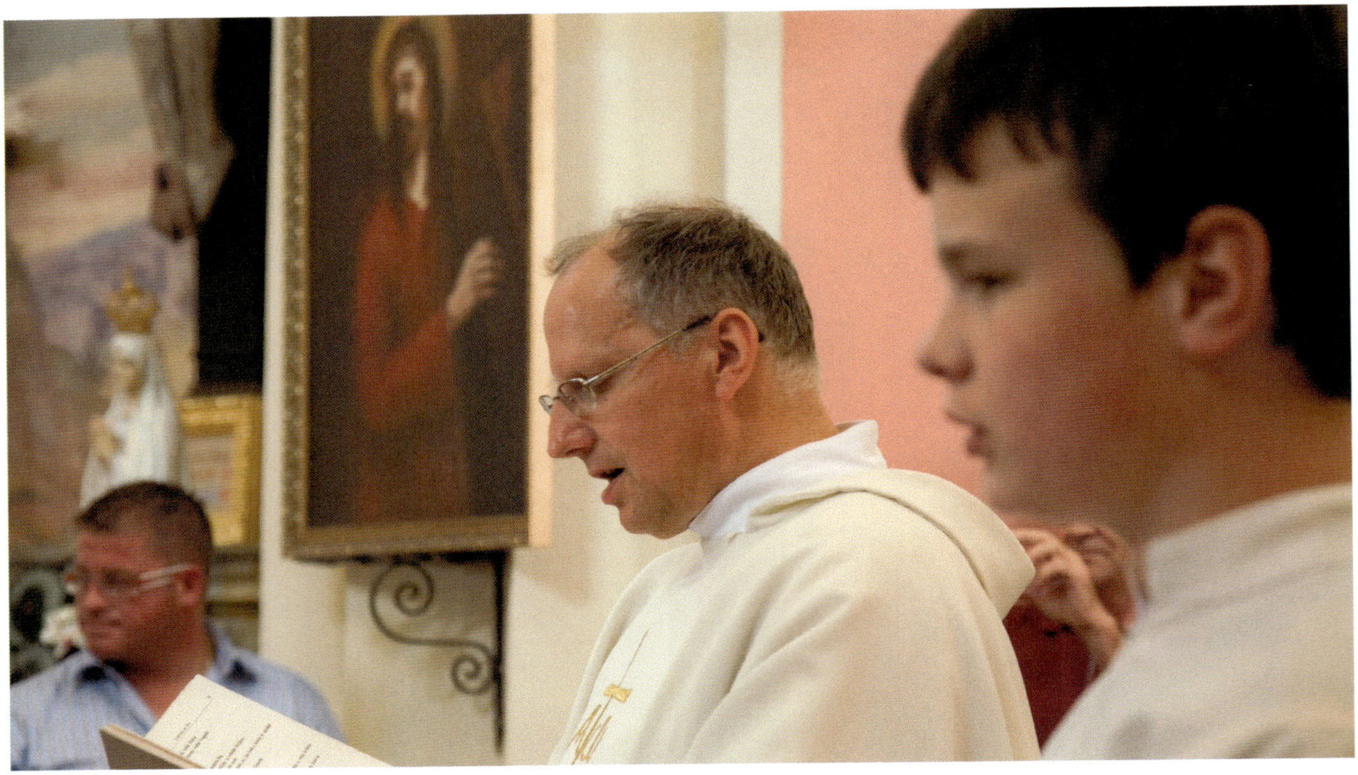

Centre focal point selected, focus is on the priest

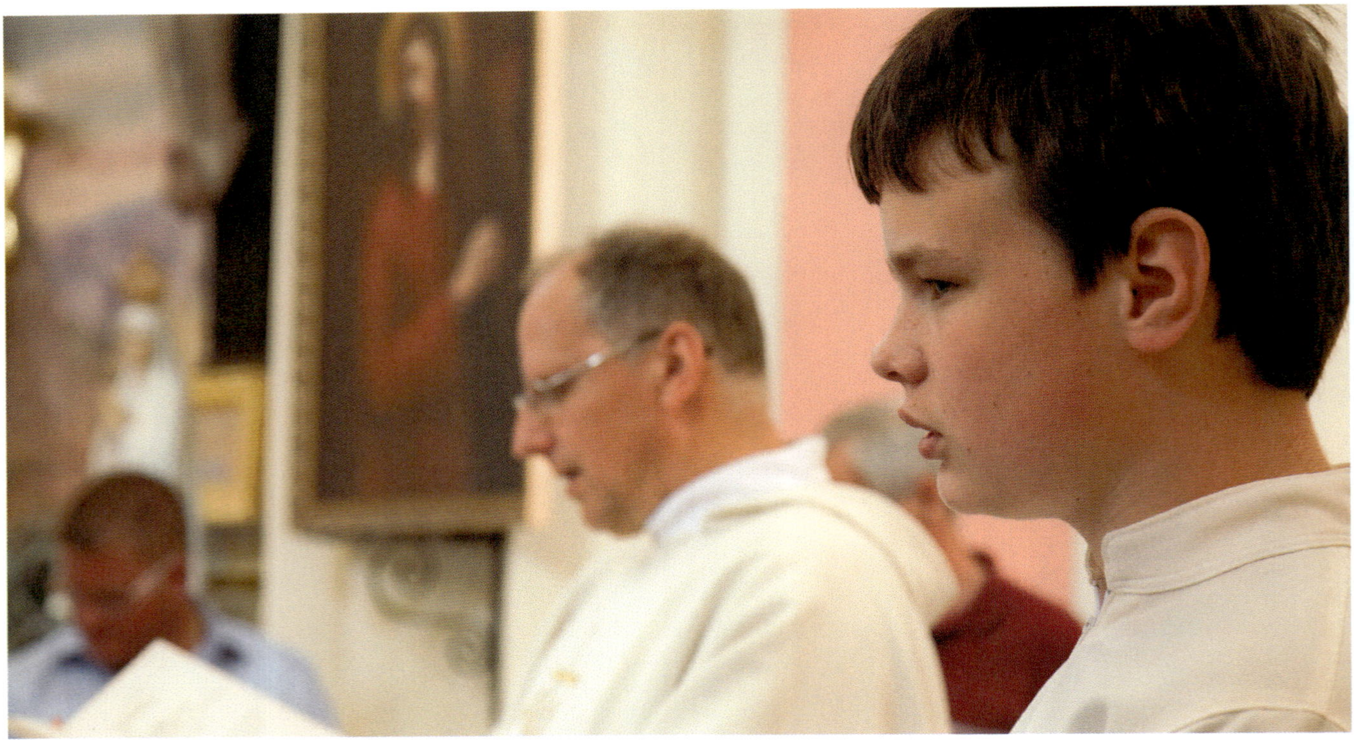

Right focal point selected, so focus is now on the altar boy

Focusing modes

Most digital SLRs and some advanced compacts allow you to choose from three focusing modes:

One shot: Different cameras may have different names for this, as seen in the table below, however the principle is the same. When you choose this mode the focus will lock on your subject when you half press the shutter button and remain locked in that position as long as you hold the button half down. You are then free to move your camera without altering the focus position. This is ideal for static subjects that are out of range of the focus points. You can lock the focus and then re-frame your shot to place the subject elsewhere within the frame.

Tip: Be careful not to move the camera back or forth because you will alter the distance between you and the subject, which in turn will render your subject out of focus and you will have to re-focus. When recomposing, ensure you only make the side to side movements, and keep them to a minimum.

Continuous shooting: This mode will lock on to your subject and track it while you are holding down the shutter halfway. The AF continues to autofocus until you press the shutter completely. This mode is typically used on moving subjects so as to ensure that the subject stays in focus.

One shot / continuous: This is an in-between mode, where the camera locks the focus but will re-focus should the subject move any significant amount.

Focus mode	Use
One shot: Canon cameras - One shot Nikon cameras - (Single servo AF-S)	Static subjects, landscapes
One shot / continuous: Canon cameras - AI focus Nikon cameras – Auto servo AF-A)	Static subjects that could move a little
Continuous: Canon cameras - AI servo Nikon cameras – Continuous servo AF-C)	Moving subjects

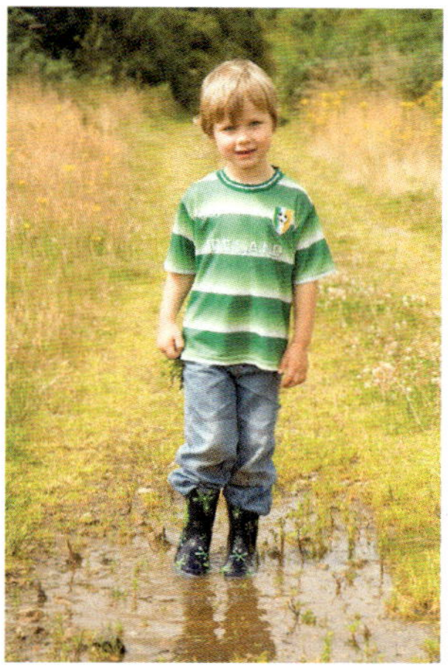

One shot mode
As the boy was standing still here, one shot mode was all that was needed.

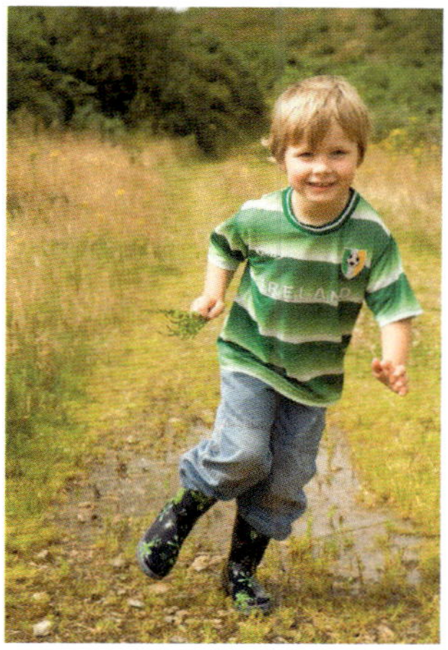

Continuous mode
Here the boy was running through the puddle, and more importantly, running towards me. That meant the distance between the camera and him was changing. By using the continuous autofocus mode, I was able to shoot a number of photos continuously, with the camera continuously focusing and tracking, so the boy remained in focus in each photo.

Part 5
The exposure triangle
(Shutter speed, aperture, ISO)

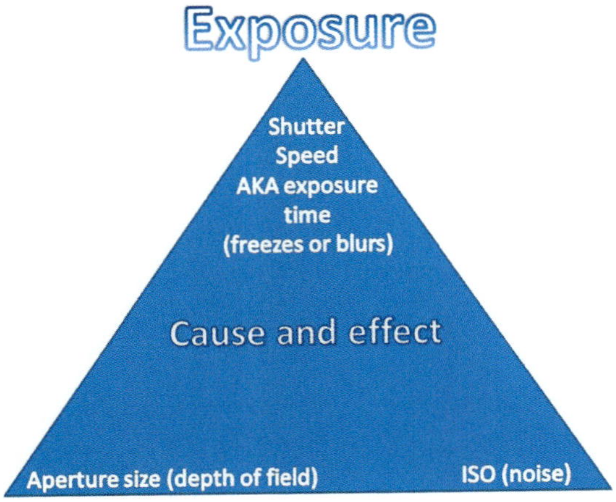

The three elements:

In order to capture our image onto the sensor or film we must expose it to light. This is known as exposure. There are three elements to consider when exposing for a photo. All three work together in a kind of cause and effect manner. In order to get the photo right, when you adjust one, you have to adjust another; whether this is done automatically by the camera, or manually by the photographer. It's not as simple as choosing each setting and firing away. Adjusting each element also has an effect on the image itself:

- **Shutter speed** (determines how moving objects will appear in your image. A fast shutter speed will freeze movement, while a slow shutter speed will blur it.)
- **Aperture** (affects "depth of field", which will determine how much of your background is either sharp or out of focus.)
- **ISO** (increasing this will also add more noise into your image.)

So to understand this, we need to look at each one in turn. As shutter speed is the most obvious (this is the clicking sound you hear when you take a photo) we will start with this.

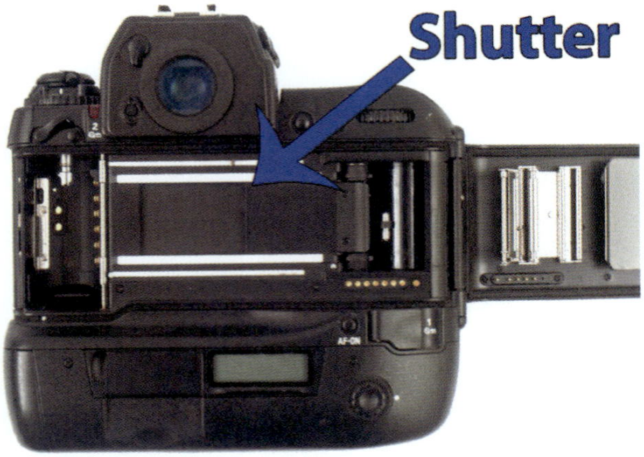

© ProductionPerig | Dreamstime.com

Shutter Speed (AKA - Exposure Time)

Naturally, as our eyes are seeing constantly moving images, our retina is permanently exposed to the light.

However, this is not the case with photography. In order to capture an image you must expose the sensor or film to the light for a period of time, known as exposure time.

Inside your camera there is a shutter that acts as a kind of curtain. When the shutter button is pressed the curtain is pulled back and light is allowed to fall upon the sensor/film. The shutter is then closed and the image is frozen in place. In essence, for the duration that the sensor/film is exposed the image is drawn upon it. With film the roll is moved on to another empty frame, and with digital the image is then transferred to the memory card and saved.

Shutter speed (exposure time) is measured in the time that the shutter is open, usually in a fraction of a second such as:
1/125 second (125th of a second).

Shutter speed adjustment is measured in stops:

- Full increments (double or half the previous speed)
- Half (1/2 a stop)
- Third increments (1/3 of a stop)

So for a shutter of 1/125,
Shutter

- One stop slower is 1/60
- One stop faster is 1/250

The table to the right shows this.

Shutter speeds (stops)			Shutter speeds (stops)		
Halves	Whole	Thirds	Halves	Whole	Thirds
	1/8000	1/6400		1/15	1/13
1/6000		1/5000	1/10		1/10
	1/4000	1/3200		1/8	1/6
1/3000		1/2500	1/6		1/5
	1/2000	1/1600		1/4	1/0.3
1/1500		1/1250	1/0.3		1/0.4
	1/1000	1/800		1/0.5	1/0.6
1/750		1/640	1/0.7		1/0.8
	1/500	1/400		1 sec	1.3 sec
1/350		1/320	1.5 sec		1.6 sec
	1/250	1/200		2 sec	2.5 sec
1/180		1/160	3 sec		3.2 sec
	1/125	1/100		4 sec	5 sec
1/90		1/80	6 sec		6 sec
	1/60	1/50		8 sec	10 sec
1/45		1/40	10 sec		13 sec
	1/30	1/25		15 sec	20 sec
1/20		1/20	20		25 sec
				30 sec	

Shutter speeds are a classic example of how the light draws the picture. Therefore, how long you expose for can make a huge difference to how your image looks. Any moving objects will be drawn according to the length of exposure.

Thus when there is movement in the scene:

A slow shutter speed (long exposure) will record this movement into what is called "motion blur", but onto one image.

A fast shutter speed (short exposure) will freeze the movement.

While in some low end compact or phone cameras you may not get the option to adjust shutter speed. many cameras today allow you at least some control. Even if they don't, knowledge of how this works will help you understand why your photos are blurred in some cases, especially when photographing moving subjects when the light is low.

Here are some examples of shutter speeds and their uses:

At a glance - Effects:
Slow speed = blur
Fast speed = freezes

Shutter Speed	Example Use
1 - 30+ seconds	Night and low-light photos on a tripod. Also used for misty/silky effect on sea or other flowing water.
2 - 1/2 second	To add a silky look to fast flowing water. Landscape photos on a tripod for enhanced depth of field.
1/2 to 1/30 second	To add motion blur to the background of a moving subject. Carefully taken handheld photos with image stabiliser.
1/50 - 1/125 second	Typical handheld photos with short focal lengths. Rule of thumb for handheld is minimum speed must equal the focal length. Eg: 50mm = 1/50sec + 100mm = 1/100 +
1/250 - 1/500 second	To freeze everyday sports / action subject movement. Handheld photos with long focal length (telephoto lens).
1/1000 - 1/4000 second	To freeze extremely fast, up-close subject motion.

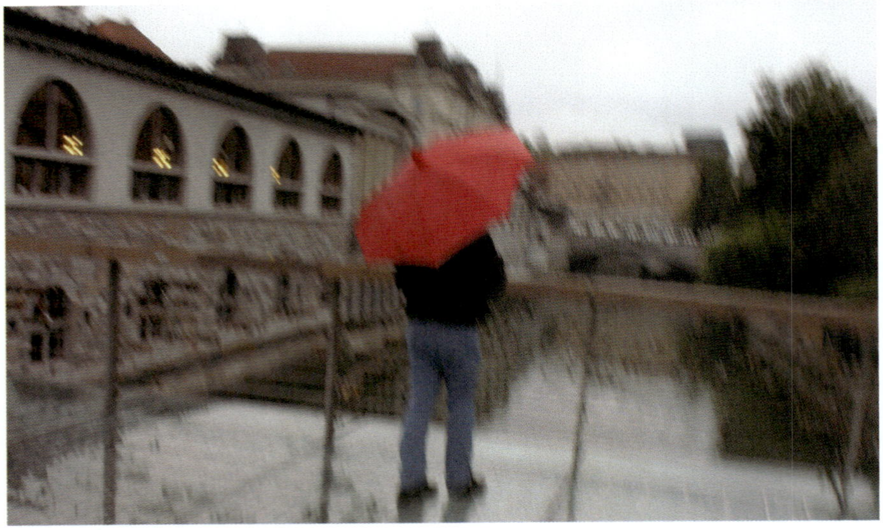

Camera shake: It's important to note that slow shutter speeds cannot be done handheld because your photo will be blurred due to vibration from camera shake. No matter how steady you think you are holding your camera, it's probably not enough.

Shutter speed 1/50 sec - This image was shot handheld. See how the slow shutter speed has resulted in a blurred image.

Minimum handheld shutter speed = 1/125 sec
This is what I consider to be the best speed to use handheld. But a lot also depends on your equipment, and the conditions you are working in.

- If it's cold, you will shiver.
- If your equipment is heavy (big long lens), you will struggle to hold it still.
- If you are working in an awkward place, or your having to stand tiptoe or crouch down for your shot, it will be harder to hold the camera steady.

Long lenses

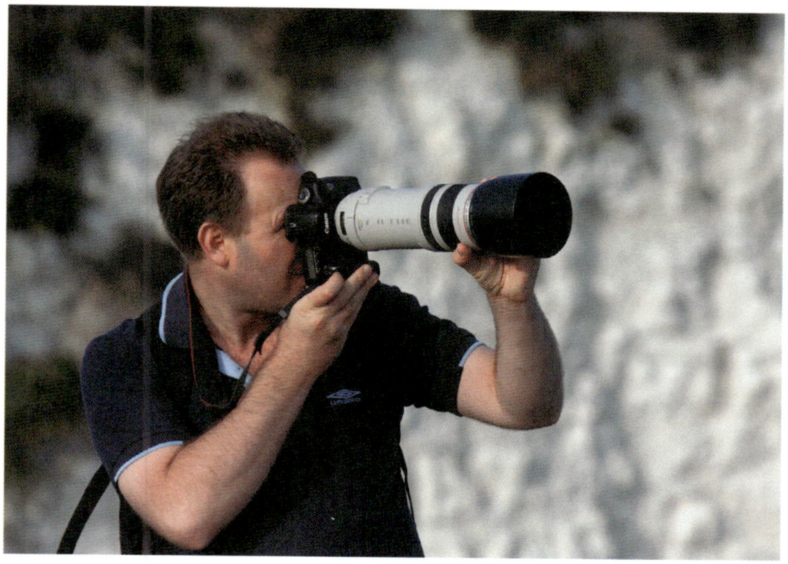

For zoom or telephoto lenses, the rule of thumb is to shoot at a shutter speed equal to or higher than the focal length.

IE: 500mm = 1/500 sec

But of course it also depends on the type of lens. A cheap lightweight zoom will be easier to hold still than an expensive top of the range lens, which is larger and heavier.

The image below was shot handheld at 1/400 at 380mm using the lens in the photo to the right. It's a heavy lens, and so is the camera, so I took no chances.

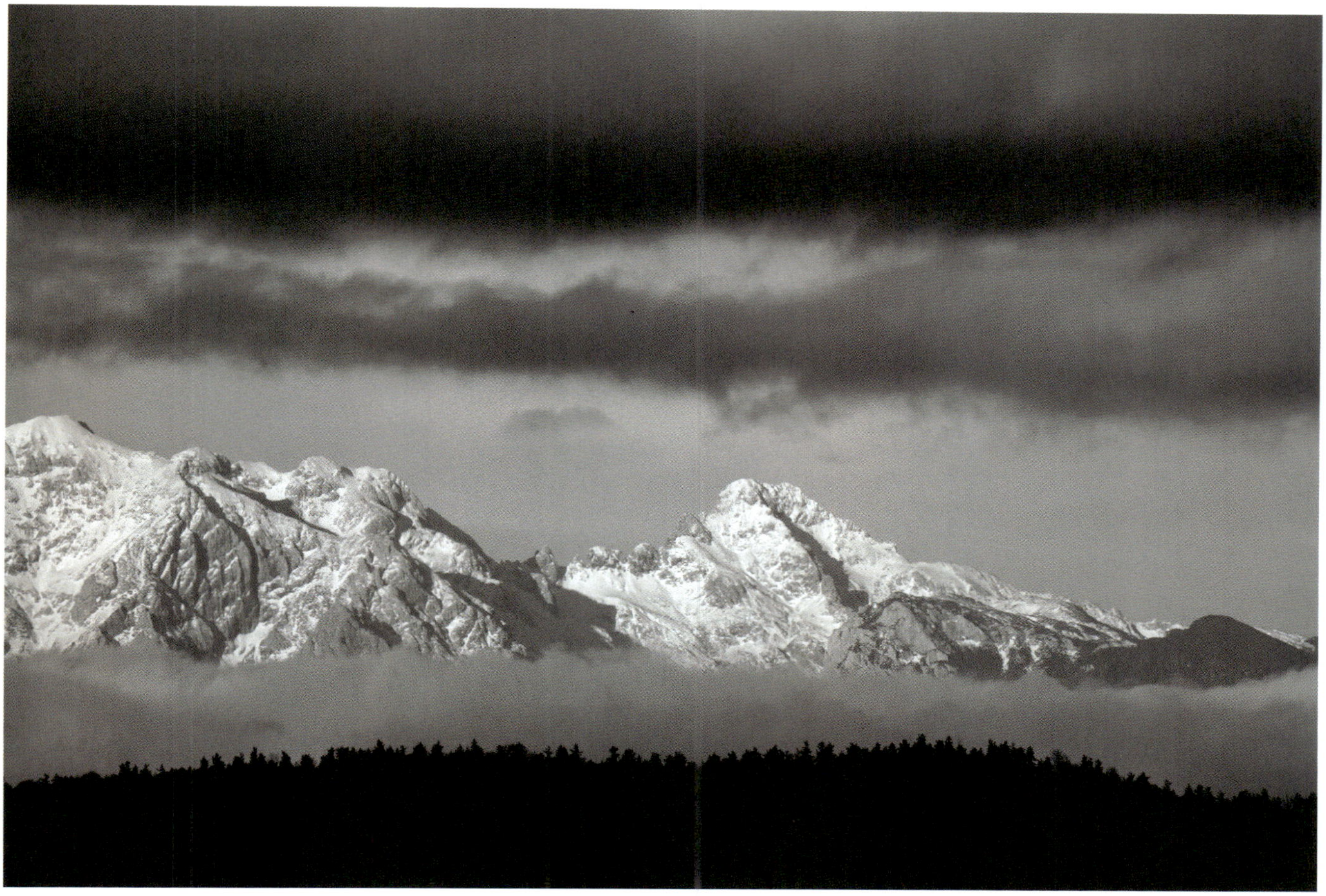

Image stabilisation/Vibration Reduction

Some more expensive lenses have the above feature which allows you to shoot handheld at slightly lower shutter speeds. However, it usually only allows about two stops below normal, and again comes with a compromise: *Softens the image.* This might be acceptable for some portraits, but definitely not for landscapes.

Tripod or increased shutter speed?

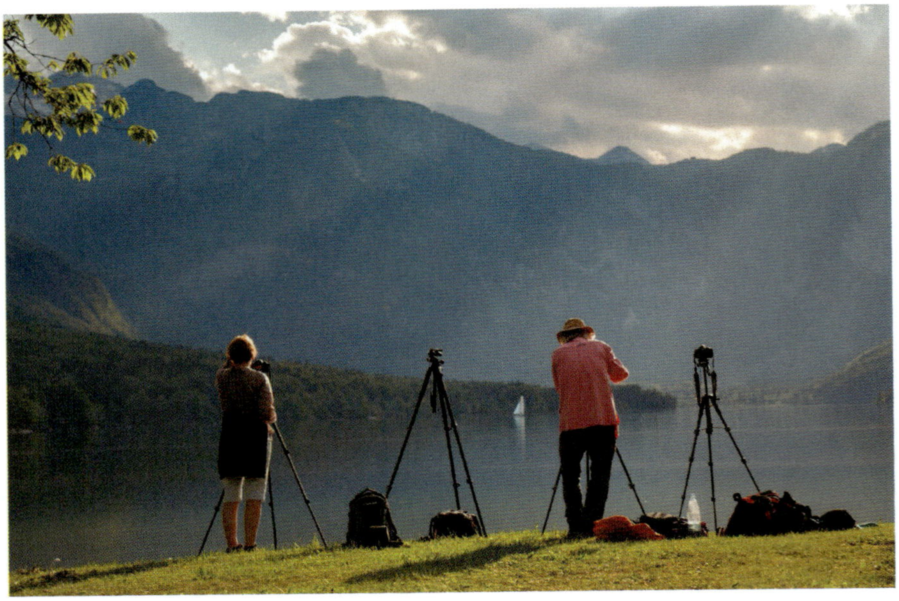

Shutter speeds below around 1/125 sec (depending on how steady your hand is or how heavy your camera is) typically need a tripod, or some other form of support to keep the camera from moving. Even the slightest movement or vibration will cause unwanted blurring in your image and a loss of sharpness.

You can also use a beanbag when shooting over walls, from car windows or on the floor. When shooting in low light or in conditions that require a long exposure, we want to keep the image sharp and free from blurring due to vibration. So the only way to do this is to increase the shutter speed, or use a tripod.

However, a tripod can only be used if your scene is still. If people are in your scene then they will be blurred, even if they are standing still. Like with holding a camera still, people cannot stand perfectly still no matter how hard they try.

Also watch out for leaves or grass blowing in the wind, or boats floating on water (unless you want this effect). Study your scene to see if using a tripod will work, or whether you have to increase the shutter speed.

Important note: If you are using a fast shutter speed, a tripod or other support, make sure you turn off the image stabilisation function. If you don't then image sharpness will be compromised because the camera assumes there is camera shake when it's on and tries to compensate regardless. So it actually creates some.

Unwanted Motion Blur

Although setting the right shutter speed avoids camera shake blur, there is also the problem of motion blur when it's not wanted. When people, especially children and babies, are moving then you need to consider how fast they are moving and increase the shutter speed accordingly.

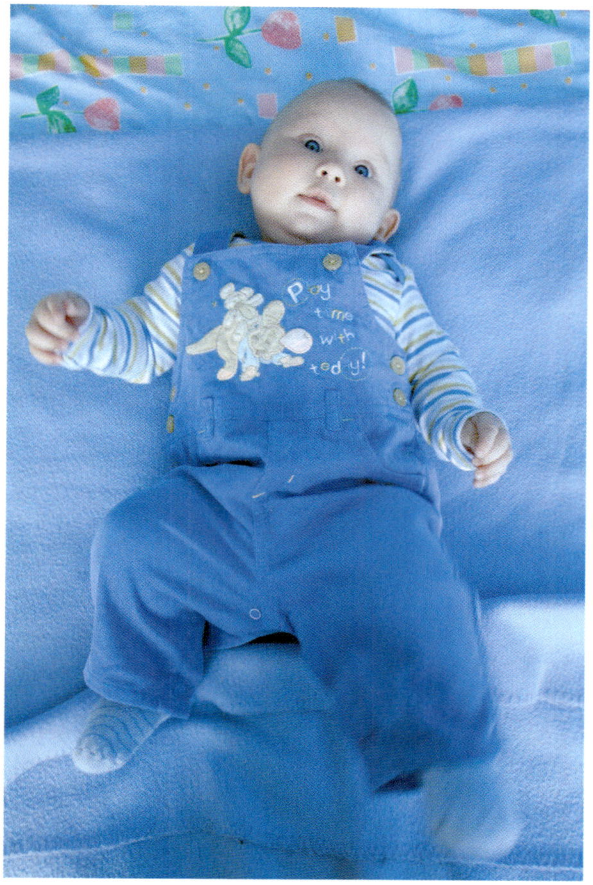

1/60 sec (moving foot and hand are blurred)
Although this was shot with the image stabiliser switched on to avoid camera shake, moving subjects can also cause blur when the shutter speed is too slow.

You either need to increase the shutter speed to at least 1/200 sec in a situation like this, or keep the subject still (not so easy with babies!)

Avoiding Unwanted Motion Blur

In order to avoid this problem, you either need to increase your shutter speed to freeze the movement, or like I did here, be patient and wait for the movement to stop, then be ready to quickly take your shot. Sometimes the situation won't allow for a faster shutter speed.

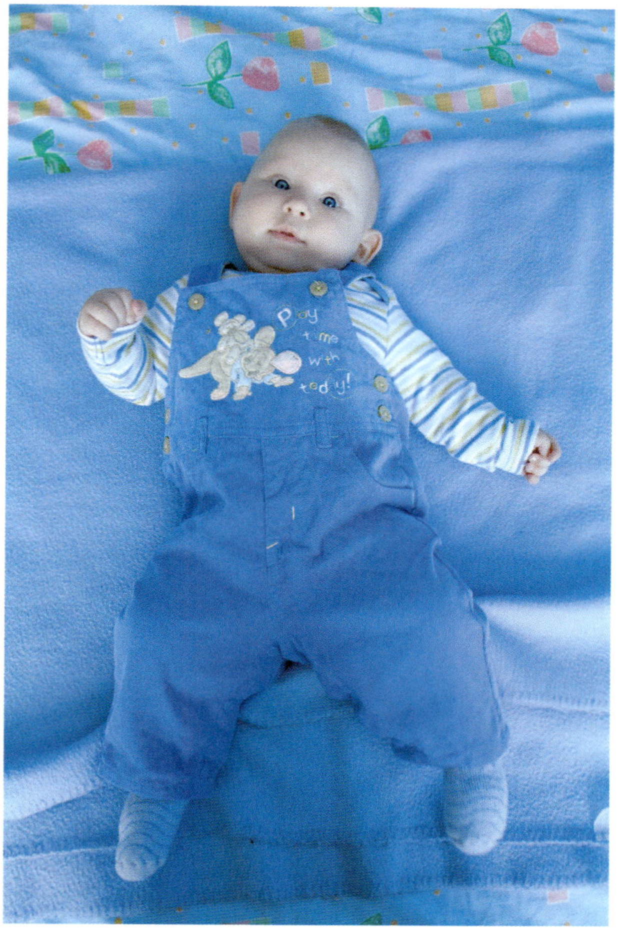

Unavoidable Motion Blur

Sometimes it's simply not possible to avoid. On this photo I needed to make a long exposure because it was dawn and the light was very low. Even though it was morning and the lake was still, the boats were drifting slightly.

I exposed for 20 seconds praying for as little movement as possible. Only the boats on the far left and right moved enough to create some blur. But overall I think the effect worked quite well.

20 second exposure

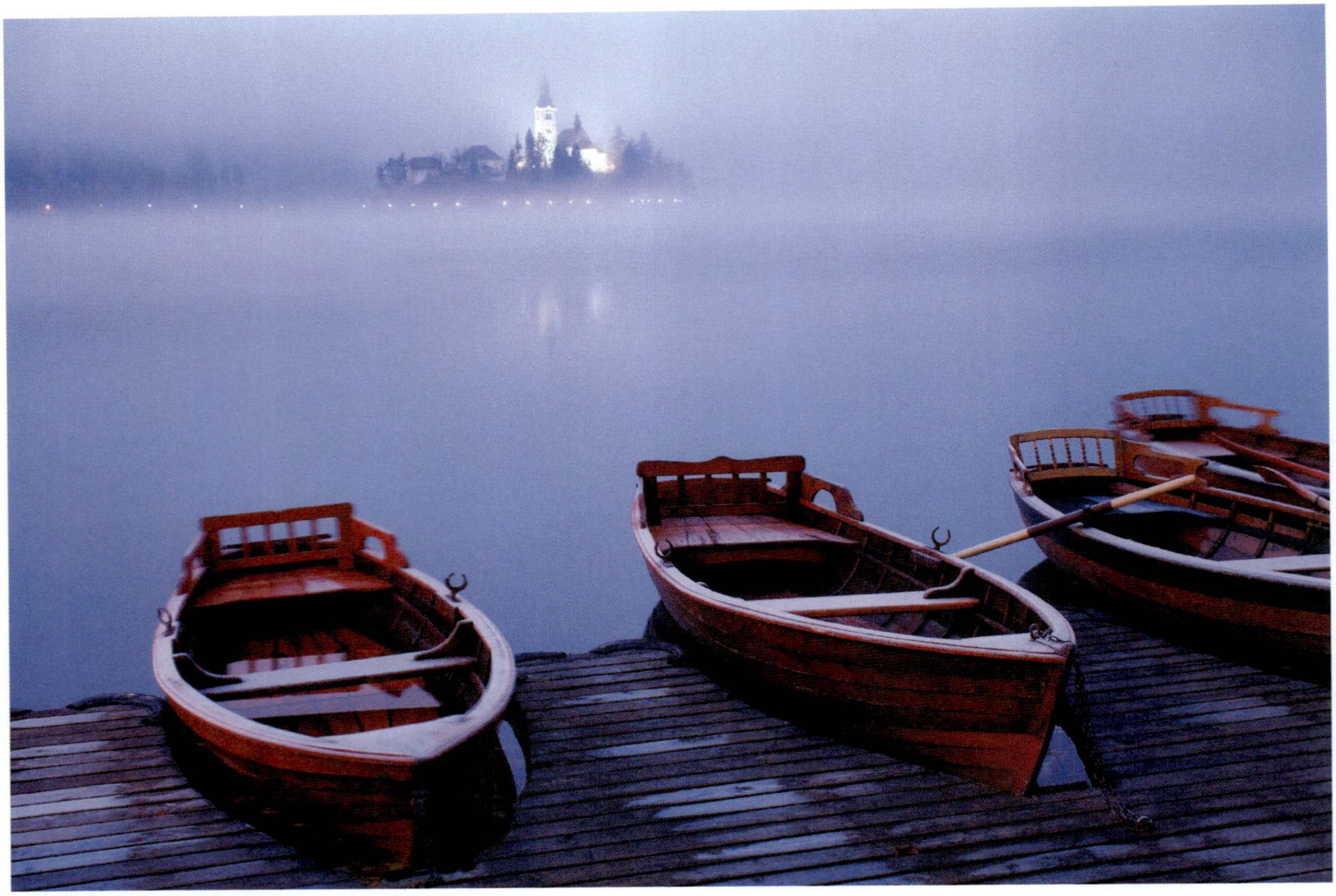

Long exposures (creative blur)

Sometimes we want to use blur in our images to creative effect. This is especially true with water, clouds and even people or vehicles. Below are a few examples, again all shot on a tripod. You can also do this with your compact camera if you place it on a tripod. This is not the magic of expensive cameras, it's all down to slowing down the shutter speed.

Fast flowing water becomes smooth and silky during long exposures

1/0.3 sec

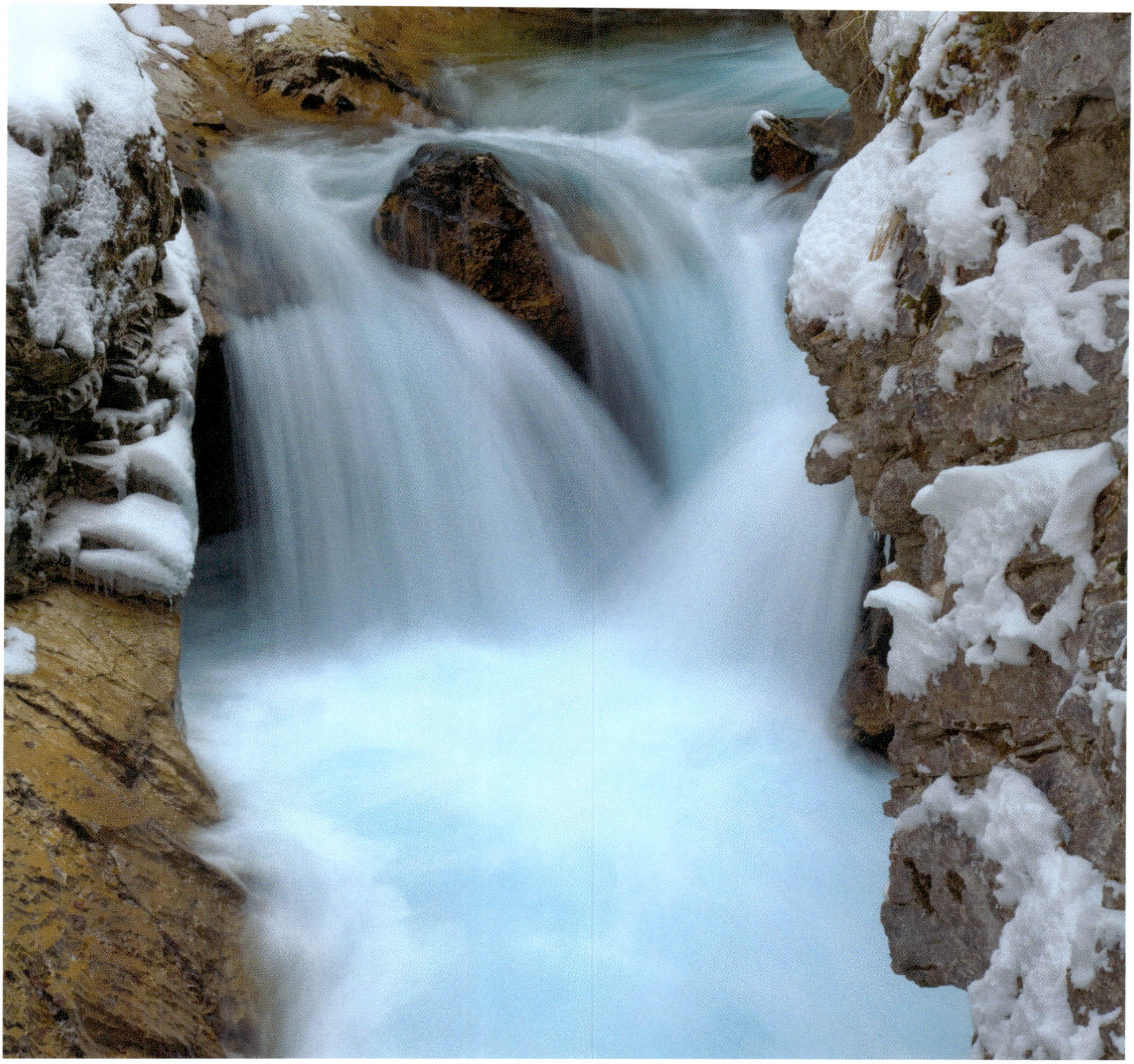

1/30 sec

This shorter exposure (faster shutter speed) has partially frozen the water but still left some sense of movement.

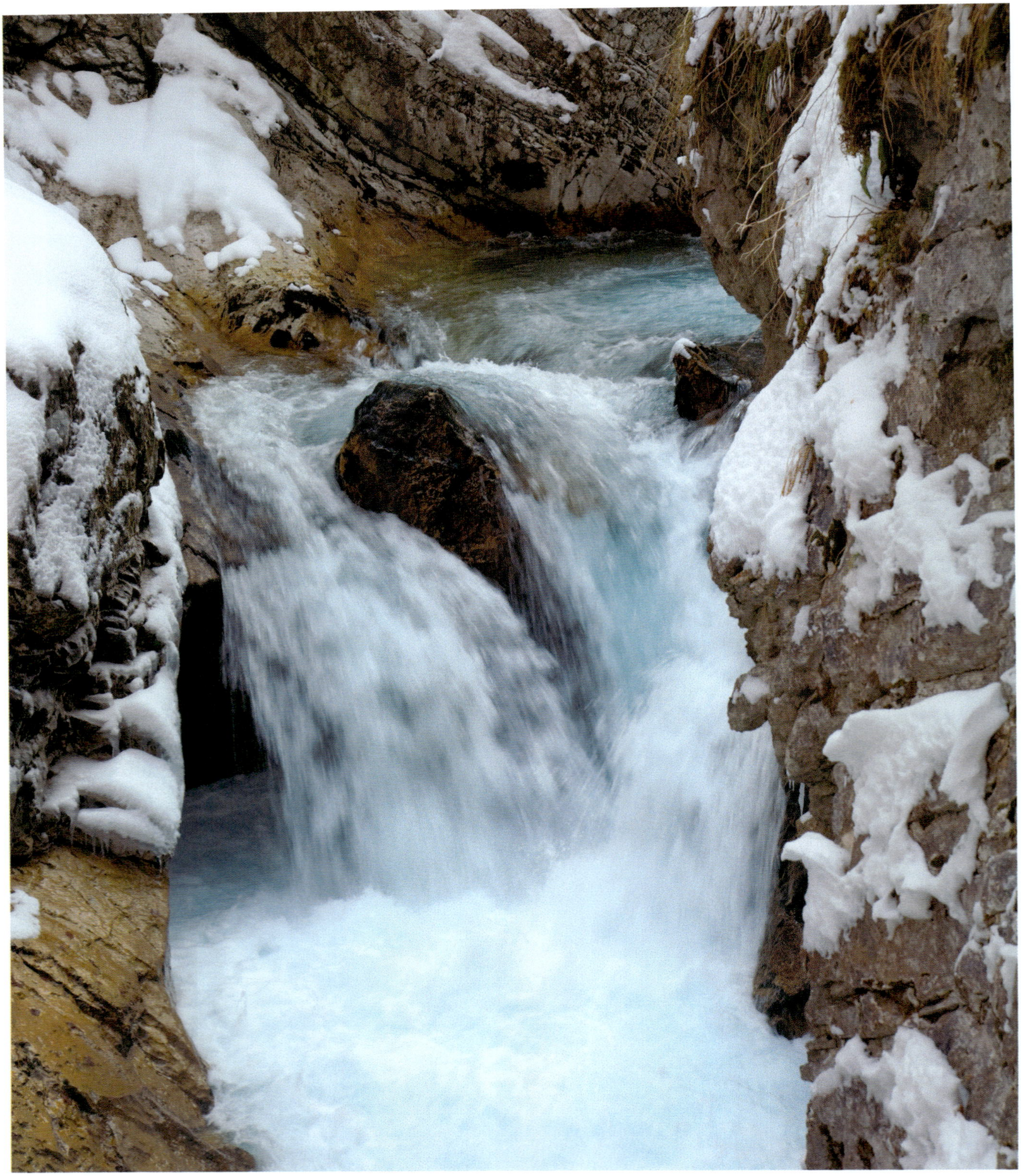

15 sec

This much longer exposure (slower shutter speed) has created a dreamy effect on the water.

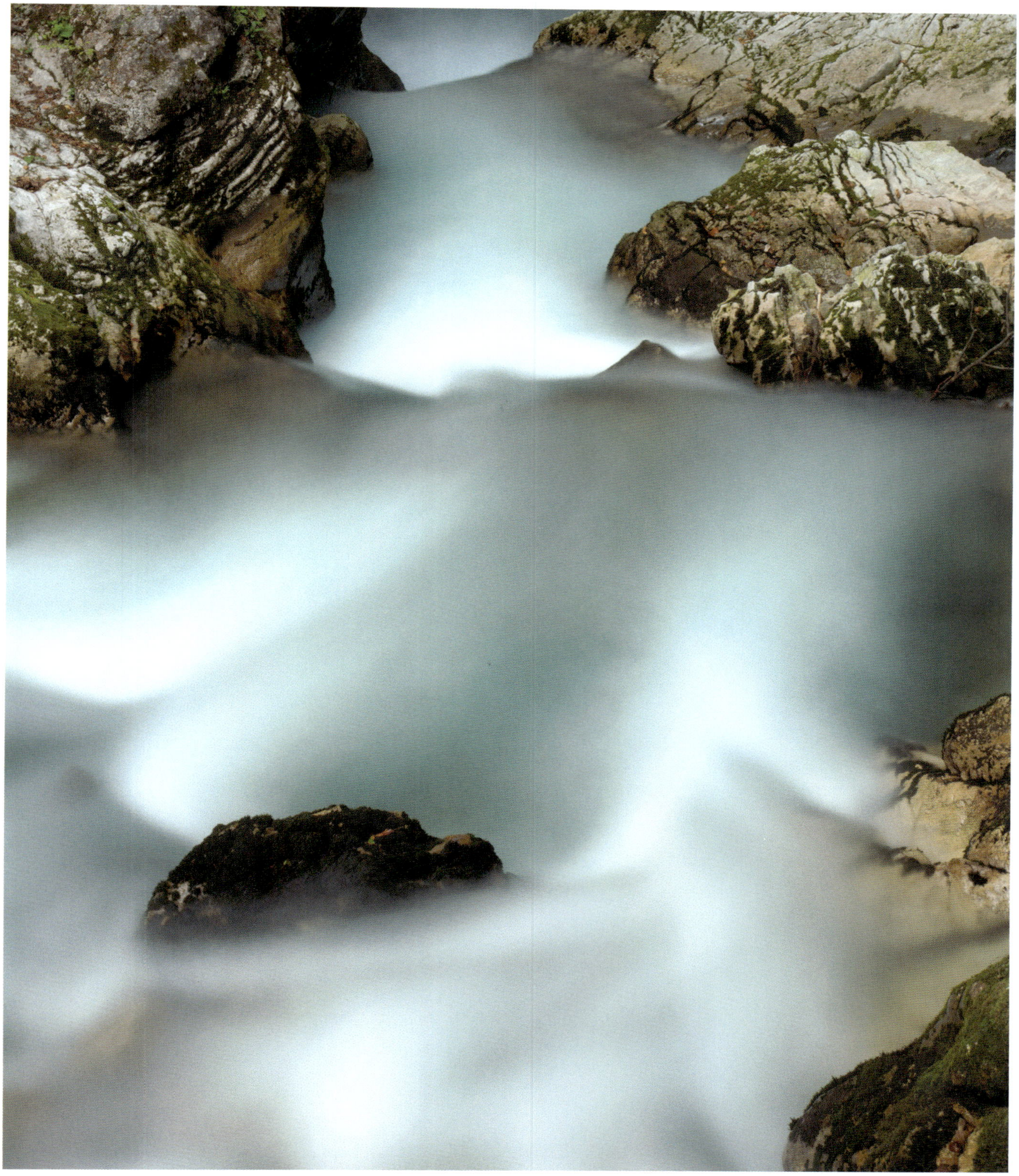

10 secs

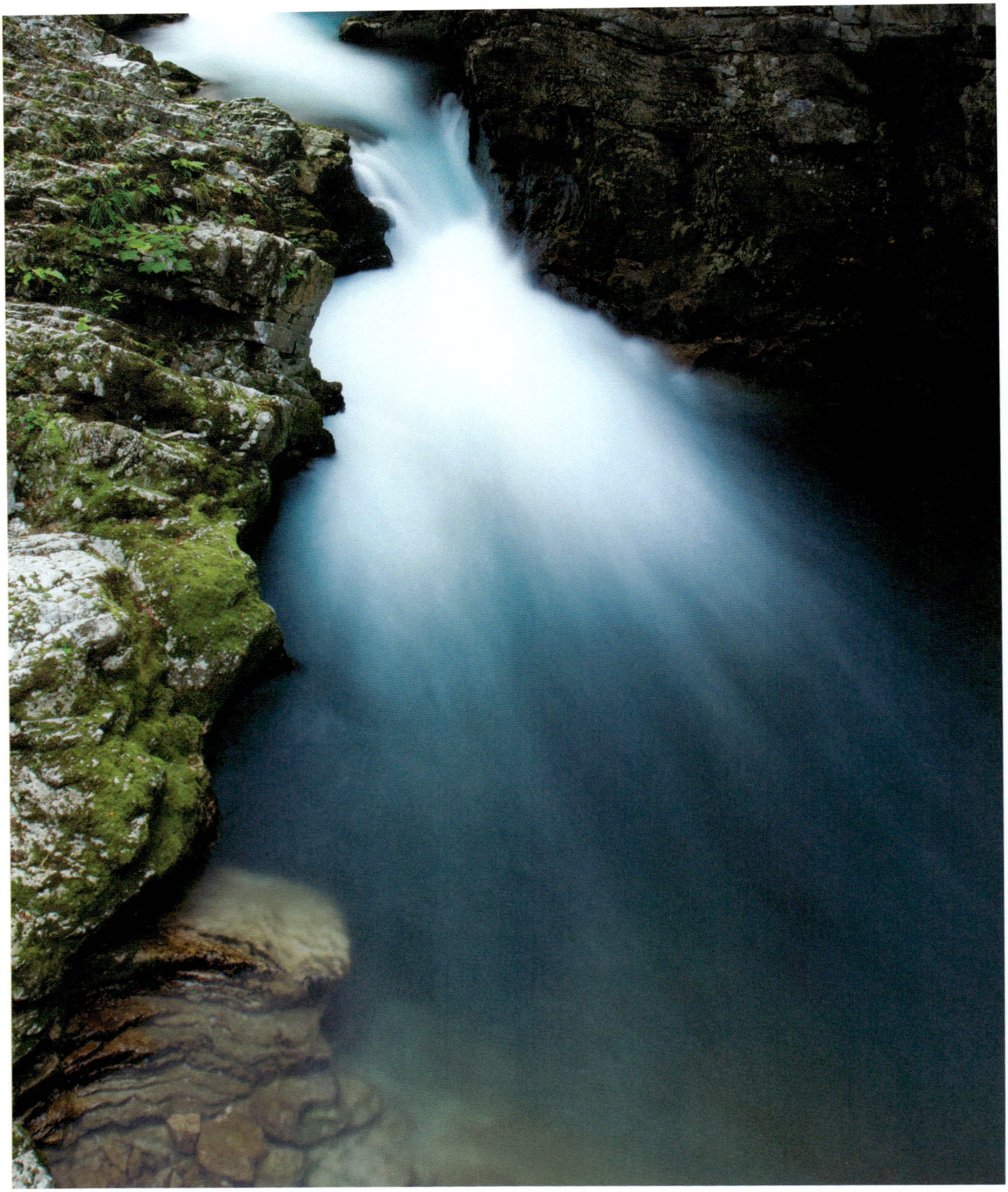

1/4 sec

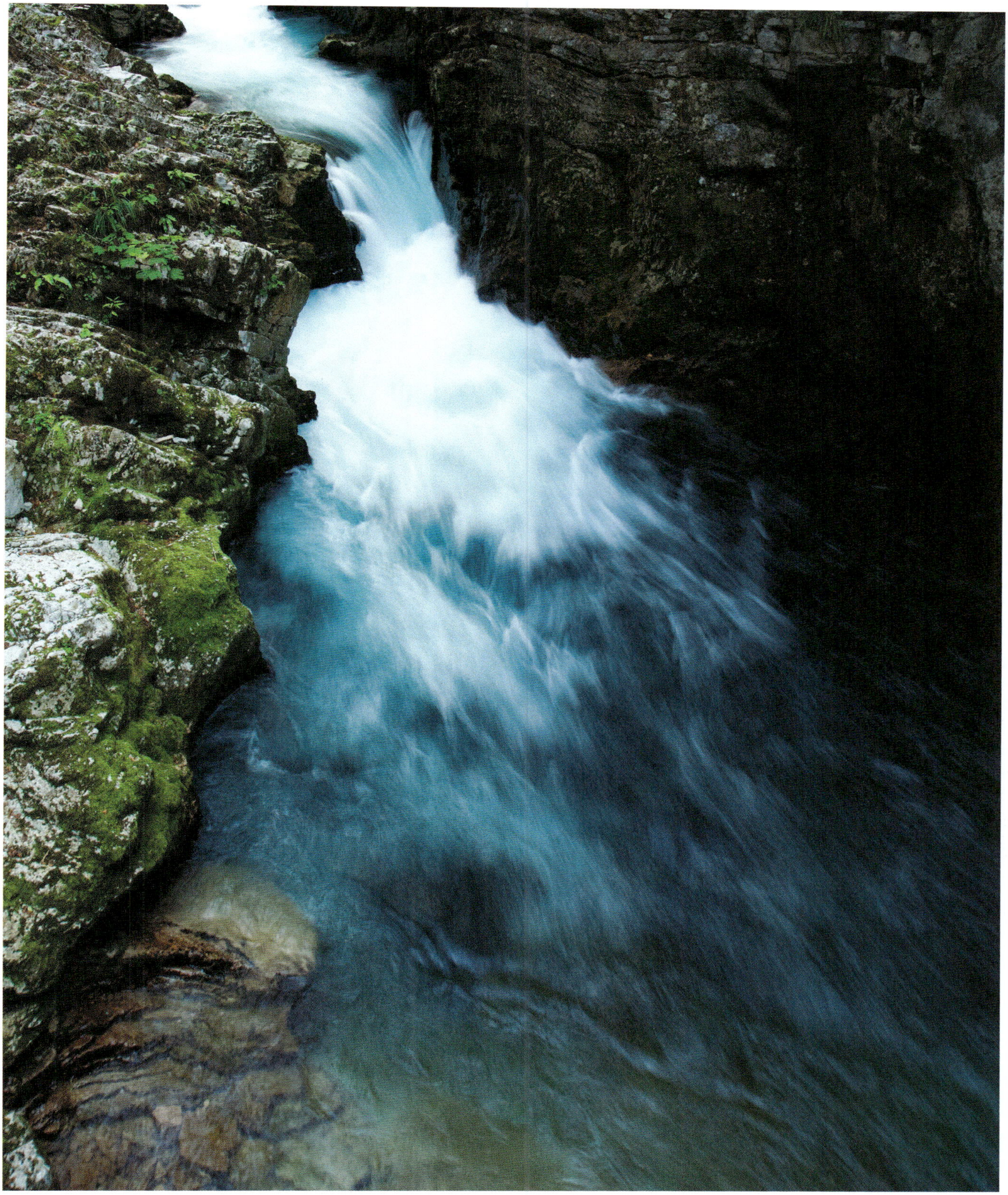

8 sec

Long exposures create a misty effect from the crashing waves on the sea.

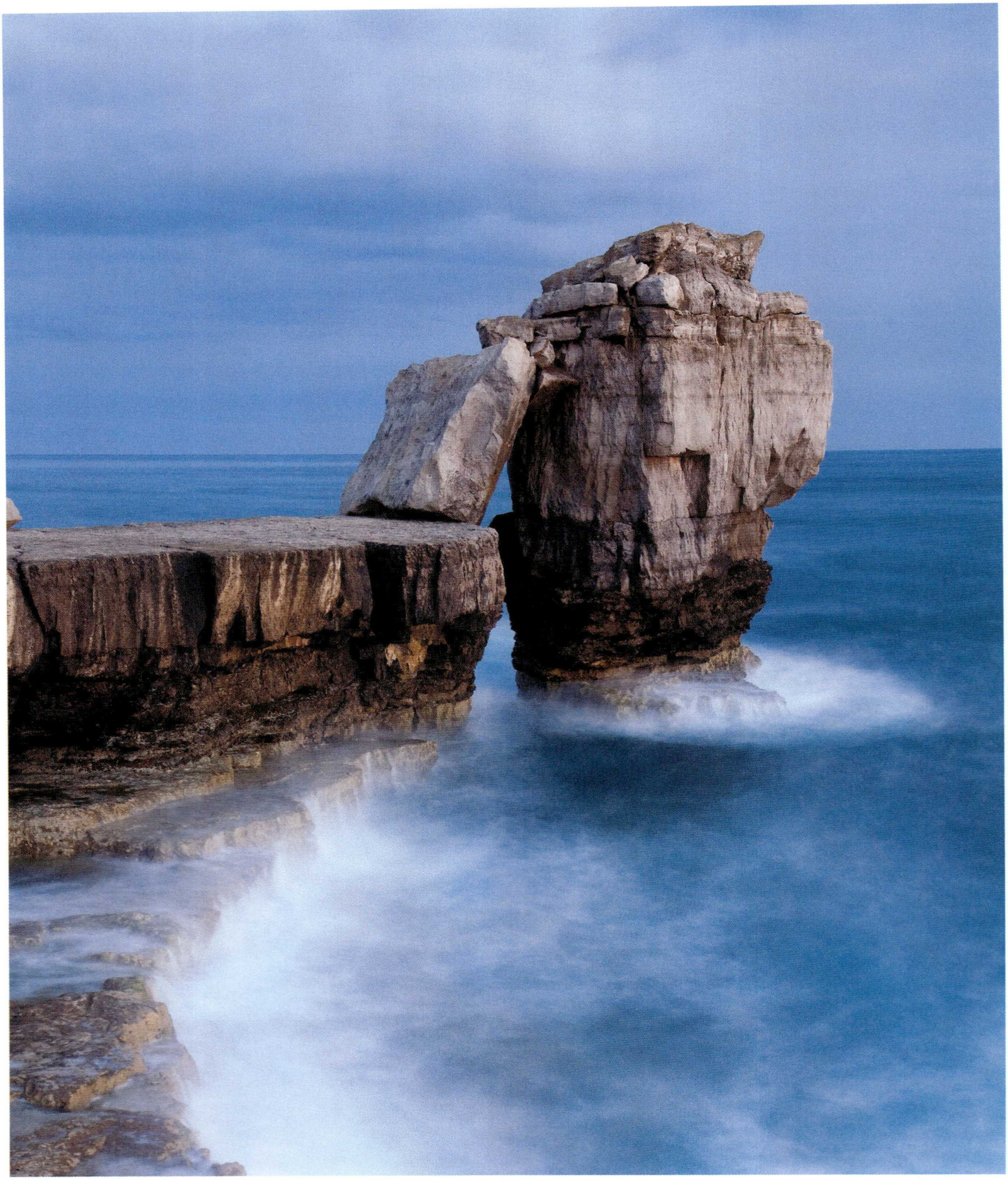

30 sec

The longer exposure also added cloud movement. Notice how there is no difference to the sea. The previous exposure of 8 secs was long enough to create the misty effect and exposing for longer has made no difference. But it has made a difference to the clouds, because the clouds are moving more slowly so a longer exposure was necessary to capture their motion effectively.

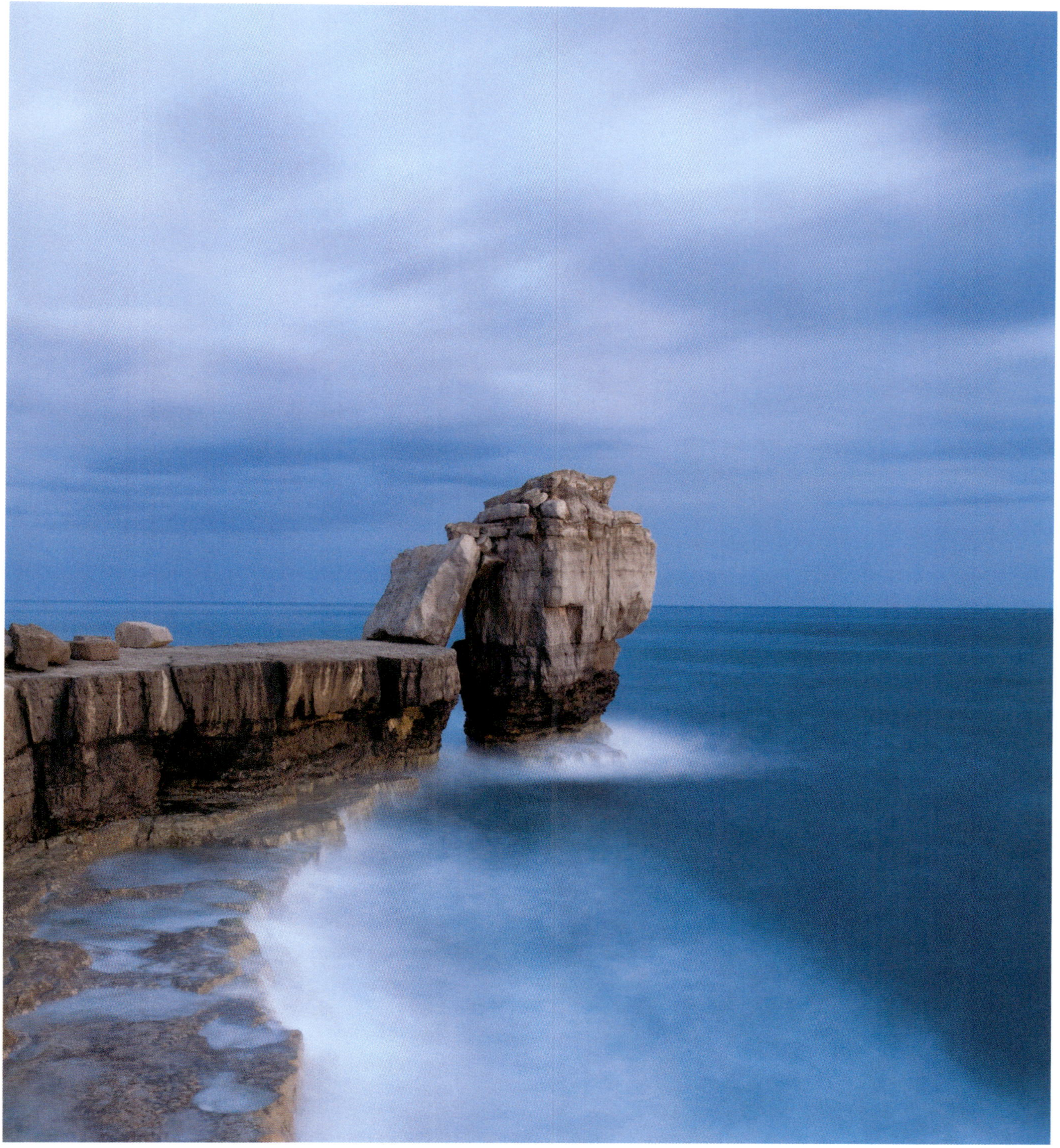

324 sec

This very long exposure has created super long cloud movement and some star trails.

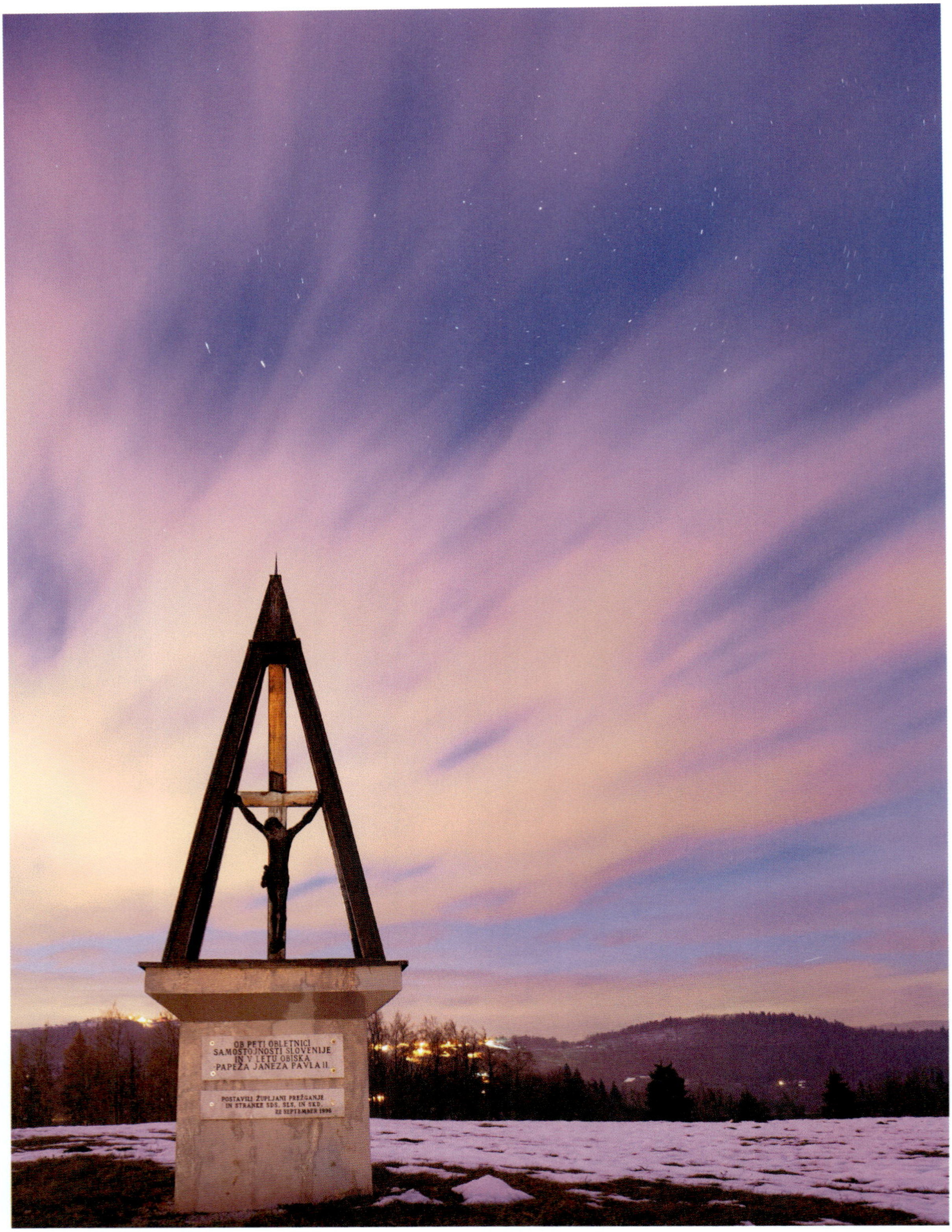

1/400 sec

Even though this is a fast shutter speed, as the duck's wings are beating extremely fast this was just the right speed to create a slight motion blur on the wings. This helps give a sense of movement in the image.

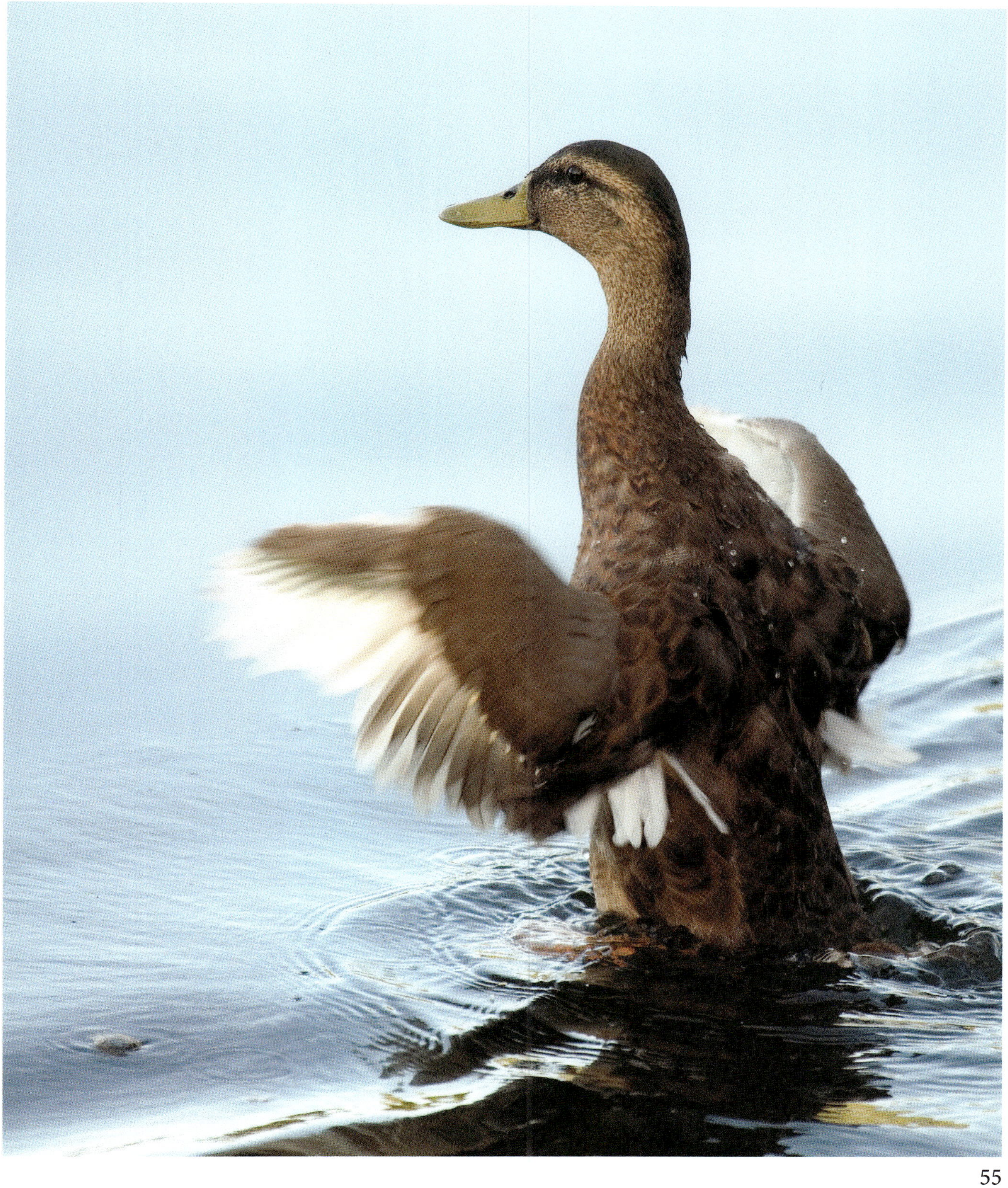

1/60 sec

Medium shutter speed along with panning produce dramatic sports/action shots.

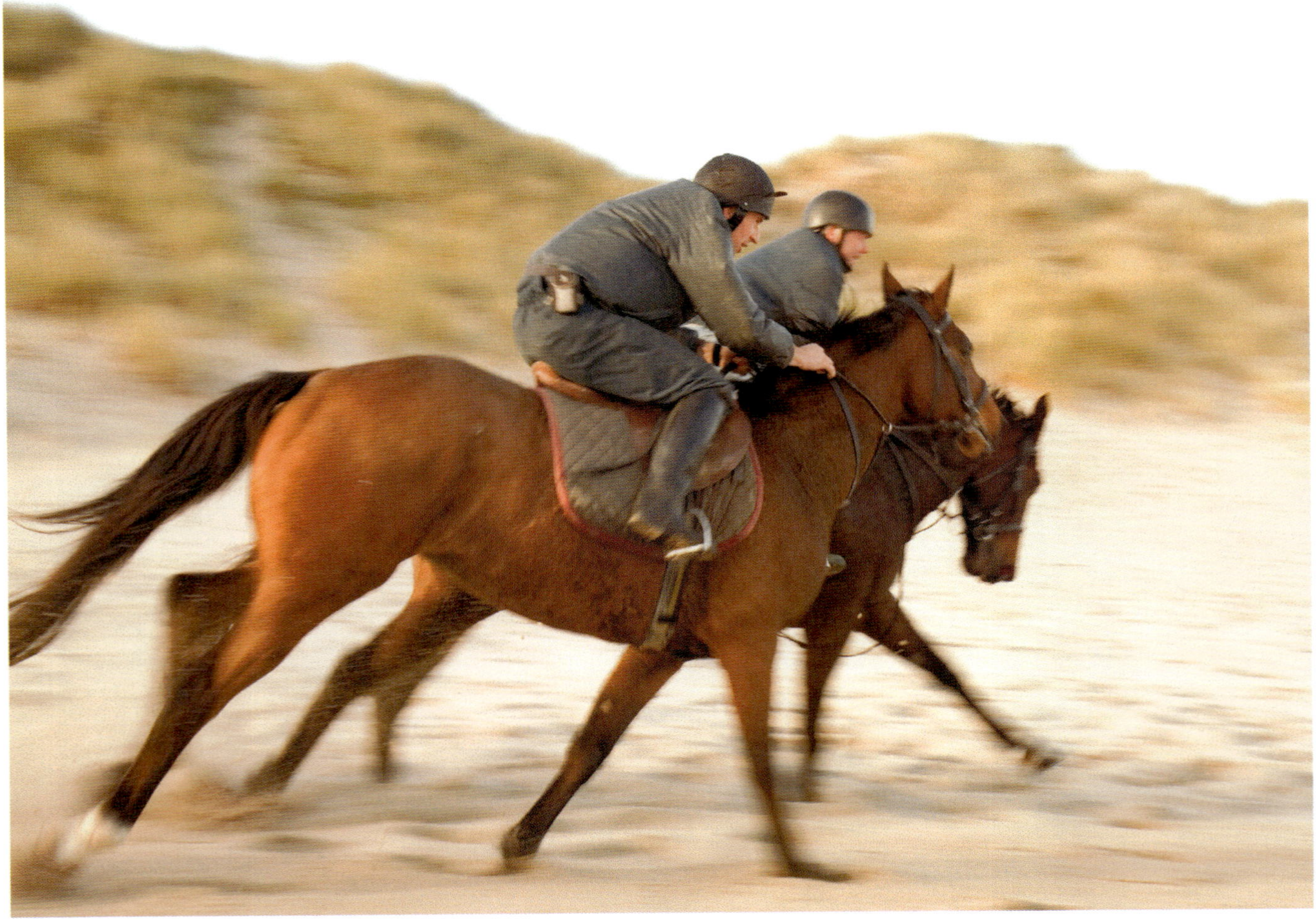

10 secs

The slow shutter speed here has not only been used to smooth out the sea, but also to blur the grass blowing in the wind.

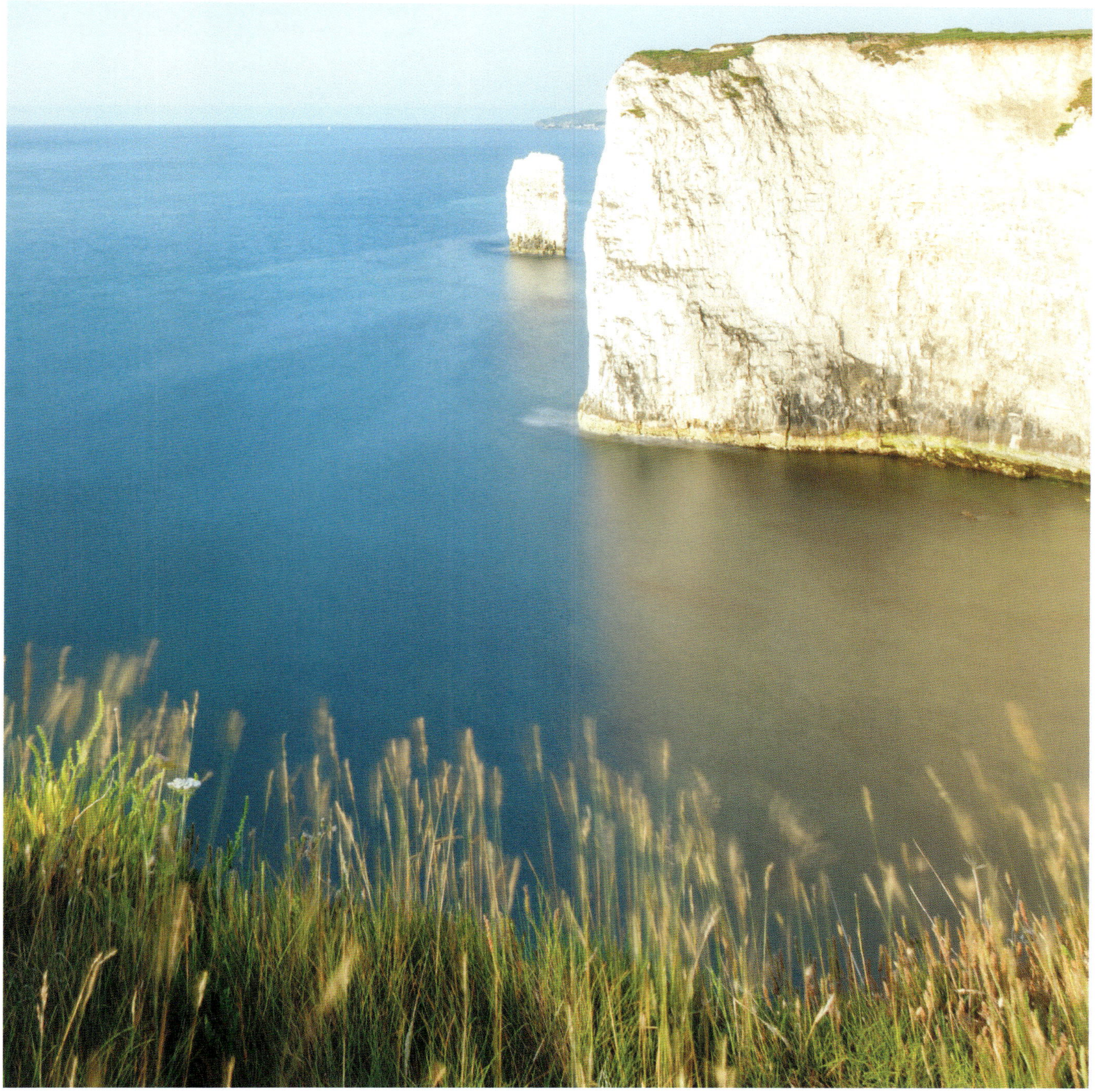

A Great example of how light draws our image

Ghost image – During a long exposure when a subject is not in the frame for the full exposure period then we can get ghosting.

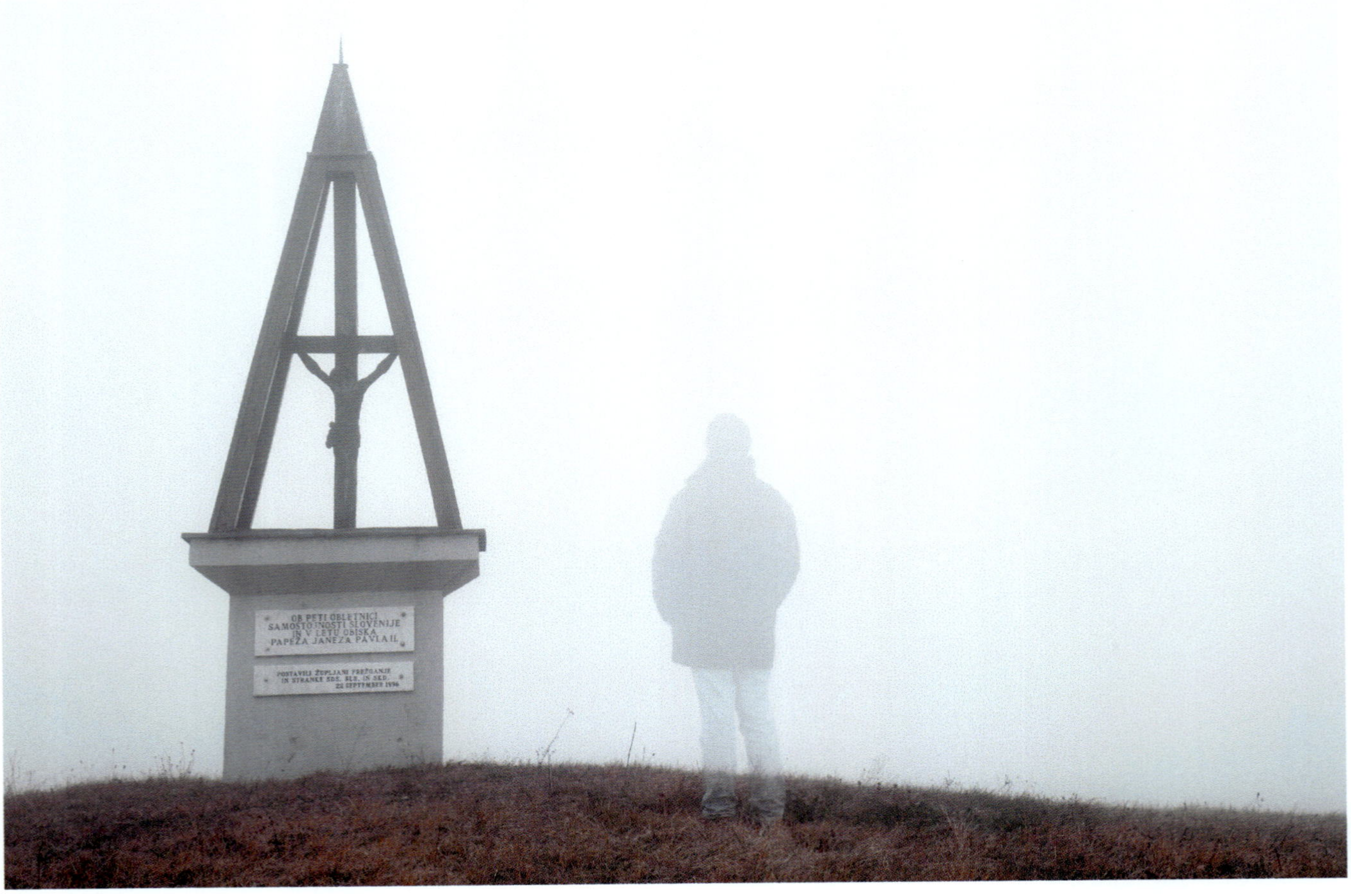

During this 30 sec exposure I stood in the frame for about 25 sec then moved away (very fast). As I was present for most of the exposure the light had started to draw me on the sensor, but because I moved away before the exposure time was up, it started drawing what was behind me. Therefore we ended up with an opaque picture of me in the scene.

However for ghosting or blurring to happen, the subject must be in the frame for enough of the exposure time, otherwise the person or people will be erased or not drawn. For example, if you set up a tripod in a busy train station where people are constantly walking past, and use a very long exposure then the result will be a picture of an empty train station. Also when shooting a street at night and someone walks in front of the camera, they will not appear on the photo if the exposure was long, say several seconds.

Practice effects like ghosting at night or in the evening, using yourself as the subject. Use the camera's timer to start.

Fast exposures – freezing your subject

1/1000 sec:

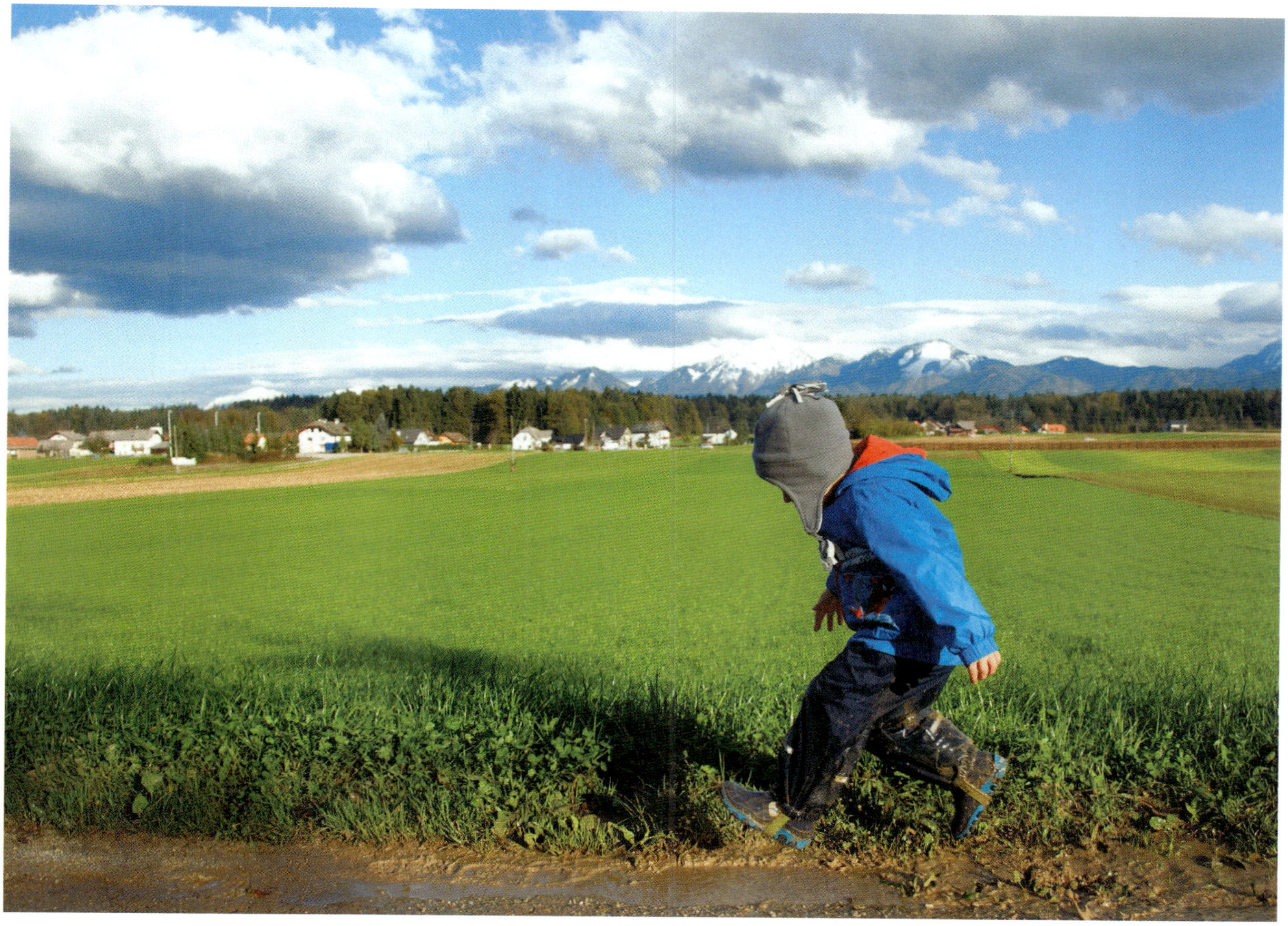

Fast shutter speeds will freeze any movement in your photo. How fast a shutter speed is required very much depends on the following things:

- How fast your subject is actually moving
- How fast it appears to be moving

The latter may sound a bit strange, but it's all about perspective. Next time you are out get a friend to run, first parallel to you (across the width of the frame, like the boy in the photo), then towards you at the same speed. You'll see that when the person is coming towards you, it doesn't seem so fast.

Different perspective

1/800 sec

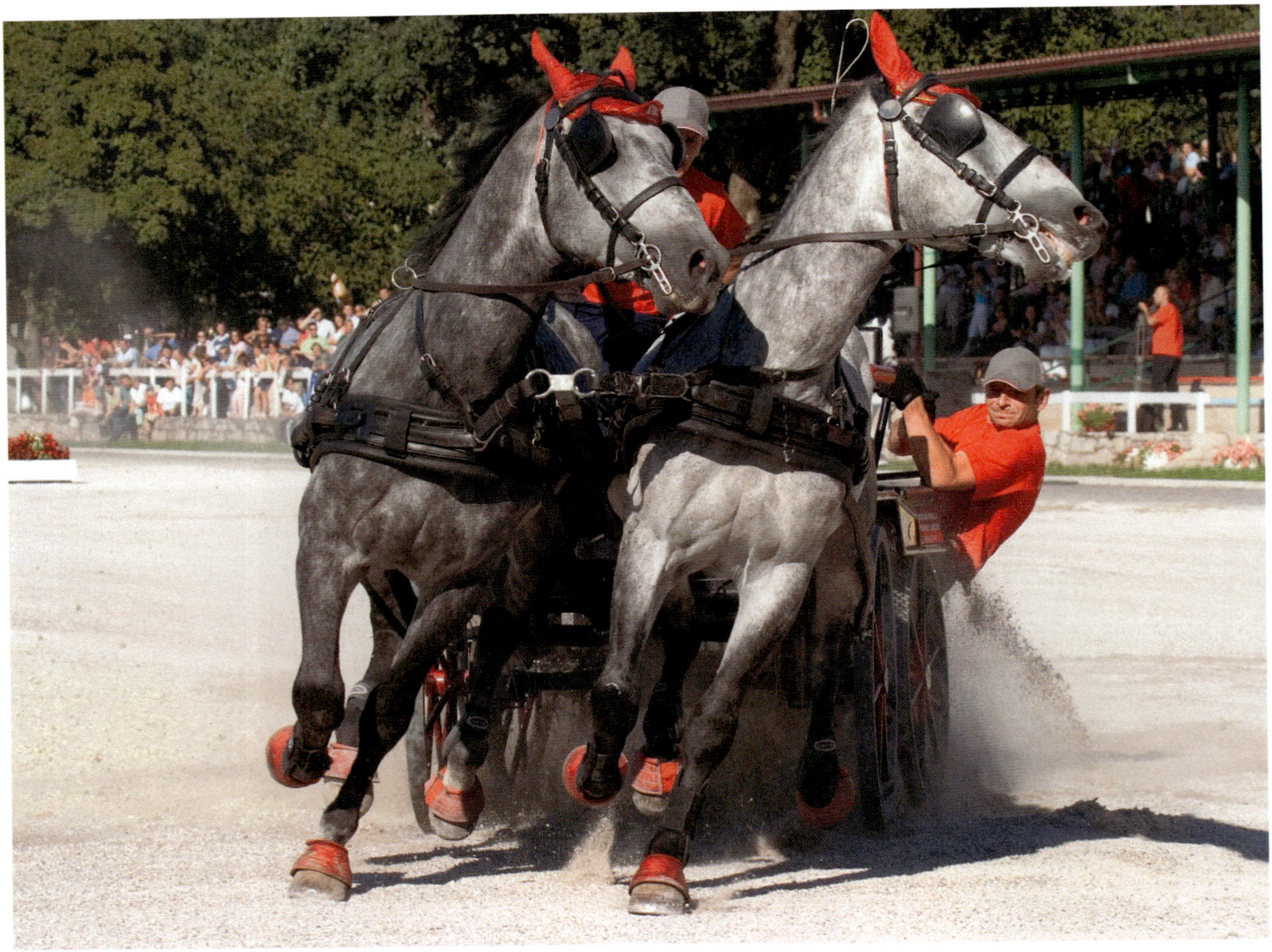

Obviously the horses were running much faster than the boy, but as they were moving in my direction, towards me, 1/800 sec was fast enough to freeze the action.

1/500sec

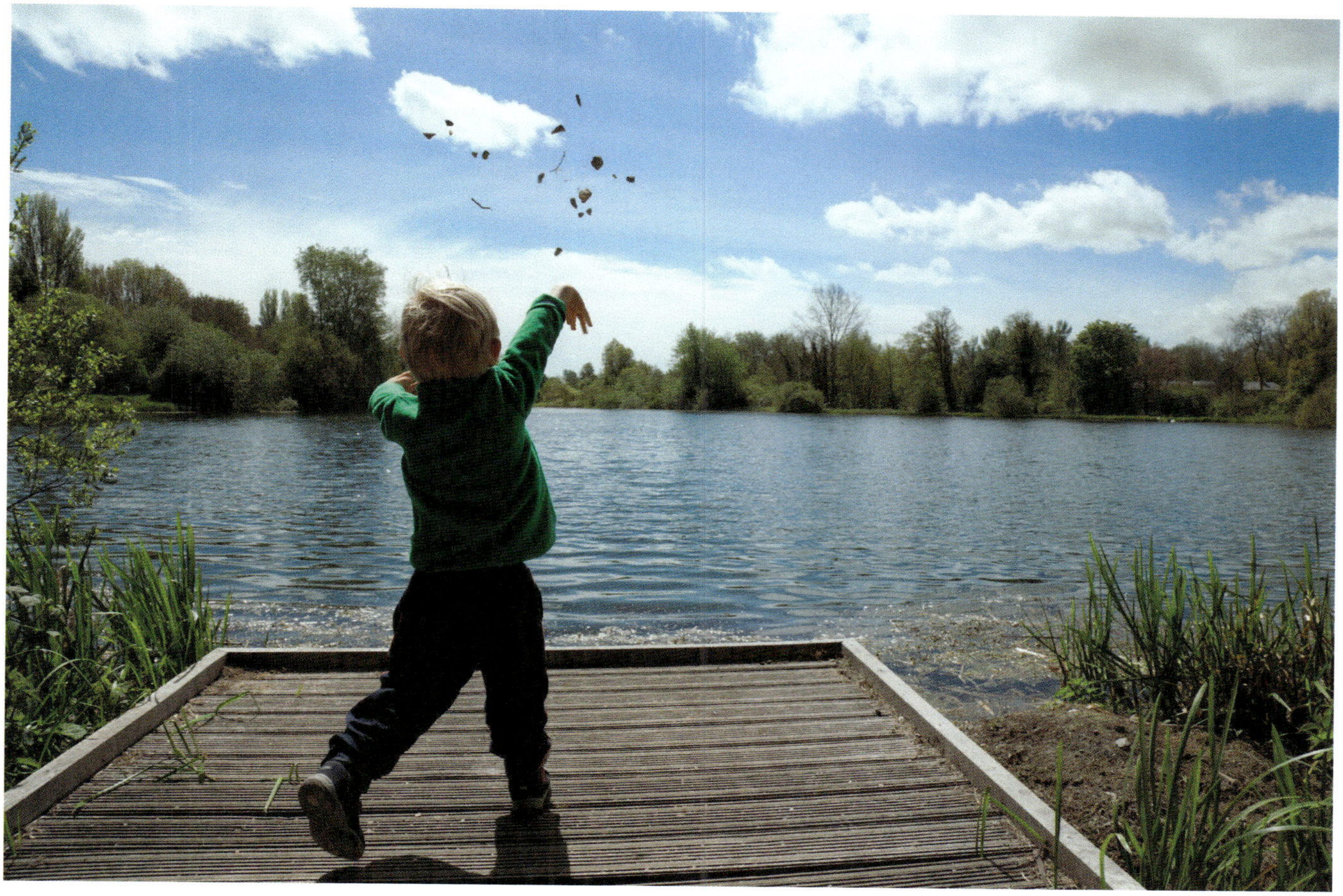

1/1250

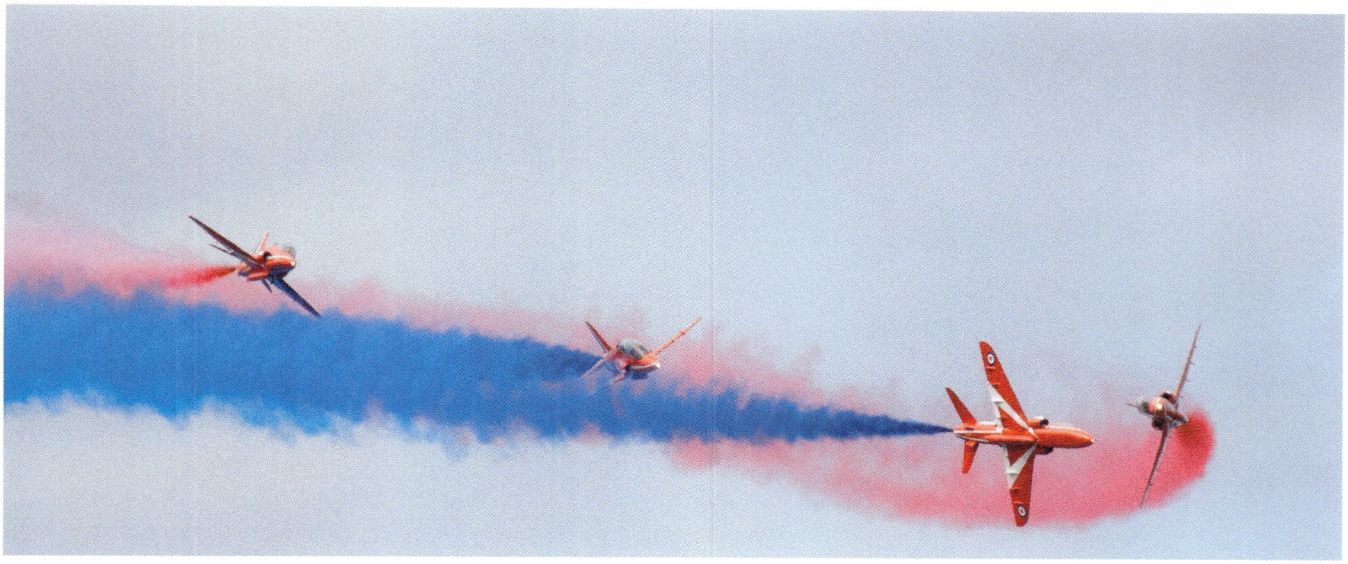

Camera settings

Many cameras have preset modes you can select which do the work for you and usually comes in the form of subject matter. In the case of shutter speed here are the options available:

Preset Modes

Sports mode: In this case for fast action photos requiring a fast shutter speed, sports mode should be selected.

Creative mode (let's you take some control)

The other mode is creative mode, where the photographer has some control over the settings. This comes in the form of a priority.

TV (Time Value) or S (Shutter): Shutter priority means that the user chooses the shutter speed and the camera then takes care of the aperture settings. This way you have full control over how much you freeze or blur your subject.

Aperture

In order to understand the camera's aperture, it helps to compare it to the pupil in our eye.

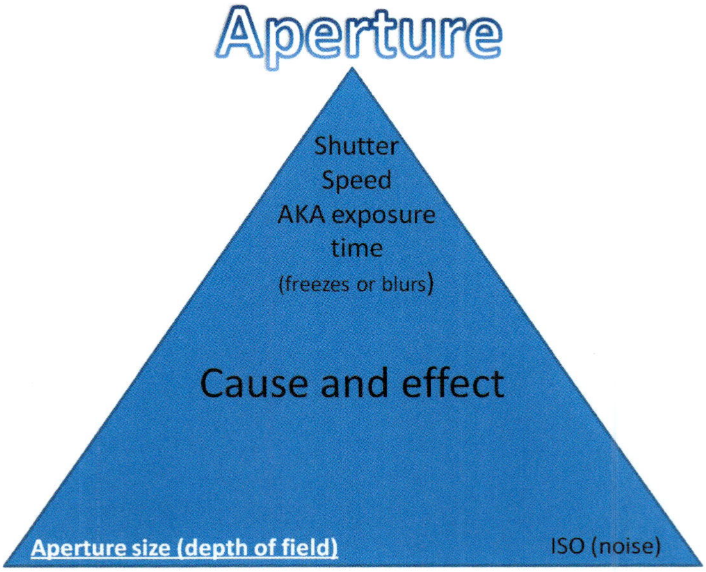

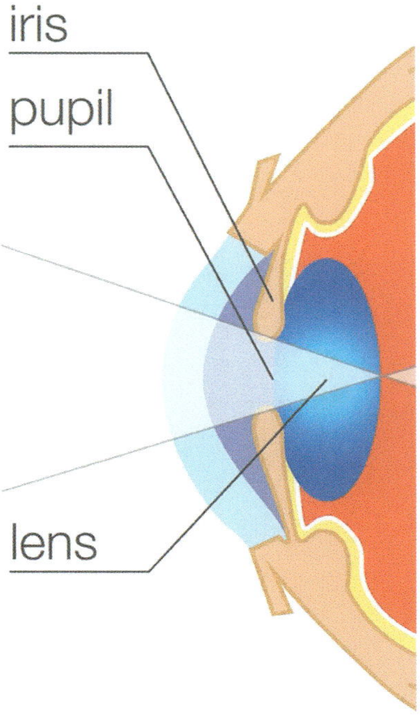

Our eye: - Iris and pupil

In our eye light enters via the pupil. The iris covers our pupil and
adjusts its size according to the brightness of the light. In bright light it expands to cover the pupil, thus the pupil is small and restricts the amount of light that enters the eye. In low light the iris retracts, thus the pupil is large and allows more light to enter the eye.

Small pupil in bright light

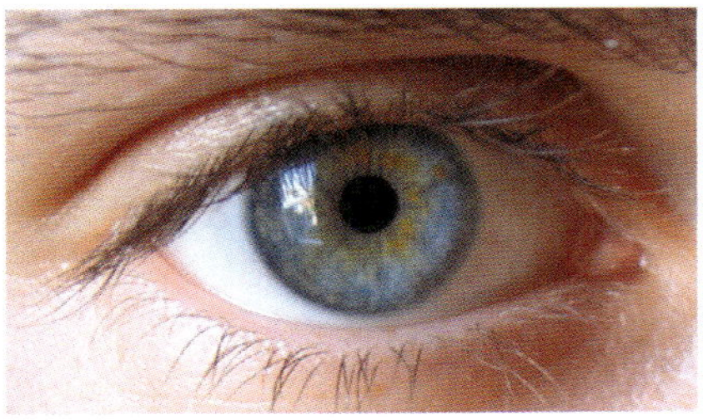

© Rhys Lloyd (freeimages.com)

Large pupil in low light

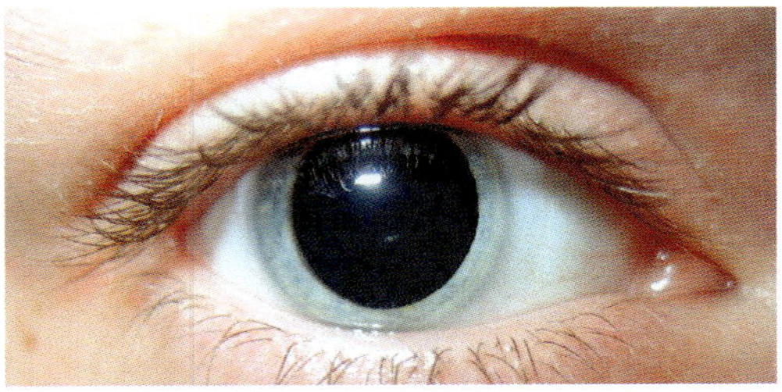

© tutnh (freeimages.com)

The camera's aperture

Like our eye, the camera also has a method of increasing or restricting the amount of light that passes through its lens. Instead of a pupil, it has an aperture, a hole if you will. It works in a similar way to our iris and pupil. A mechanical iris works to set the size of the aperture hole. When you press the shutter to take your photo, the aperture blades close in to set the aperture just before the shutter is opened.

You can see this by pressing the depth of field preview button on your lens (if you have one)

Aperture sizes:

Aperture sizes are determined by f + number (also known as f-stop)
The higher the number, the smaller the aperture. See below:

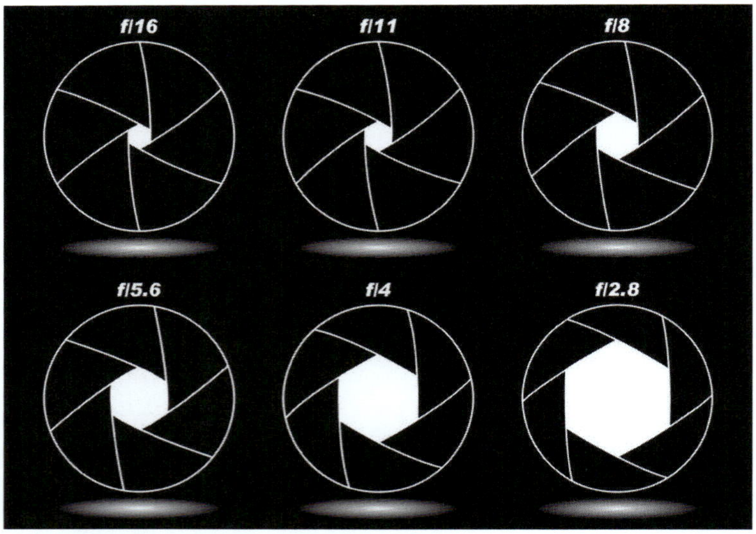

F -Stops		
Halves	Whole	Thirds
	F2.8	F3.2
F3.3		F3.5
	F4	F4.5
F4.5		F5
	F5.6	F6.3
F6.7		F7.1
	F8	F9
F9.5		F10
	F11	F13
F13		F14
	F16	F18
F19		F20
	F22	F25
F27		F29
	F32	

Example apertures and a size chart

To the right you can see a chart depicting the range of apertures available. Just like with the shutter speeds, you can use whole stops, half stops and third stops. The range of apertures available will very much depend on the lens you have. In a DSLR the aperture ring is in the lens, not the camera. Most lenses start at around F4.5 - F5.6 and go up to F22. The F2.8 size is usually found on much more expensive lenses. Smaller apertures of F32 upwards are usually found on expensive zoom and telephoto lenses. My Canon L series 100 - 400mm goes up to F40.

Aperture and focal length:

Although apertures come in f numbers, the actual dimension of the hole depends upon the focal length. The dimension can be calculated thus:

Focal length divided by F stop

Therefore the aperture of a 50mm lens at f/8 will be a circle with diameter of 50/8 = 6.25mm
The aperture of a 100mm lens at f/8 will be a circle with diameter of
100/8 = 12.5mm

Effect: - Depth of field

Depth of field is the distance in front of and behind your point of focus that will also be in focus. The aperture setting affects the depth of field as follows:

A smaller aperture (f16) will result in a larger depth of field, so more of the scene will be in focus (great for landscapes)

A large aperture (f4 will result in a small depth of field, so less of the scene will be in focus. (great for portraits)

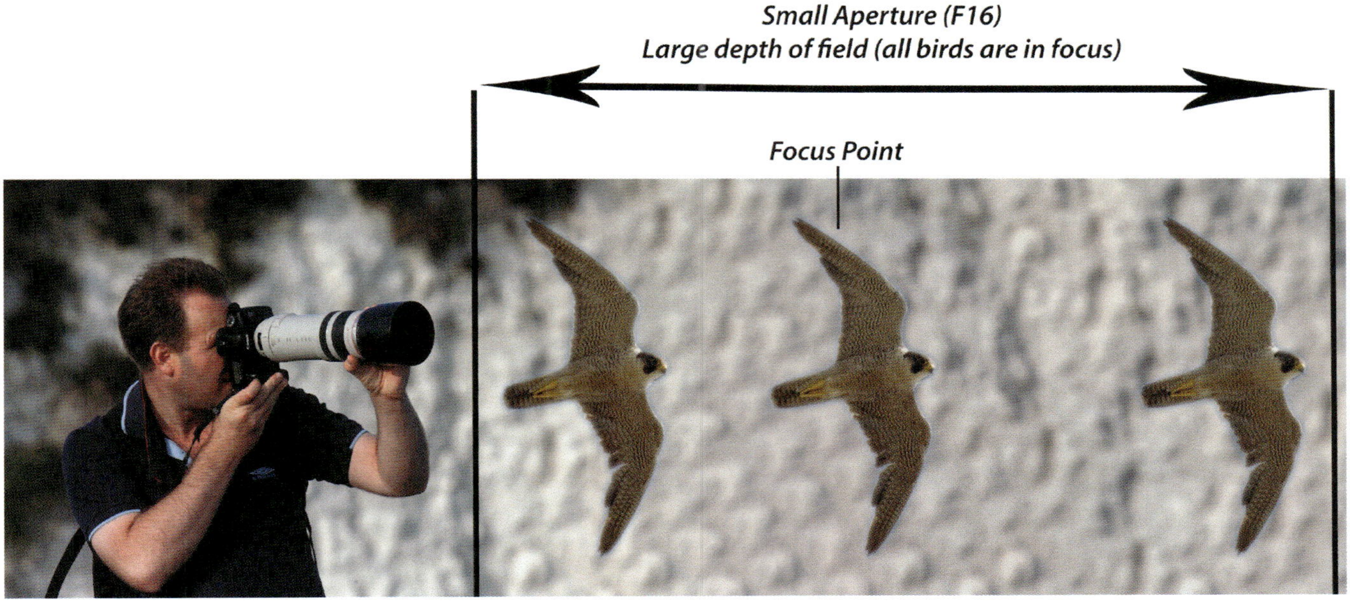

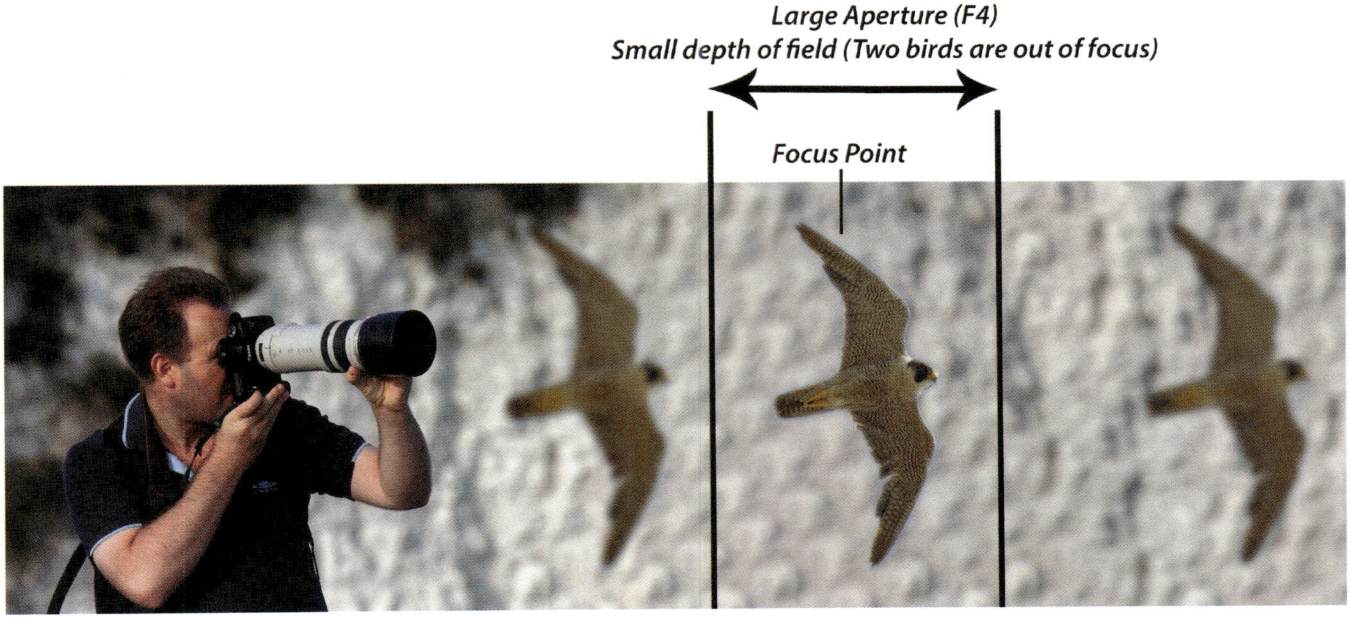

Two other things affect depth of field

Focal length – longer focal lengths reduce the depth of field even more because as we saw earlier, the longer the focal length, the larger the hole. So although the F number is the same, the hole is actually bigger. This means that the depth of field you get from an F16 at 50mm, is larger than an F16 at 200mm.

Distance from your point of focus – the closer you are to the point of focus, the more the depth of field is reduced. Conversely, the further away you are from the point of focus, the larger the depth of field.

At a glance – F-stop vs Aperture size	At a glance – F-stop vs Focal length
Large number (F16) = small hole = large depth of field	Short focal length = smaller hole = larger depth of field Ex: at 50mm at F8 - 50/8 = 6.25mm
Small number (F5.6) = large hole = small depth of field	Long focal length = larger hole = smaller depth of field Ex: at 200mm at F8 - 200/8 = 25mm

Hyperfocal point:

The depth of field is not equal on both sides, and is actually shorter at the front than at the back of your point of focus. Depth of field extends rough 1/3 in front of your point of focus and 2/3 behind. This is important to remember when taking landscape shots where you want to maximise your front to back sharpness. The simple way to do this is to focus about 1/3 of the way into your scene. For even more accuracy you can use a hyperfocal point chart, or special software which you can download for free at: www.dofmaster.com See below for an example:

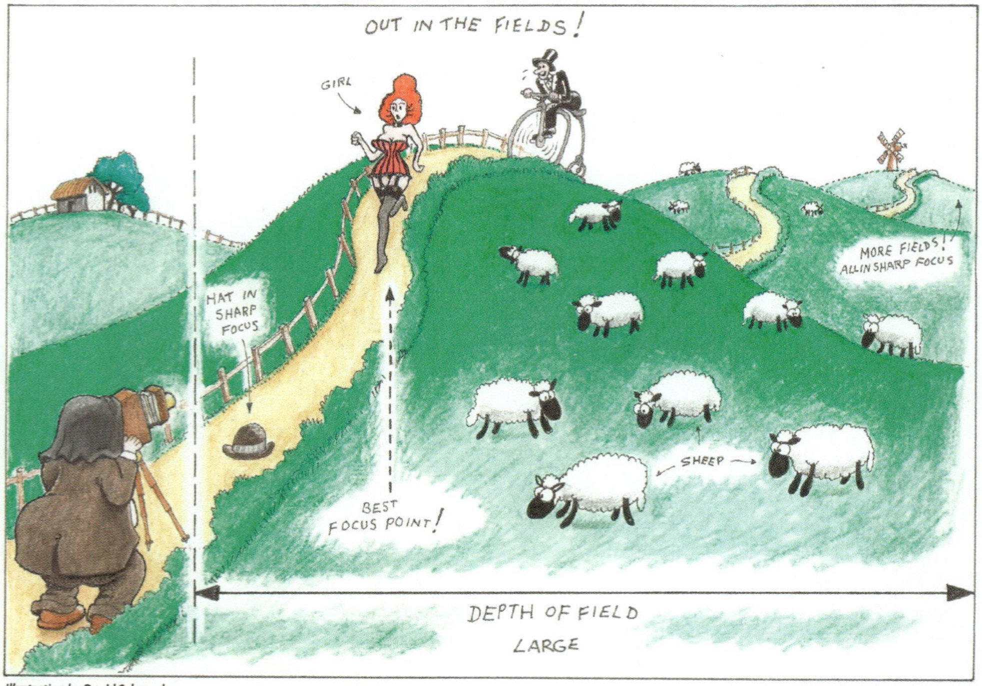

Illustration by David Selwood

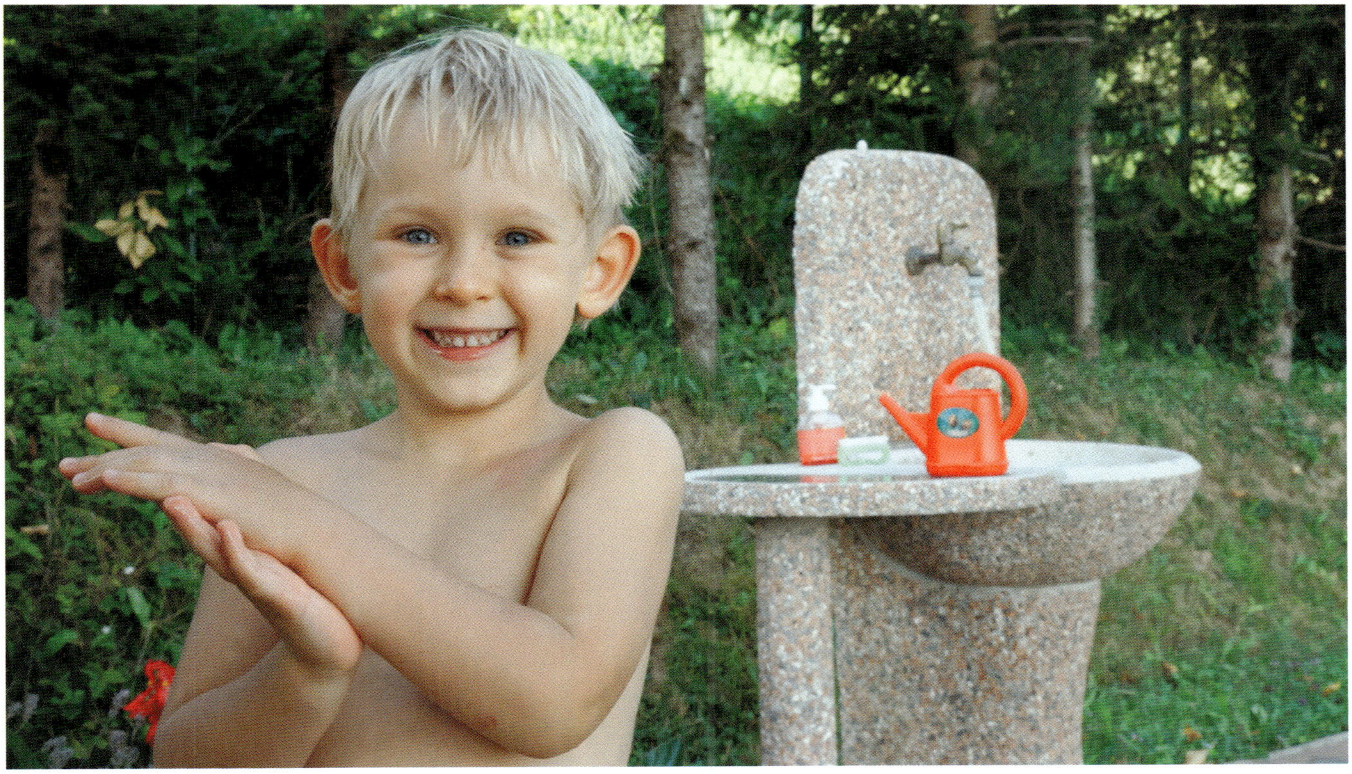

F16 at 50mm
Large depth of field has kept the object behind acceptably sharp

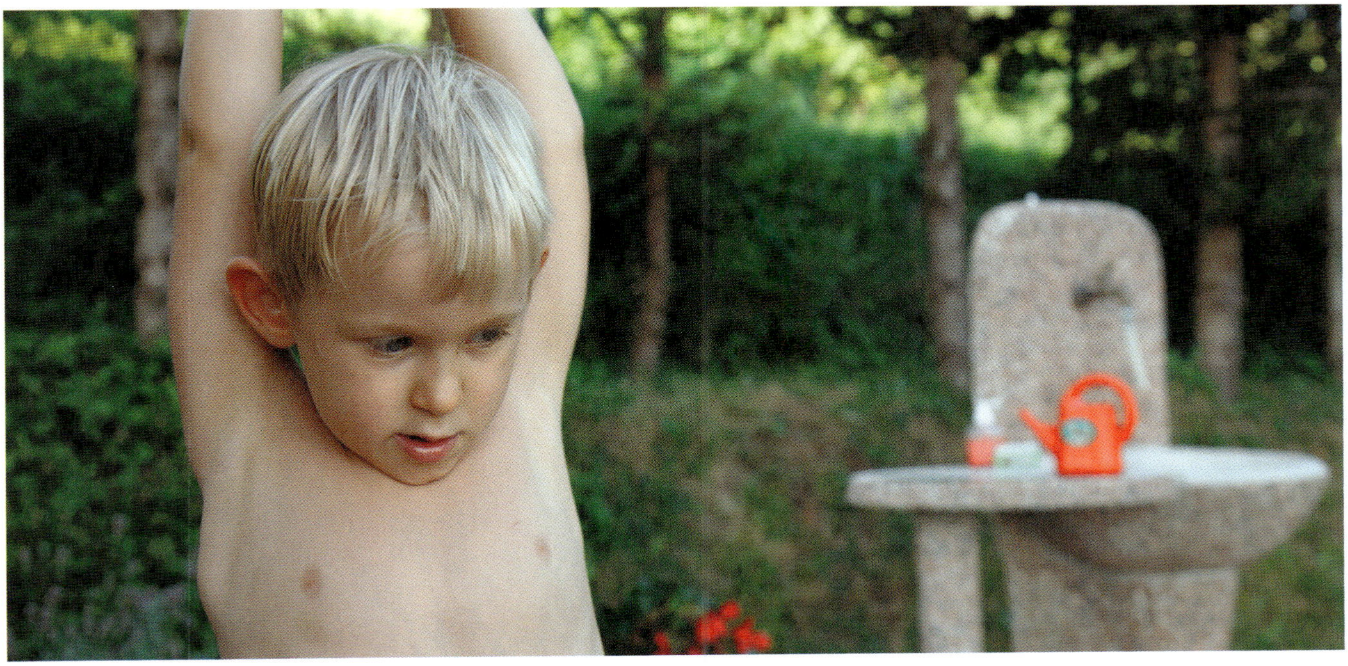

F5.6 at 50mm
Narrow depth of field plus the slight increase in distance between the boy and the object has thrown the background more out of focus

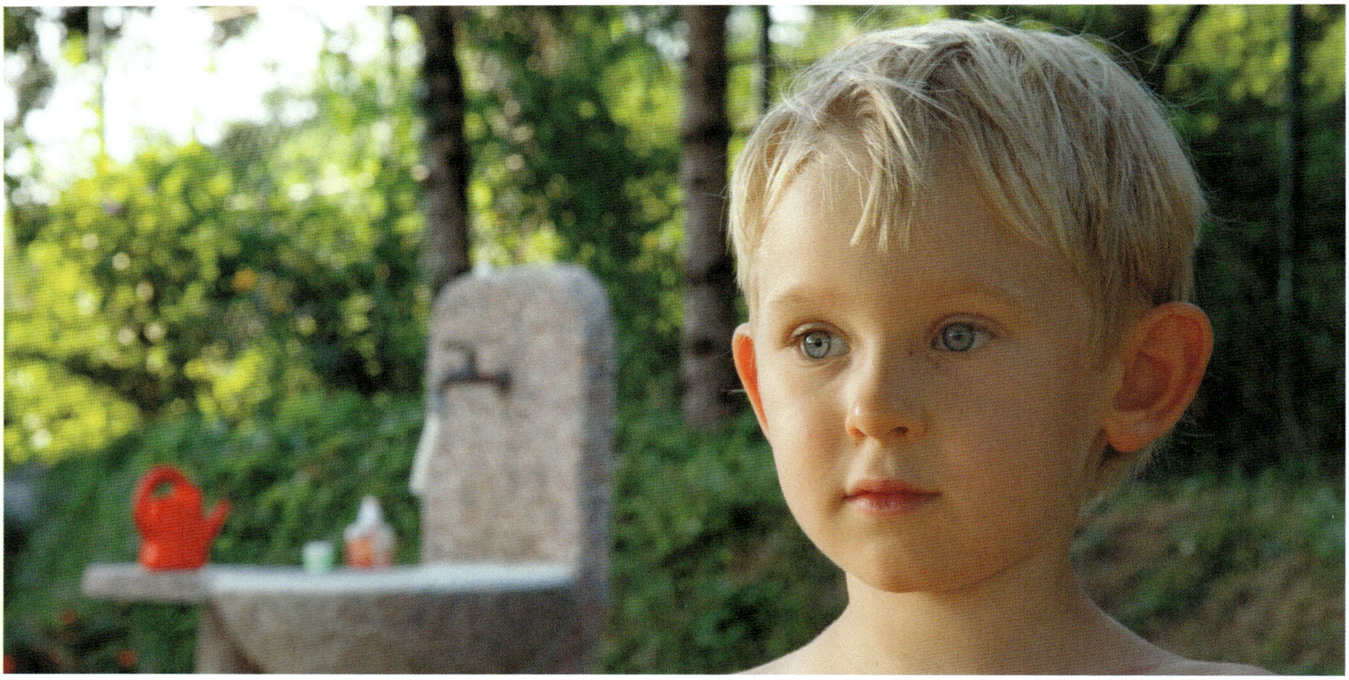

F16 at 105mm
At a small aperture the increased focal length and distance between the boy and the background object still throws everything out of focus

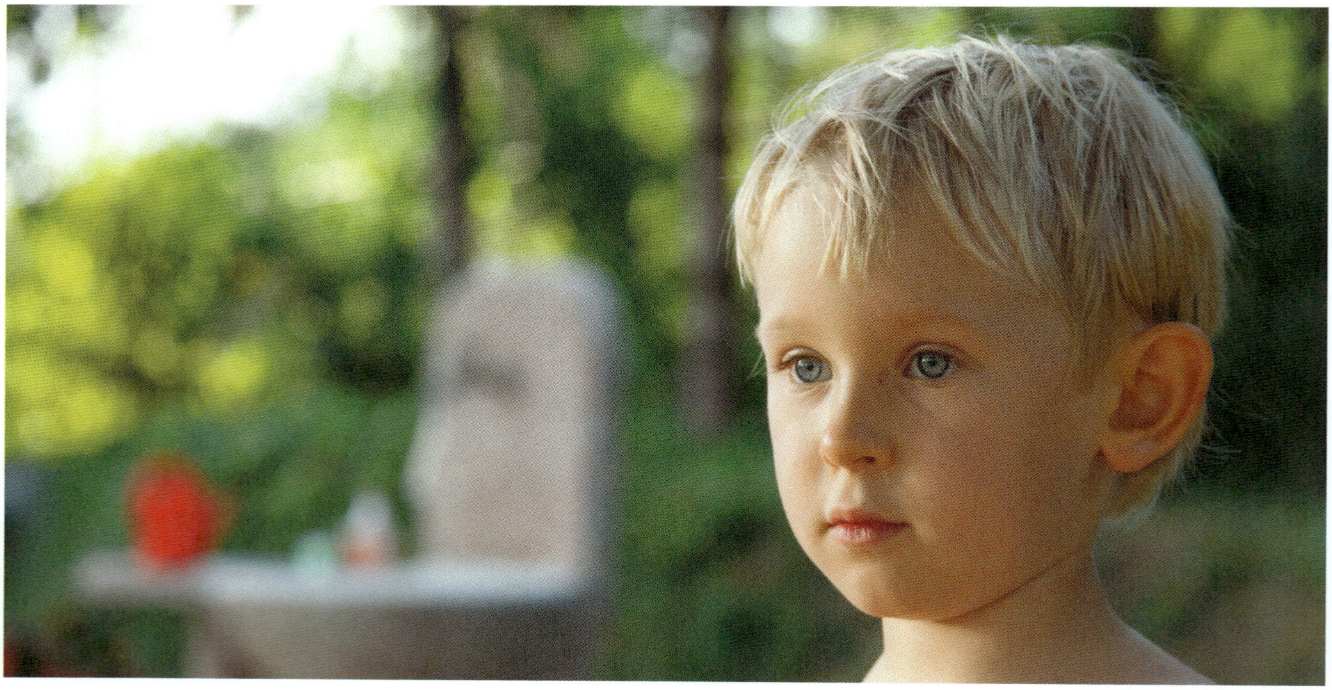

F5.6 at 105mm
A longer focal length and larger aperture increases the background blur even more.

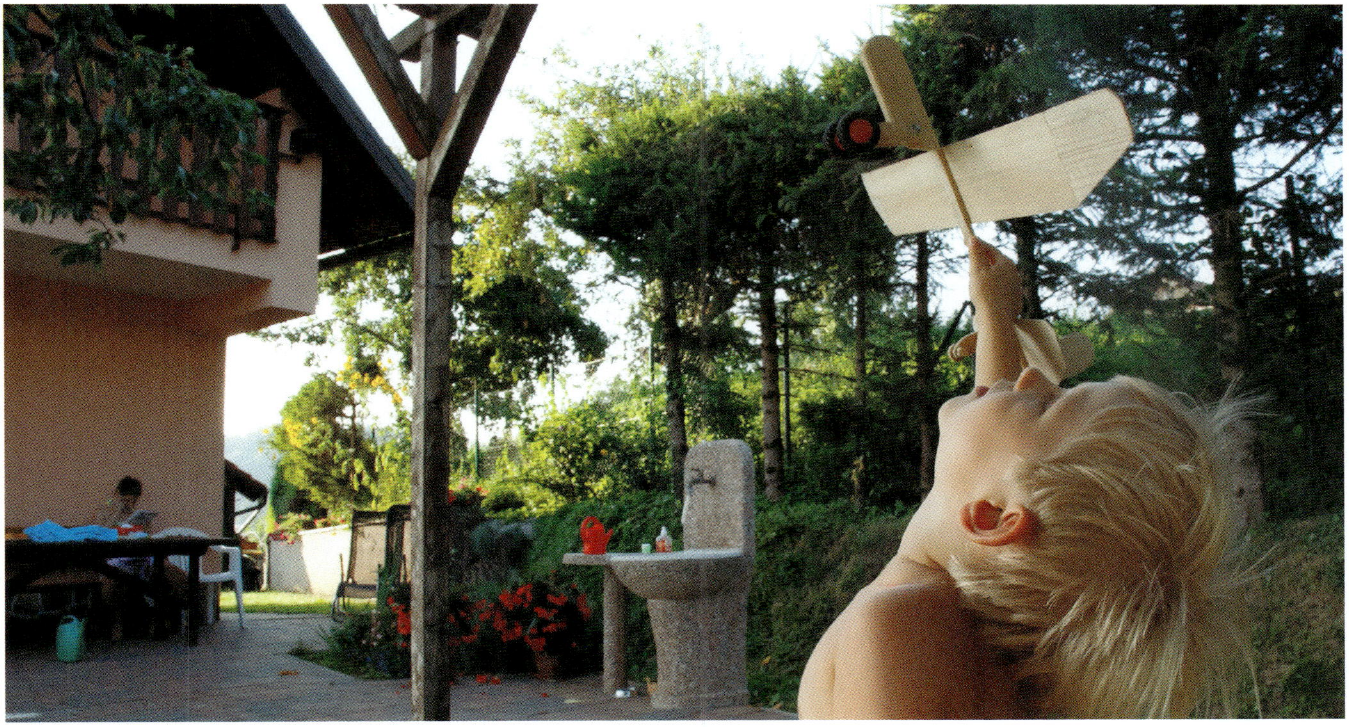

F16 at 24mm

Conversely, at shorter focal lengths (wide angle in this case) we can increase the depth of field when background objects are further away. Notice how the background is sharper in this image than in the previous one shot at F16 at 105mm

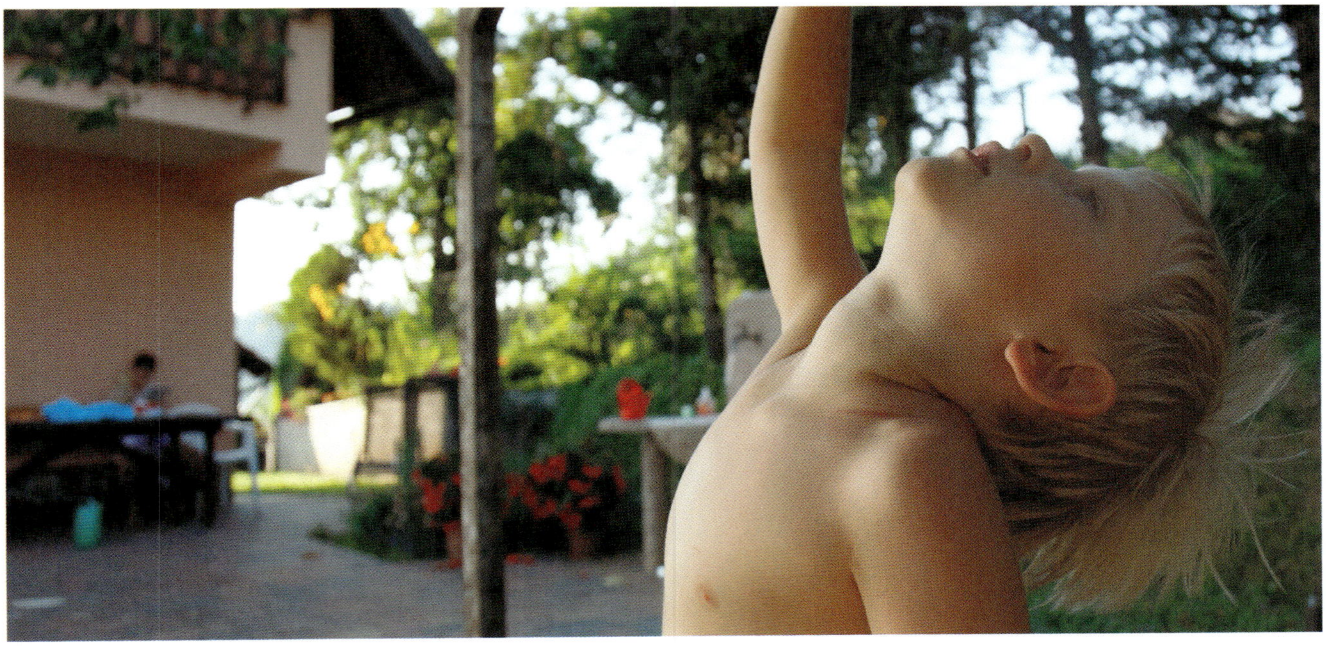

F5 at 25mm

Again, notice how the background is not as blurry as the photo taken at F5.6 - 105mm

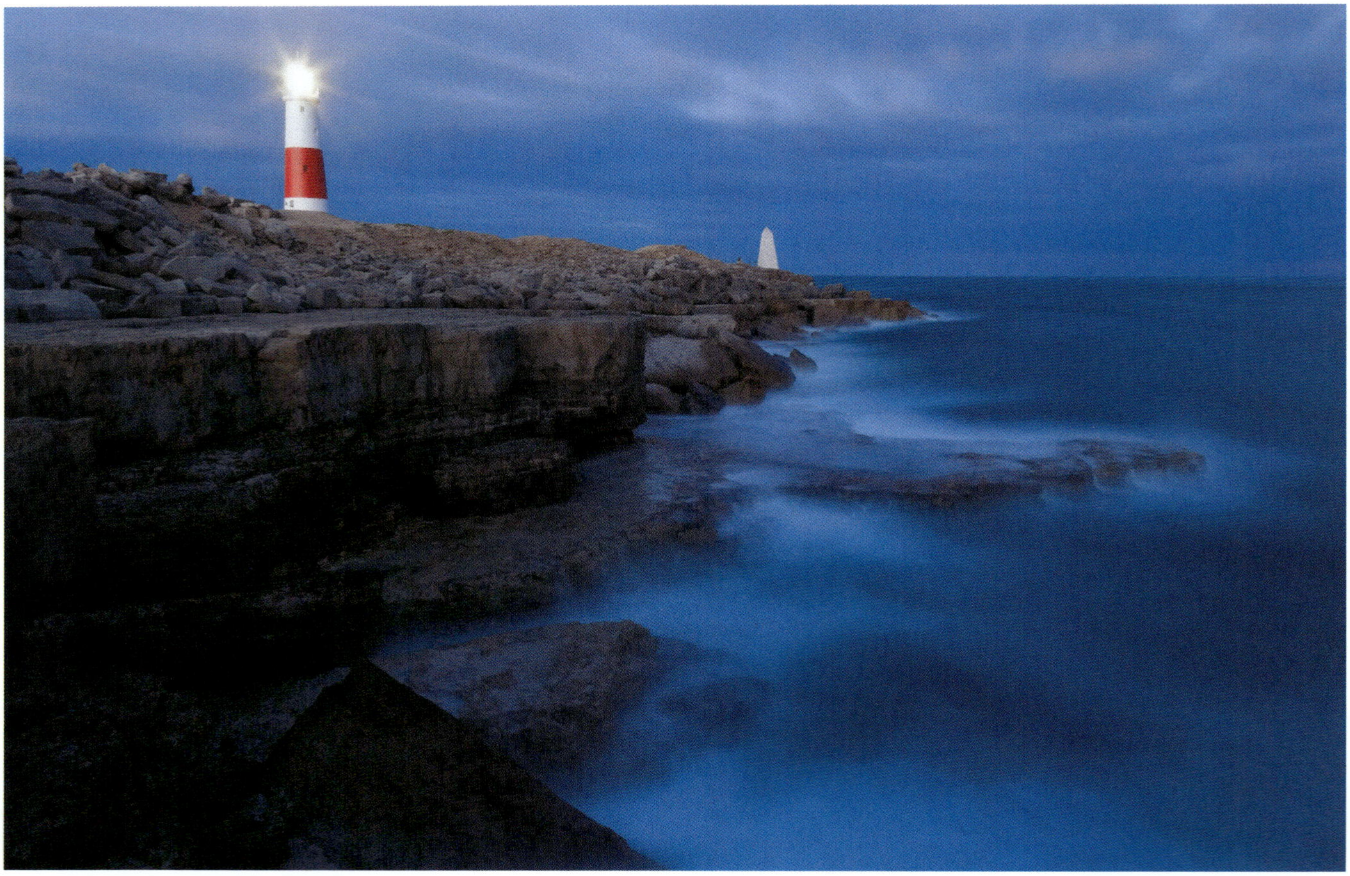

Aperture - f16 Focal length - 24mm
For landscapes we want a large depth of field to get maximum sharpness across the scene

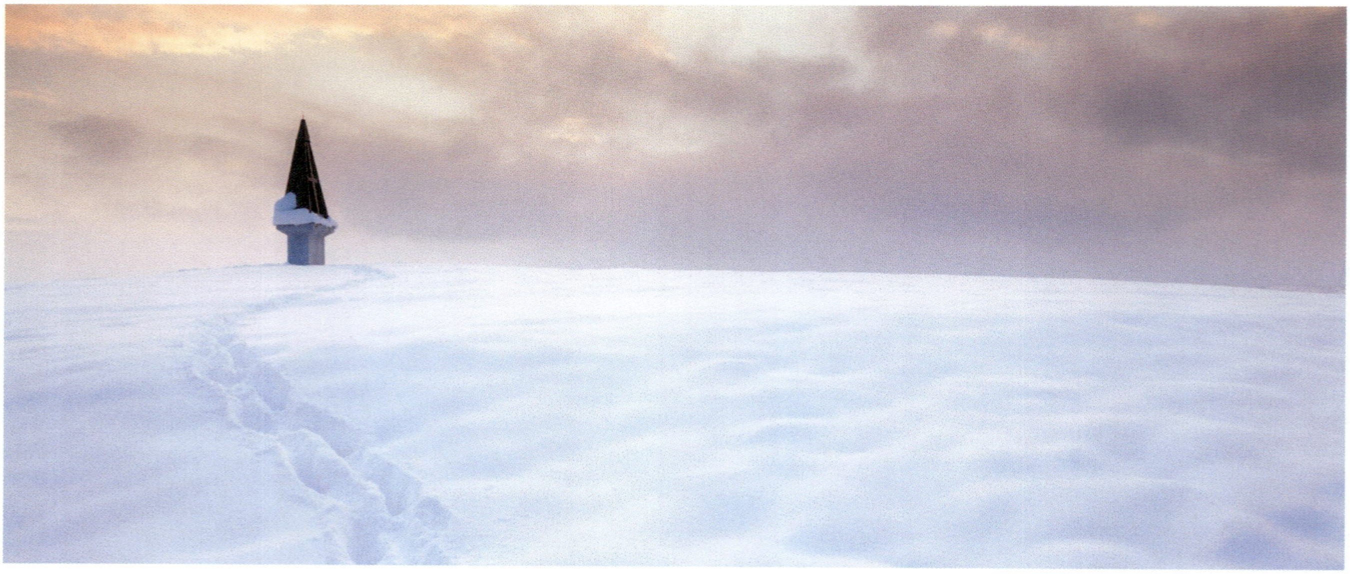

Aperture - f20 Focal length - 24mm

Great for portraits

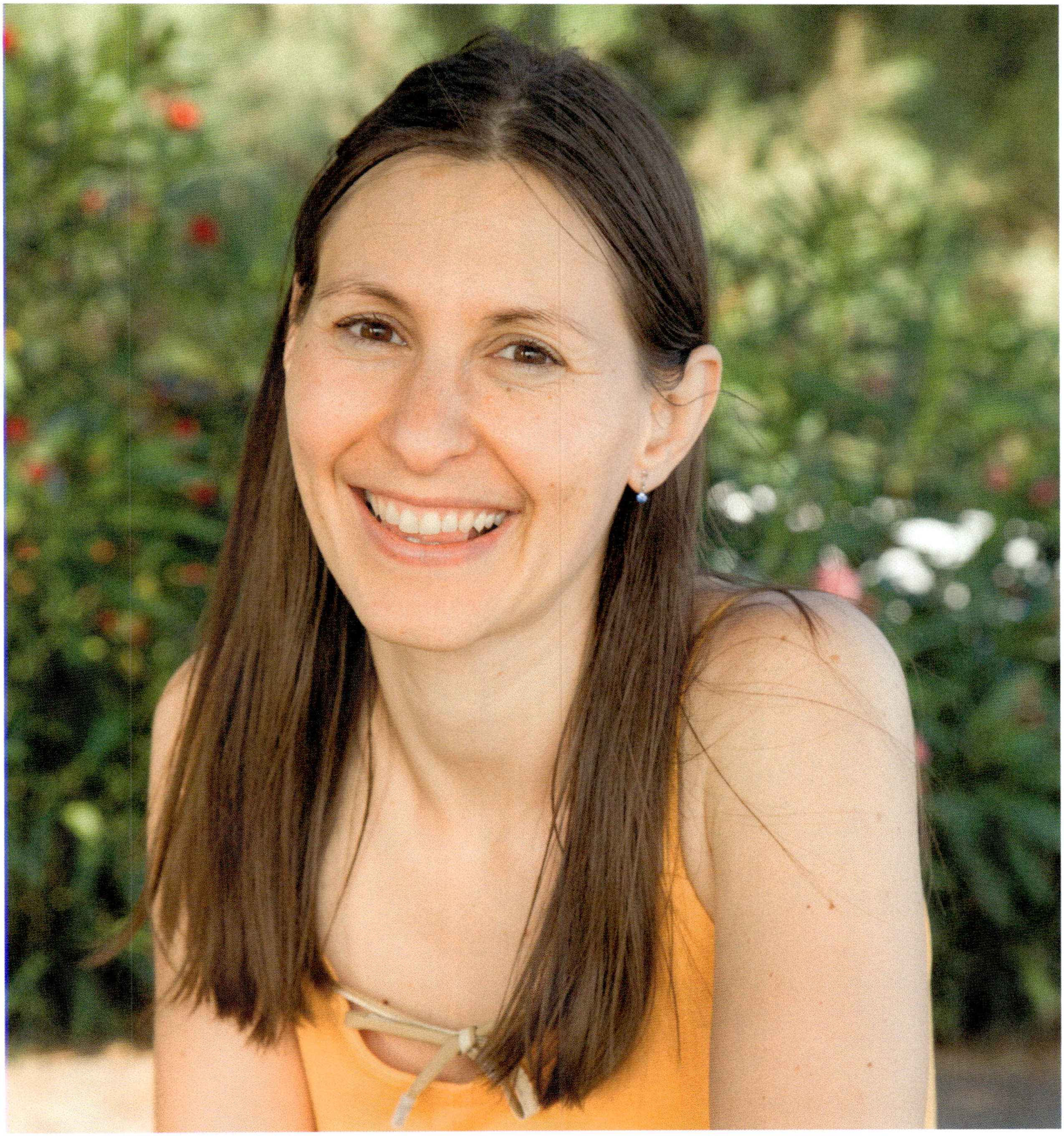

Aperture f7.1 – Focal length 82mm

A narrow depth of field has resulted in:

- The focal point, the woman, being sharp
- The rest of the scene is blurry.
- This effectively isolates our subject from the background and makes it stand out

Choosing where to focus

It's not only where you stand, but where you focus that determines
how much of the background is in or out of focus

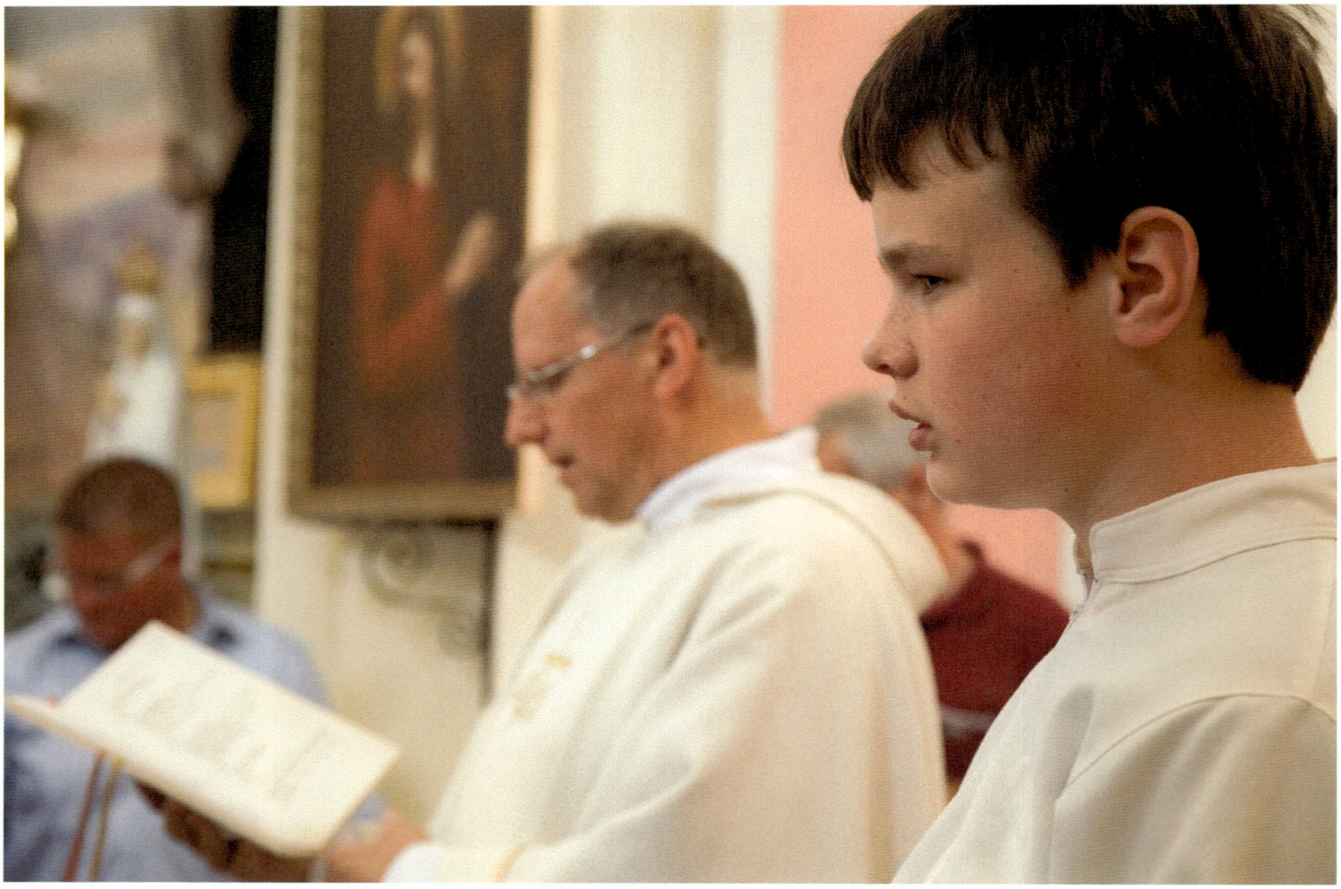

Aperture – f5.6 - Focal length - 85mm
With the focus on the boy and the large aperture, he now stands out in the photo and the priest and man behind are blurred.

Notice how the blurring increases the further back you go in the picture.

Focusing in the middle

With the focus on the priest, notice how the man in the background is now more in focus and the boy is blurred.

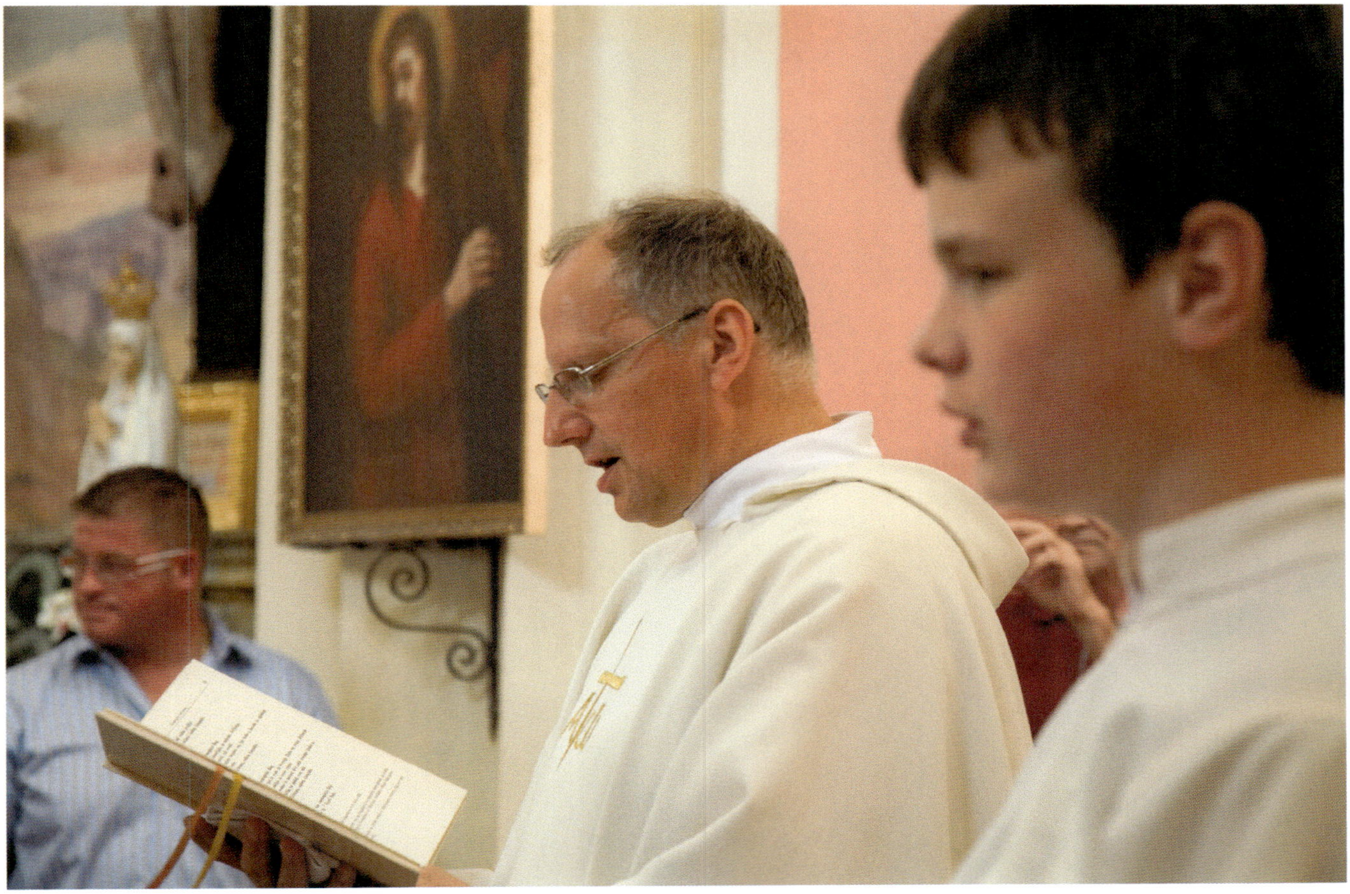

Aperture – f5.6 Focal length - 85mm

Getting rid of messy backgrounds

With an even longer focal length, we are able to further reduce our depth of field and blur the background even more. This is perfect for messy backgrounds which might otherwise distract from our subject. This way we can completely isolated our subject from the background, and, in this case, our eye is drawn straight to the kitten and not to the background.

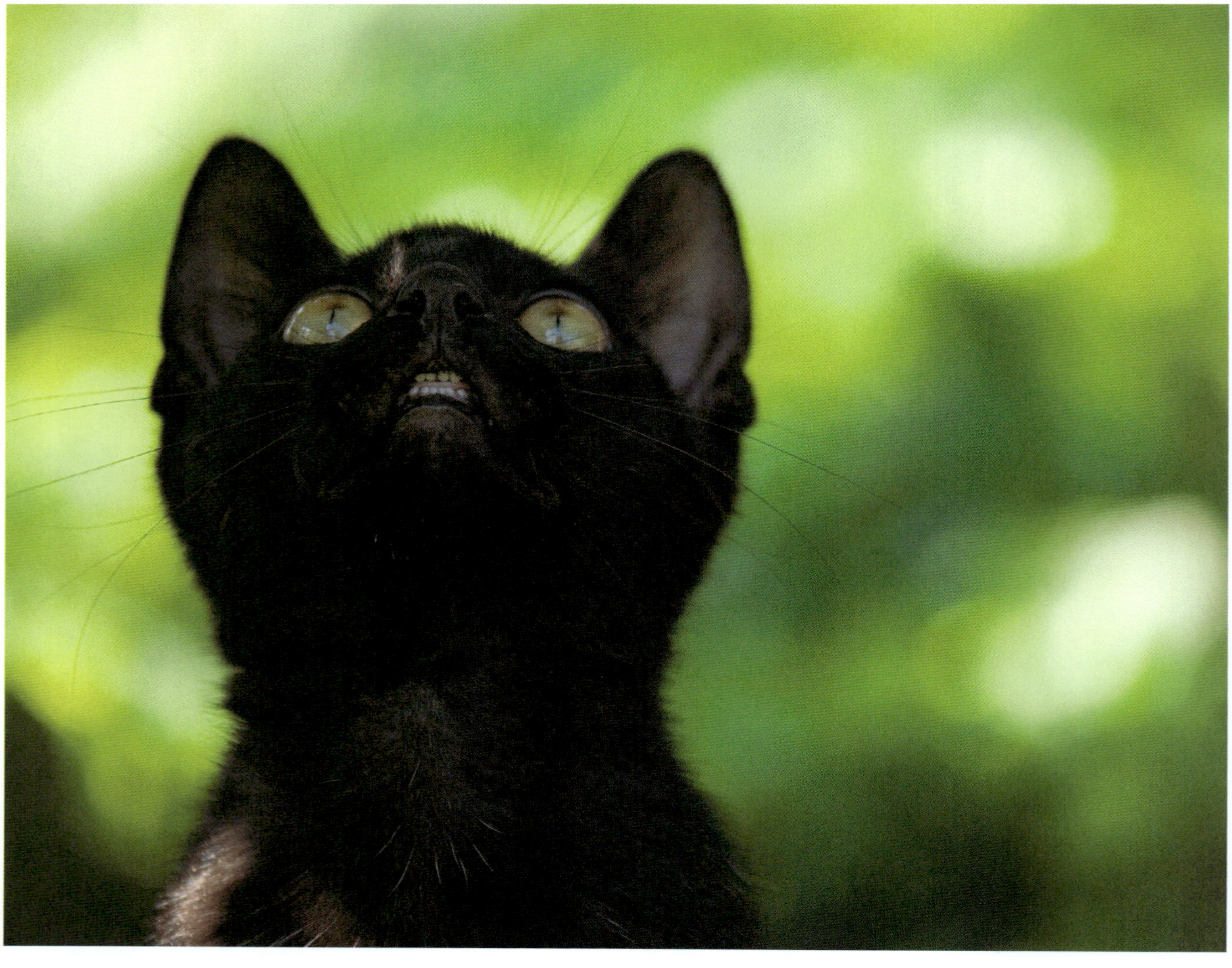

Aperture f5.6 – Focal length 400mm

Creative use of depth of field

We can also use this effect in a creative manner. With the Canada goose the grass behind has been reduced to a pure green background by the long focal length and large aperture.

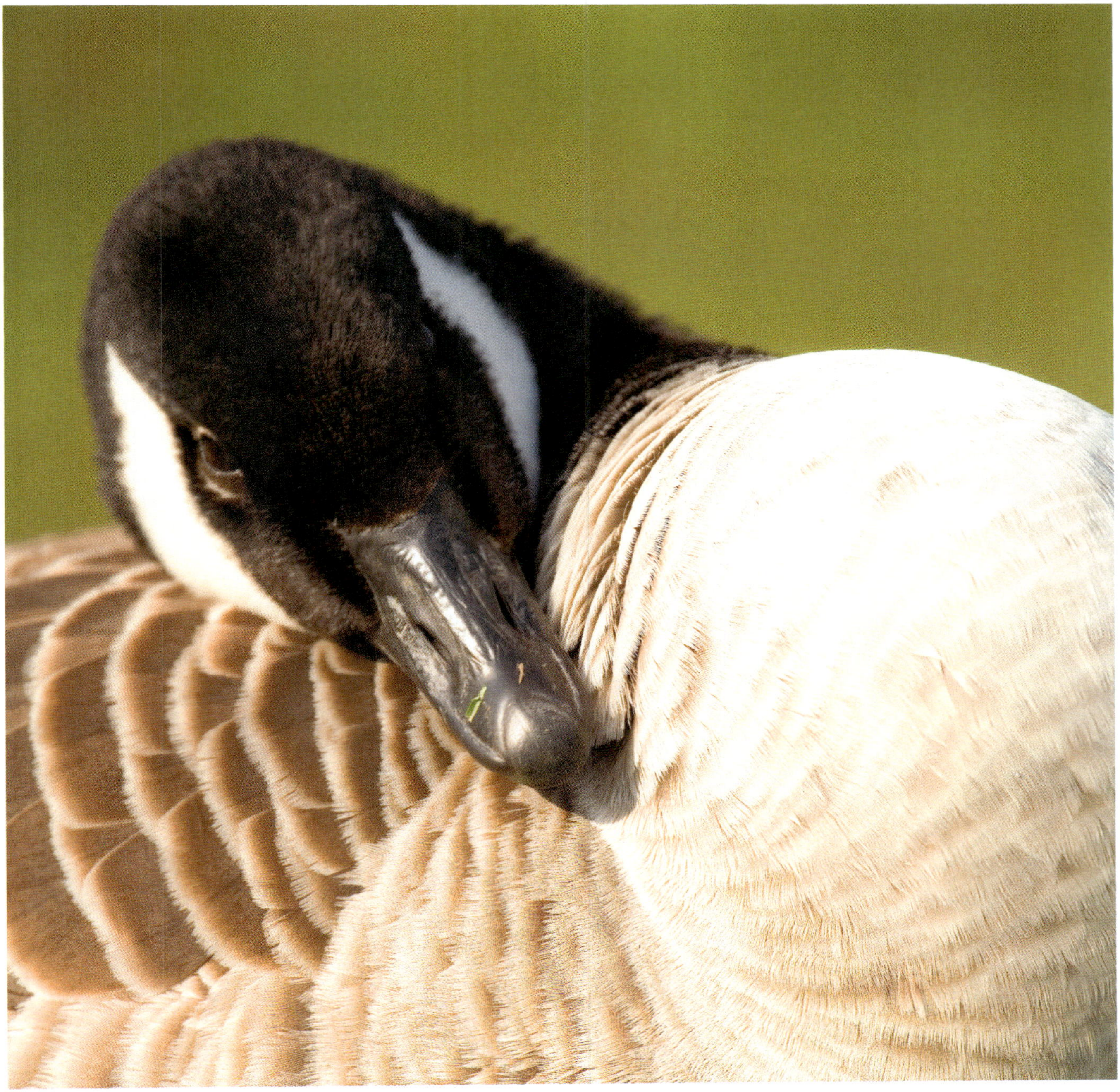

Aperture f7.1 – Focal length 400mm

Here I have focused on the cat, and the narrow depth of field has put the girl out of focus. This way our eye is drawn to the cat first, then into the scene and to the girl. The narrow depth of field has also given us a sense of distance and further enhances the image of the cat following its owner.
Aperture f5.6 – focal length 105mm

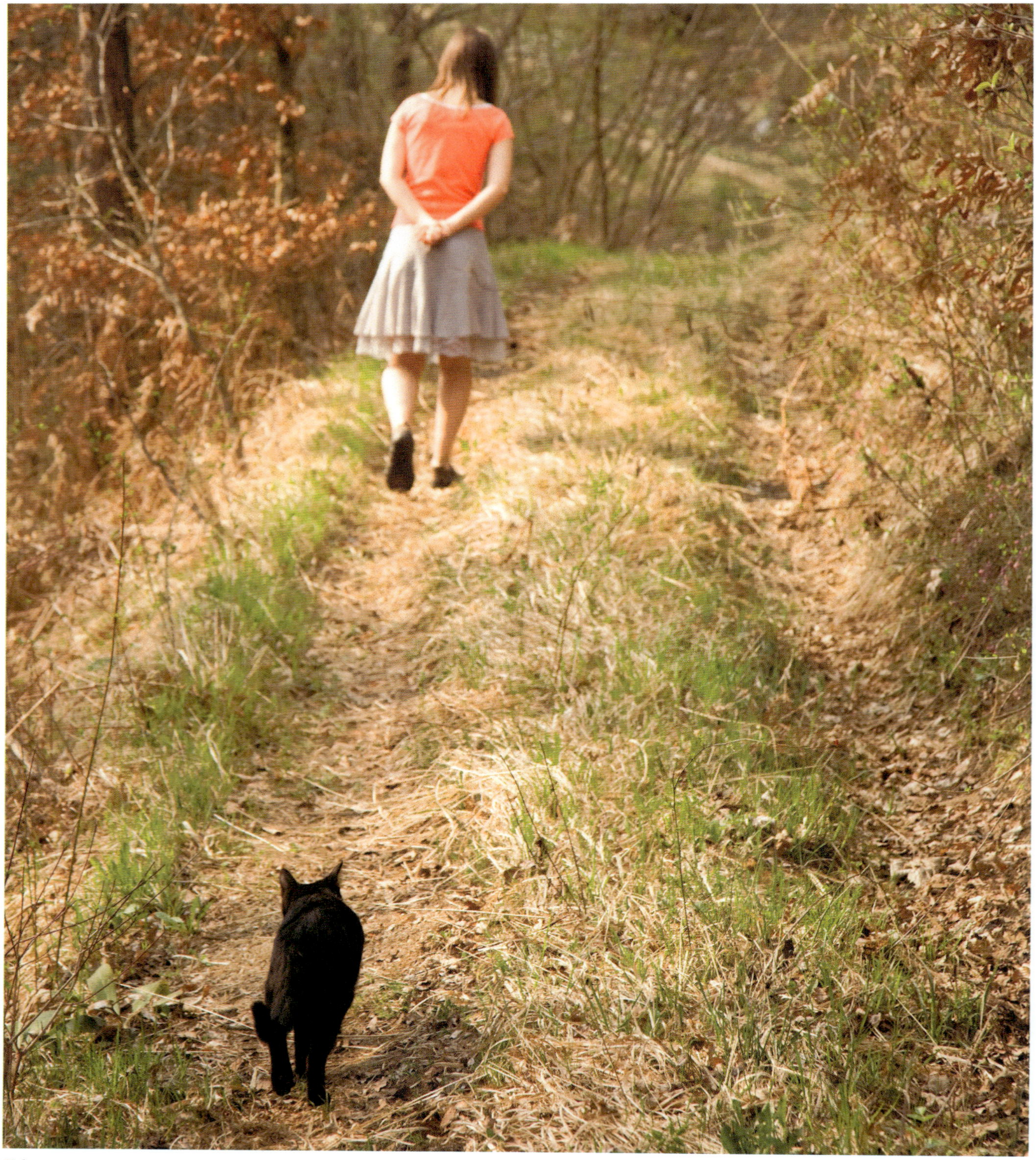

Mistakes

Think about your point of focus.
Choose your point of focus wisely when shooting with a large aperture, long focal length, and getting very close because your depth of field is greatly reduced.

BAD

Aperture f5.6 – Focal length 105mm

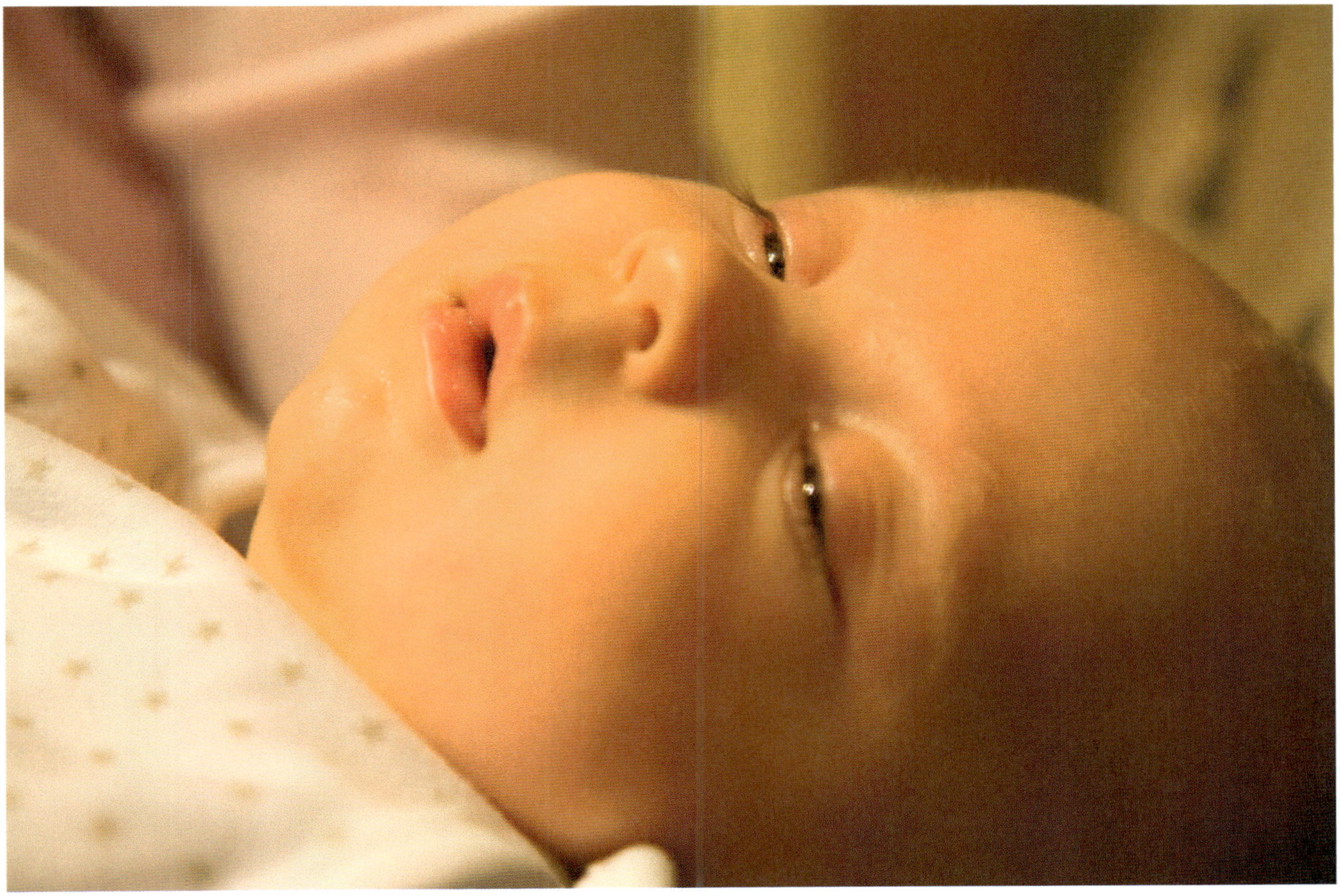

Focal point – right eye
The narrow depth of field has thrown the eye in front out of focus.

GOOD

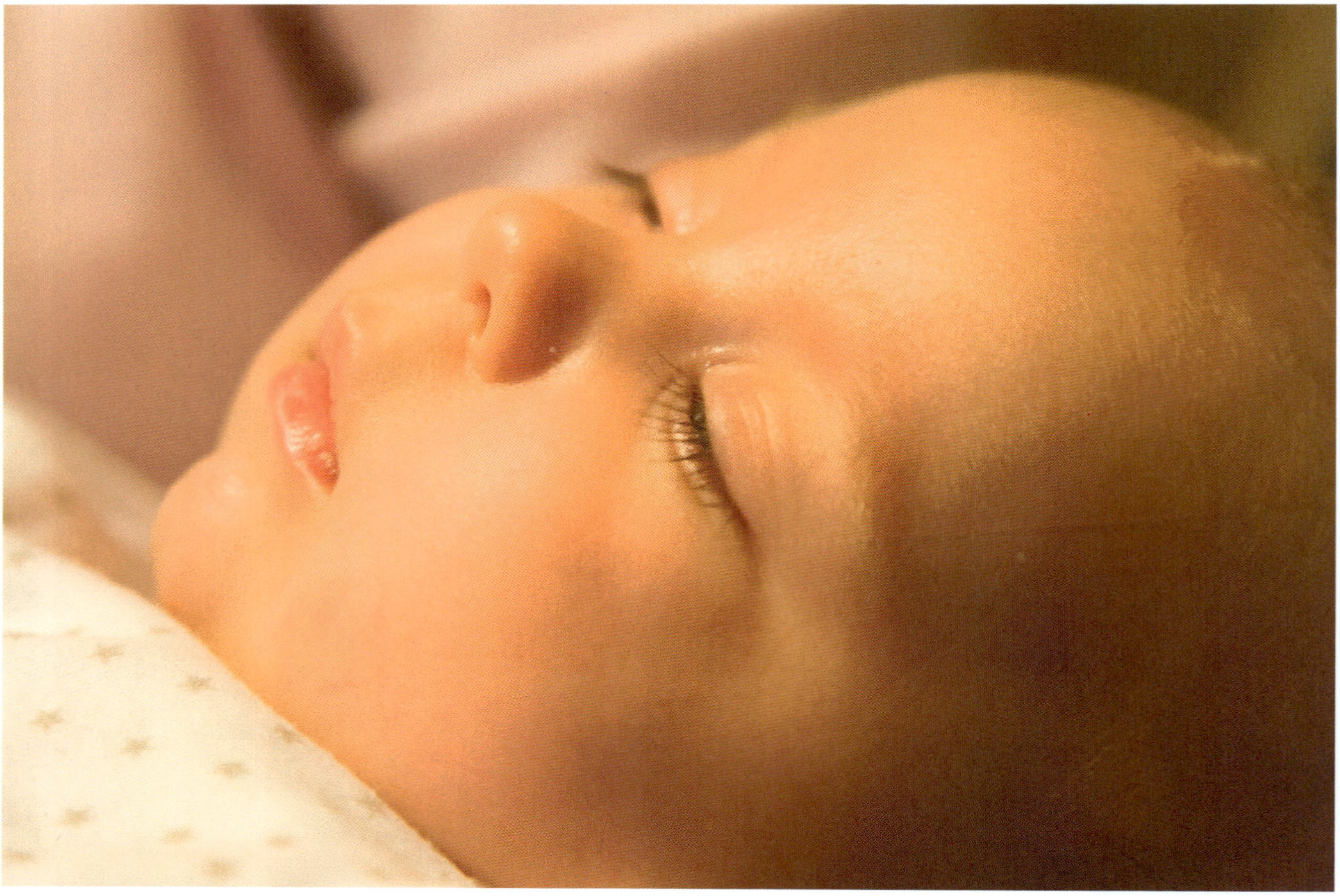

Aperture f7.1 – Focal length 105mm
Focal point – nose
The slightly smaller aperture and focus on the nose has now widened the depth of field and brought the front eye more into focus.

Think about using a smaller aperture

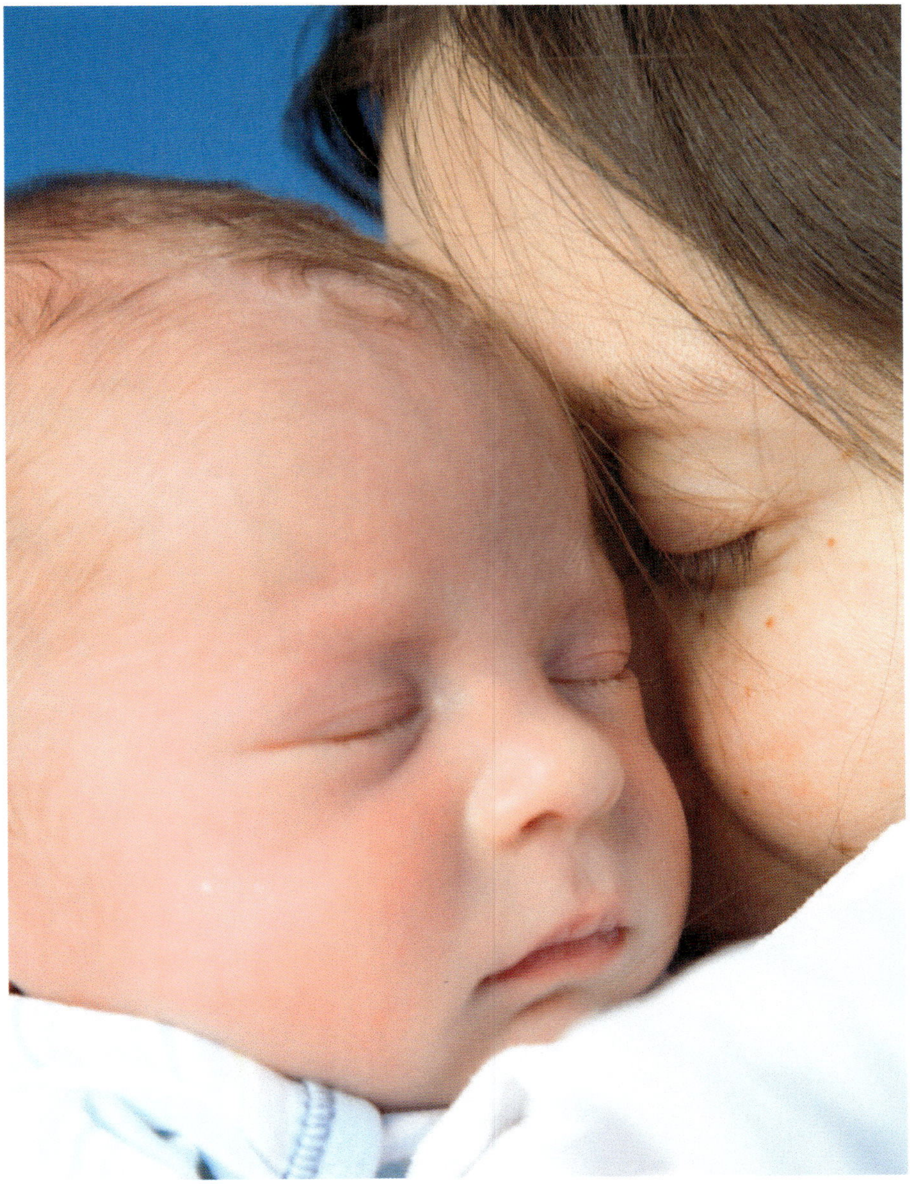

Aperture f8 – Focal length 105mm

When there are two people in your photo, think about their distance apart, not sideways but between you and the camera. Although they are standing next to each other, one might be a little closer than the other. Or, as in the photo above, when a mother is holding her baby, the baby could well be slightly in front of the mother and thus a little closer to the camera. When getting in close and using large apertures, again the depth of field is greatly reduced.

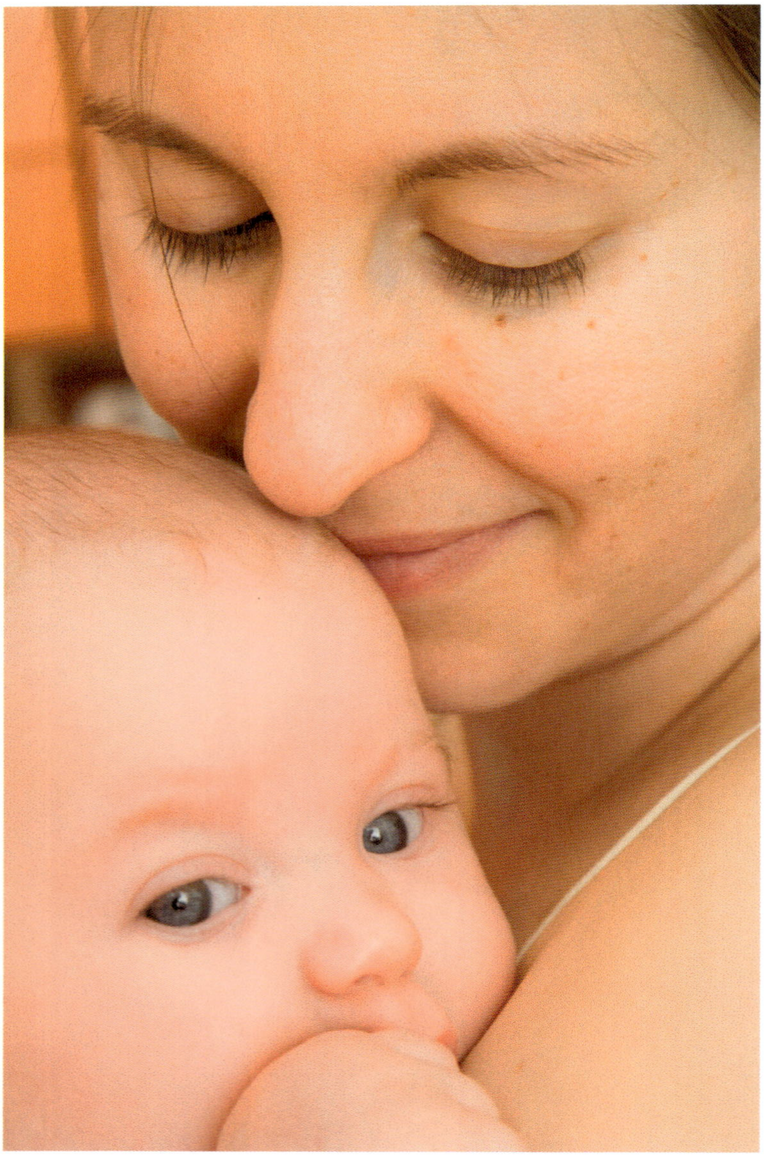

Aperture f9 – Focal length 105mm

With the focus on the mother's eyes, that extra one stop on the aperture has put the baby's face more in focus.

Camera settings

As I said before, many cameras have preset modes you can select which do the work for you and usually comes in the form of subject matter. In the case of aperture here are the options available:

Automatic Modes

Portrait Mode: This mode will set the largest aperture possible with the lowest shutter speed possible. This way the background is thrown out of focus and your subject is made to stand out.

Landscape Mode: This mode selects the smallest aperture possible under the conditions at the time to maximise front to back sharpness.

Creative Mode

AV (aperture value) or A (aperture): This comes in the form of aperture priority, meaning that the user chooses the aperture and the camera then takes care of the shutter speed settings. This way you can choose how much front to back sharpness or blur you want.

ISO

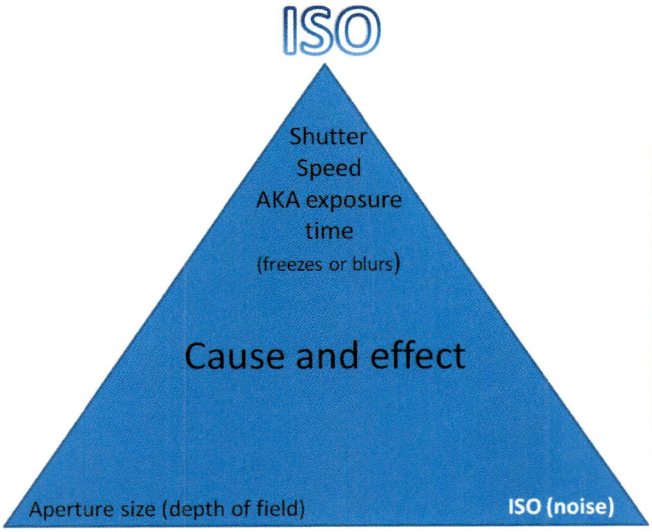

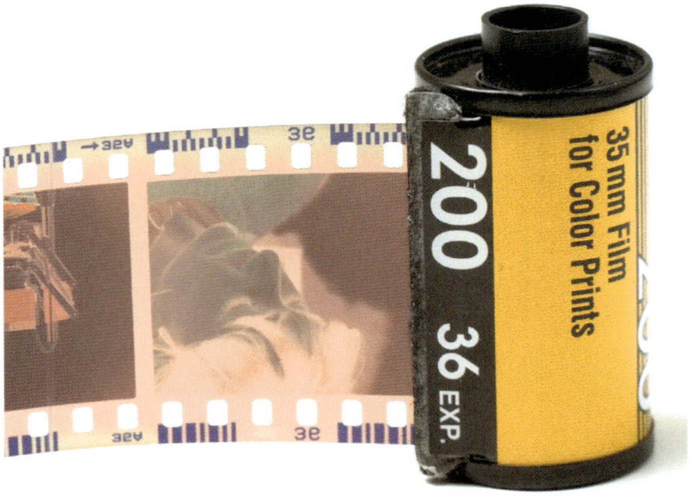

© Claudio Fichera | Dreamstime.com

In the days of film, ISO was also known as film speed. Anyone who is old enough to remember shooting only in film might also recall that when they bought film, alongside the number of photos it would also have a number such as 200, like in the photo here. This number denotes the film speed. So the roll of film here has a film speed of ISO 200.

Digital camera sensors have been designed to emulate ISO film speeds to allow photographers the same, and in fact more, benefits that increasing and decreasing the ISO brings. But in order to understand digital ISO, it helps to also understand how ISO works with film.

Image capture devices

Film

Silver Halide Crystals

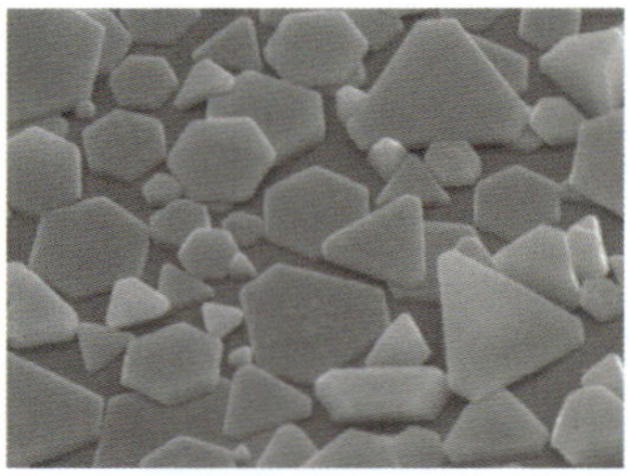

Photo Copyright © 2011 Kodak. Used with permission.

Film is coated with tiny pieces of silver halide crystals. These crystals react when exposed to light and change, depending on the amount of light that falls upon them.

Smaller pieces react slower to light and larger pieces react faster to light. The size is denoted in the film's ISO, which is a measurement of the film speed. Hence:
ISO 100 is slow film
ISO 1600 is fast film

Slow film needs more light to capture a picture, therefore is best used in bright situations. In low light the film must be exposed for longer

Fast film needs less light to capture a picture, therefore is ideal for low light situations and won't need to be exposed for as long as slow film.

Noise - the cost of using a higher ISO

Because film with a higher ISO contains larger pieces of silver halide, the larger pieces show up on the resulting image as grain, and when an image from this is blown up you will see the grain even more. On the other hand, as low ISO films contain smaller pieces of silver halide, there is less grain and the picture remains smooth and sharper even when blown up in size.

Think of it as a mosaic with hundreds of tiny pieces making up one big picture. Now imagine that one mosaic has larger pieces, while another has smaller pieces.

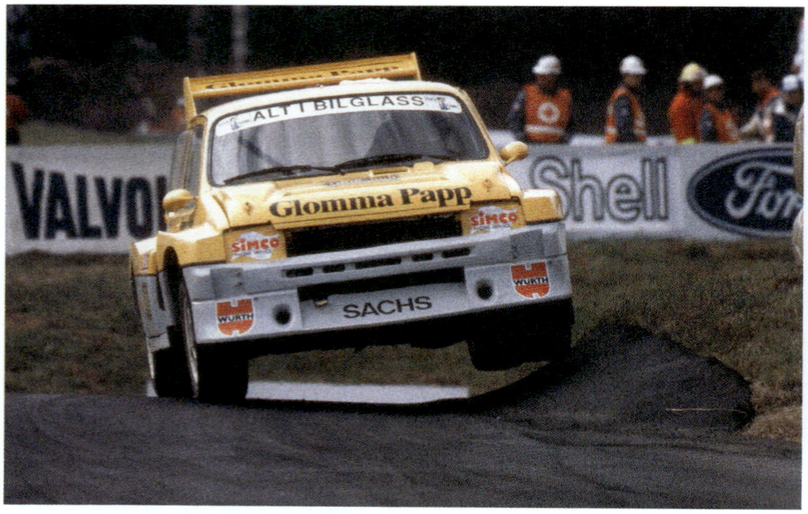

Image shot on ISO1000 film © Eddi Laumanns

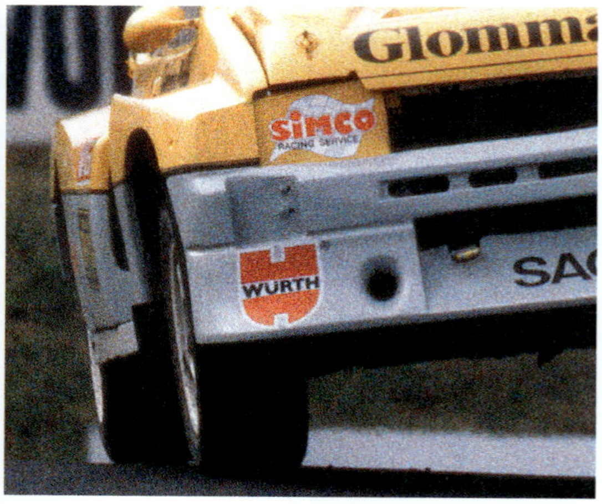

Blown up the grain becomes more obvious

Digital Sensor

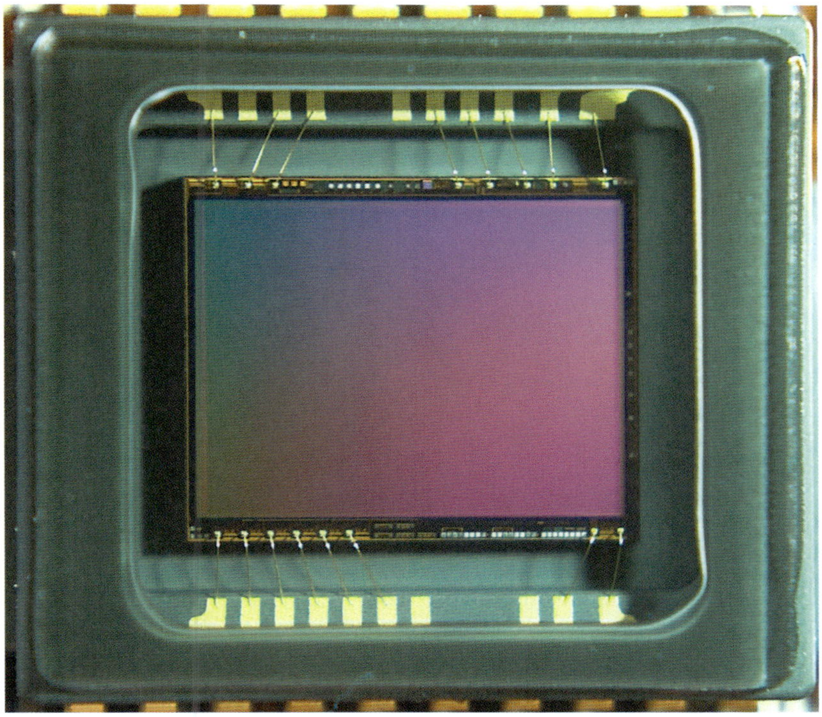
© Dom1 | Dreamstime.com

Digital sensors use tiny photodiodes that allow an electrical current to flow when light is placed upon them. Think of it as a switch that is turned on when a light is shone upon it. To make a photodiode react faster to light you must electrically increase its sensitivity. So in digital sensors ISO sensitivity is emulated, and thus allows us to change the ISO settings in the camera. An obvious advantage to this is that we can do it on a per image basis and not have to change a roll of film. Just like with camera film though, this advantage comes at a price: *noise.*

Noise and its effects

Essentially, the more you increase the sensitivity of the sensor, the more electrical noise you introduce into the signal. It's a bit like your old TV having a bad signal. The picture is fuzzy because of noise generated by electrical interference in the atmosphere.

Noise is worse with cheaper sensors, and better on larger and more expensive ones. The smaller the sensor, and the more pixels it contains, the worse the noise. However, digital camera manufacturers are making huge advances with reducing noise. There is also a lot of good software out there that can reduce noise in an image, although it does soften the image.

Noise is more noticeable on computer screens and when making large prints (depending on the quality of the noise). It's also more noticeable in dark images, or black parts of your photo. Cheaper sensors can suffer from colour noise.

Noise caused by long exposures

Extremely long exposures can also create noise in an image. It happens because the longer the shutter is open, the longer the sensor is powered and so it starts to get hot. The heat build-up also generates noise in the image. So, while with film we can expose for hours, with digital generally anything over 5 minutes will result in a nasty looking image. There is a long exposure noise reduction option in most cameras today, which takes a second photo of equal length with the shutter closed and then uses that to remove the noise from the previous long exposure. But that means you have to wait before you can take another photo. If your exposure was ten minutes long, then you have to wait another ten minutes before you can take another. Noise can also be reduced by software during processing, so it's much better to do it that way.

ISO 128000 on a Canon EOS 5D m3 (Professional SLR)

This camera not only has a full frame sensor (35mm - same as film) but is also a higher end SLR, so the noise is much less noticeable.

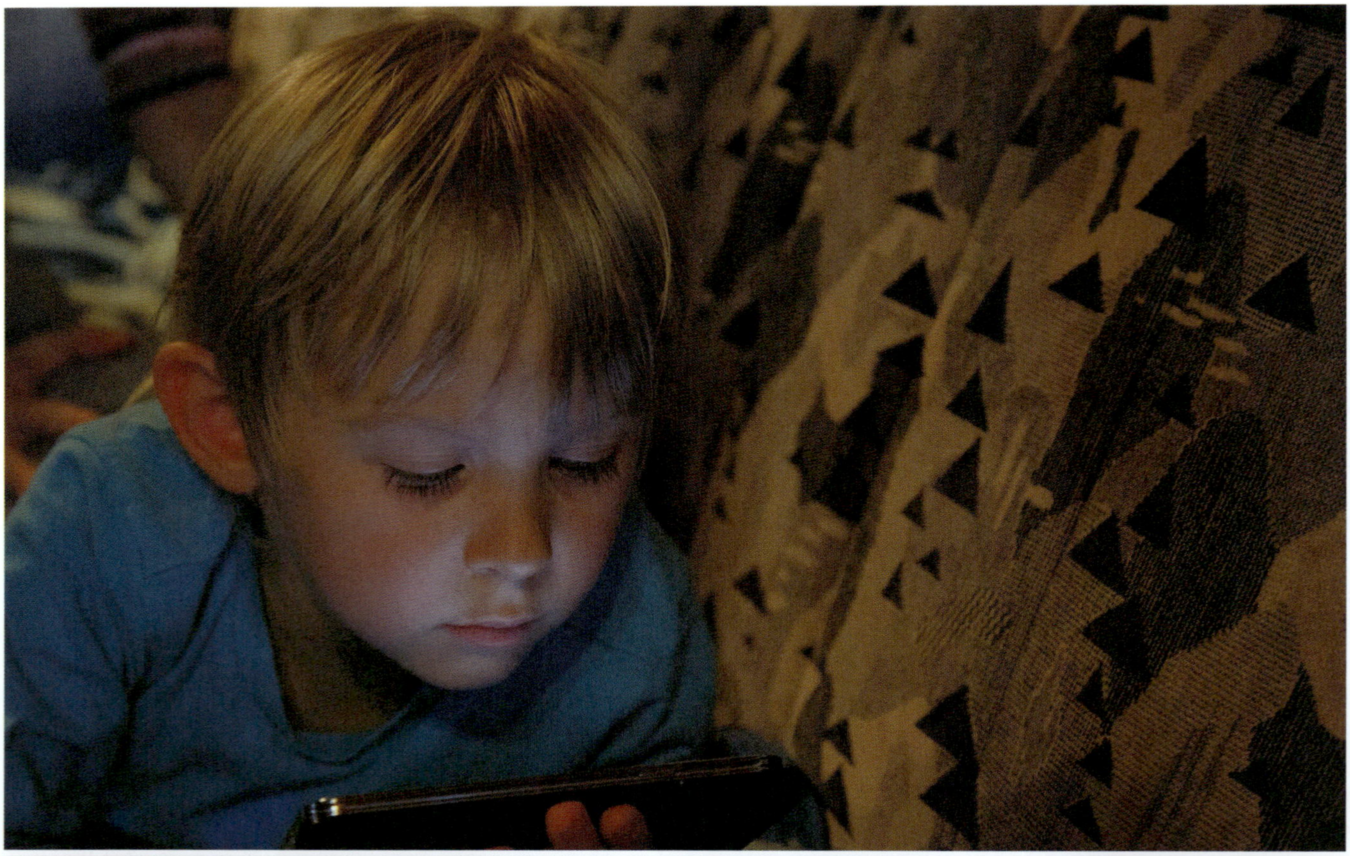

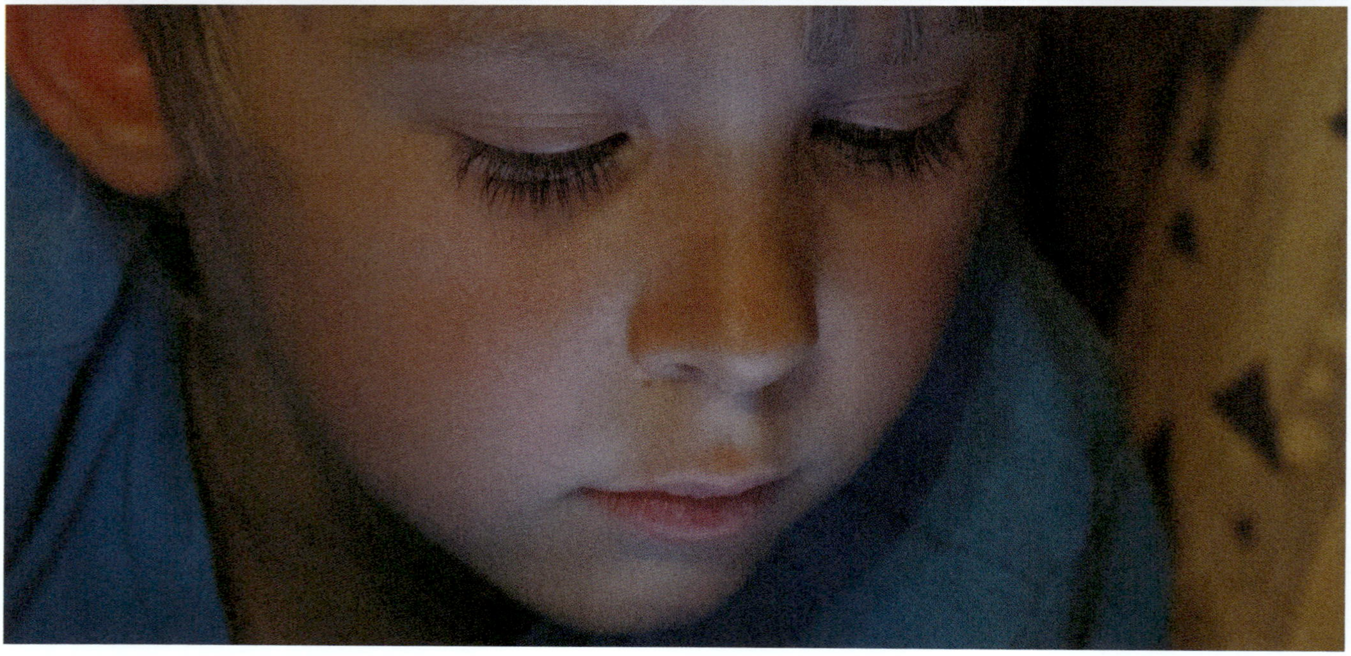

ISO 128000 on a Canon EOS 5D m3 (Professional SLR)

By using noise reduction software we can reduce the noise in an image shot at a high ISO. Again it comes at a price: *softening.* On portraits this is not such a problem as it smoothes out the skin. But it can be a problem with landscapes as we lose sharpness.

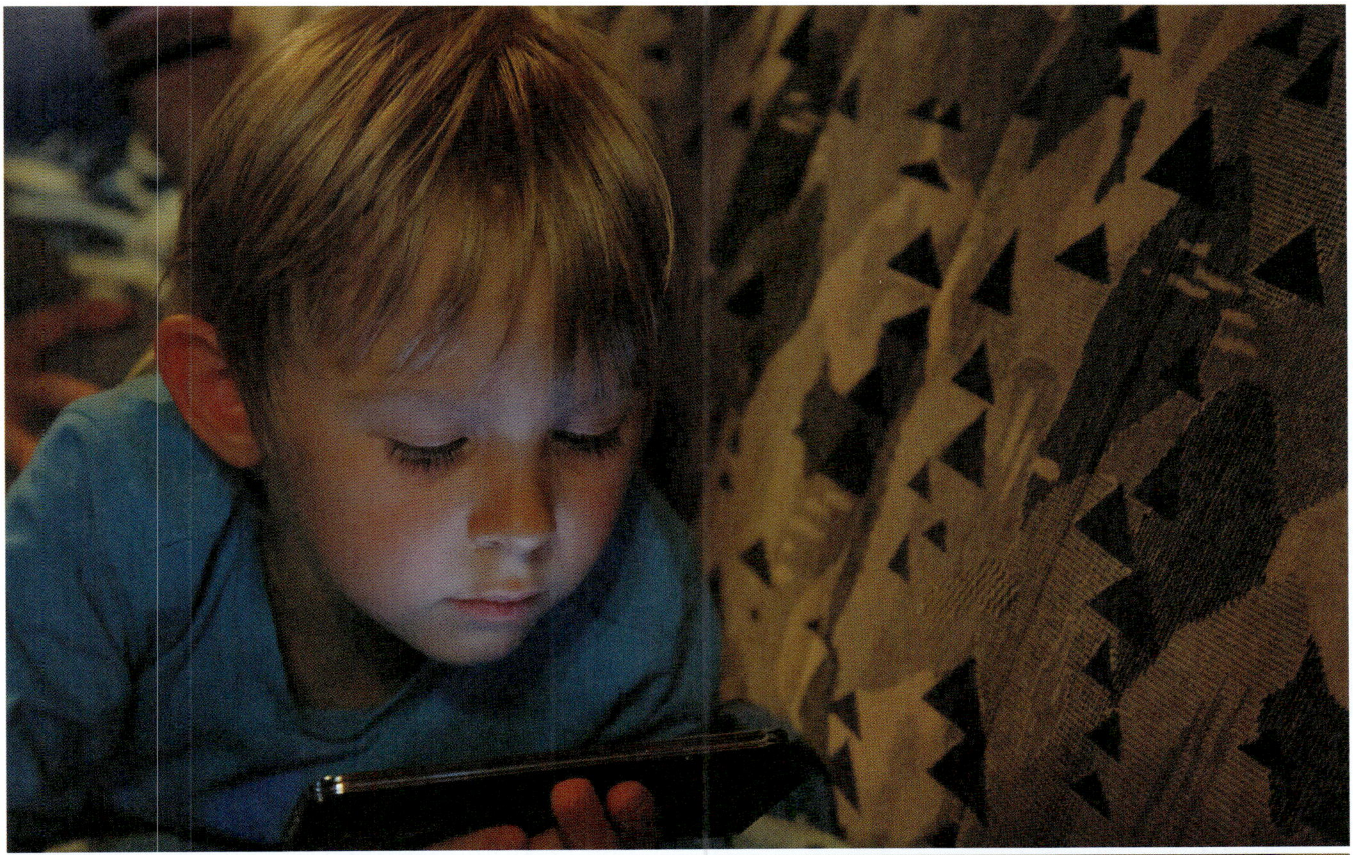

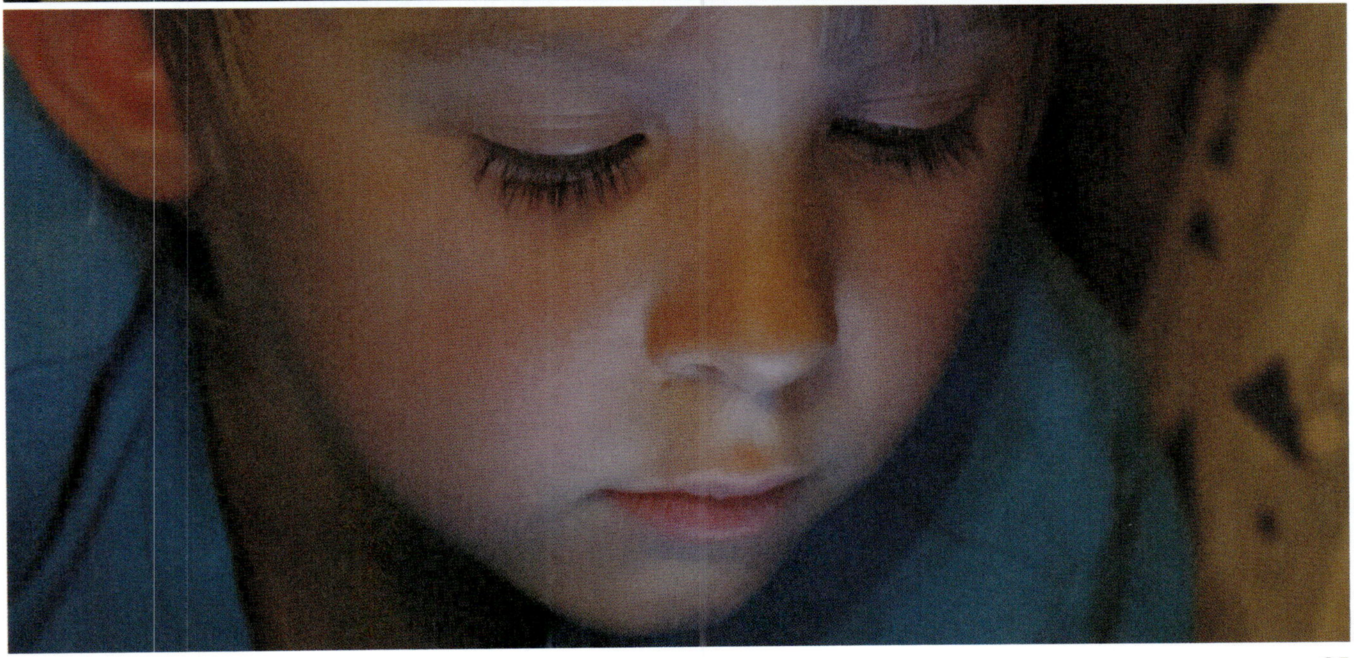

ISO Settings

ISO sensitivity	
Whole	Thirds
50	
	64
100	80
	125
200	160
	250
400	320
	500
800	640
	1000
1600	1250
	2000
3200	2500
	4000
6400	5000
	8000
12500	10000

ISO settings are measured in numbers, as indicated in the table to the left. As the number increases, so does the sensitivity.

Traditionally the camera film's ISO was measured in whole stops, one stop being double the lower stop, or half the higher stop. i.e. 50 100 200 etc

However, with digital sensors having more control over sensitivity they can now offer 1/3 of a stop, offering a much wider range of sensitivity options.

How high the ISO goes will depend on your camera. As manufacturers are continually improving their sensors, ISO ranges are ever increasing. Nonetheless, you should be careful because while your camera may offer a high ISO such as 6400, you may find that the noise at this level is awful and renders the shot unusable. Remember that noise is also more prevalent in dark or black areas, so if you are shooting at night or in a dark place, you might want to think twice about how high you set the ISO.

Tip: take some sample shots on your camera at each ISO setting to determine at what point the noise becomes too bad. Then you will know how high you can go without compromising on quality.

At a glance
Higher number = shorter exposure time = more noise
Lower number = longer exposure time = less noise

Cause and effect

As we are learning with photography, nothing is without consequence. The same applies when setting your shutter speed, aperture or ISO: they all affect one another and ultimately a compromise is required. On the following pages is a breakdown of the effects they have on one another

ISO vs SHUTTER SPEED (camera set to aperture priority mode):

As we saw earlier, increasing the ISO increases the film / sensor's sensitivity to light. In the case of shutter speed, this means that when a higher ISO is set, it will react faster to light and thus need less exposure time to create the photo. So if the camera is set to aperture priority and you have chosen your aperture size the shutter speed is automatically set. But if you increase the ISO, the shutter speed will be increased also. Conversely, if you reduce the ISO the shutter speed is also reduced.

Advantage: Increase the ISO to get a faster shutter speed without increasing the aperture or vice versa.

Reason: To avoid reducing your depth of field and keep more of the scene in focus or to deliberately reduce your depth of field and throw the background and other subjects out of focus.

At a glance

ISO effect on shutter speed:
- ISO 200 = 1/60sec
- ISO 400 = 1/125 sec

Increase ISO = Increase shutter speed
Decrease ISO = Decrease shutter speed
ISO + 1 stop = shutter speed +1 stop
ISO -1 stop = shutter speed -1 stop

Use: Freezing fast moving subjects in low light blurring them in good light. Increasing or reducing the smoothness of water.

Examples: Sports, people, flowing rivers, waves crashing against rocks or the beach.

Compromise: More noise in the photo when increasing the ISO.

ISO vs APERTURE (camera set to shutter priority mode):

Again, we have the same effect with aperture. When the camera is set to shutter priority and you have chosen your shutter speed, the aperture is automatically set. But if you increase the ISO, the aperture will decrease in size because less light is required. Conversely, if you reduce the ISO, the size of the aperture will increase.

Advantage: Increase the ISO to get a smaller aperture without having to decrease the shutter speed or vice versa.

Reason: To increase your depth of field and get more of your scene in focus, or vice versa, without having to compromise your shutter speed.

At a glance

ISO effect on aperture:
- ISO 200 = F11
- ISO 400 = F16

Increase ISO = Decrease aperture size
Decrease ISO = Increase aperture size
ISO + 1 stop = aperture -1 stop
ISO -1 stop = aperture +1 stop

Use: There may be times when you want to set the shutter speed in order to get the precise amount of motion blur or freeze, but your depth of field is too narrow or too wide. Increasing or decreasing the ISO will allow you to control your depth of field without compromising your exposure time.

Examples: Creative sports shots, people, flowing rivers, waterfalls and ocean waves.

Compromise: More noise in the photo when increasing the ISO.

SHUTTER SPEED vs APERTURE (camera set to shutter priority mode):

At a glance
Shutter effect on aperture:
• 1/125= F16
• 1/250= F11
Increase shutter = Increase aperture
Decrease shutter = Decrease aperture
Shutter +1 stop = aperture -1 stop
Shutter – 1 stop = aperture – 1 stop

With the camera set to shutter priority, we choose our shutter speed and the aperture is set automatically. But again, if you increase the shutter, you also increase the aperture size, and vice versa, because a faster shutter speed needs more light, and therefore a larger aperture is required to get it.

Advantage: Increase or decrease the shutter speed without having to adjust the ISO.

Reason: To control how much you freeze or blur your subject.

Use: Freezing moving subjects in low light or deliberately adding motion blur.

Examples: Sports, people, flowing rivers, waves crashing against rocks or the beach.

Compromise: A faster shutter speed will increase the aperture and thus result in loss of depth of field and front to back sharpness. A slower shutter speed will reduce the aperture and result in an increased depth of field and more of the scene in focus where it may not be wanted.

APERTURE vs SHUTTER SPEED (camera set to aperture priority mode):

At a glance
Aperture effect on shutter:
• F16 = 1/125
• F11 = 1/250
Increase aperture = increase shutter speed
Reduce aperture = reduce shutter speed
Aperture + 1 stop = shutter + 1 stop
Aperture – 1 stop = shutter – 1 stop

Well, by now you get the picture.

Advantage: Increase or decrease the aperture without having to adjust the ISO.

Reason: To keep your depth of field large or small and reduce noise.

Use: Maintaining front to back sharpness in a landscape scene or increasing depth of field to include multiple subjects and keep them all sharp. Reducing depth of field to deliberately throw the background or other subjects out of focus.

Examples: Sports, people, landscapes.

Compromise: Reduces shutter speed and increases motion blur or vice versa.

Part 6
White Balance

Light temperature:

As the title indicates, light has a temperature, which is why some light seems warmer (more red) and some colder (more blue). Colour temperature is measured in kelvins (K). The most obvious example of this is candlelight, which has a very low colour temperature and appears warm (more red). Tungsten light (household lightbulb) also has a low colour temperature. Below is a chart showing the colour temperatures of a variety of light sources.

Color Temperature	Light Source
1000-2000 K	Candlelight
2500-3500 K	Tungsten (household lightbulb)
3000-4000 K	Sunrise/Sunset
4000-5000 K	Fluorescent light
5000-5500 K	Camera flash
5000-6500 K	Daylight with clear sky (sun high in the sky)
6500-8000 K	Overcast or cloudy sky
9000-10000 K	Shade or heavily overcast sky

Matching the colour temperature of the light source and the camera:

Ideally we want our whites to be white. But this won't happen if we don't match the colour temperature of the light source with the camera. To do this we need to match the colour temperature setting of the camera with the light source. If our setting is higher, then the picture will be warmer (more red), if we set it lower, then the picture will be colder (more blue). We do this by adjusting something called white balance. See the examples on the following pages.

At a glance
Colour temperature of light:
• Low colour temperature, 1500K is redder
• High colour temperature, 9000K is bluer
Example:
1. Midday sun has a higher colour temperature and is cooler
2. Sun at sunset has a lower colour temperature and is therefore redder

How does it affect my photo?

Camera film is colour balanced for daylight conditions. If you ever took photos inside with the lights on and without using a flash you probably noticed you got a red colour cast over the entire image. This is because there is a difference between the colour temperature of the film and the light source. In the image below the white balance has been set to daylight, giving the same results.

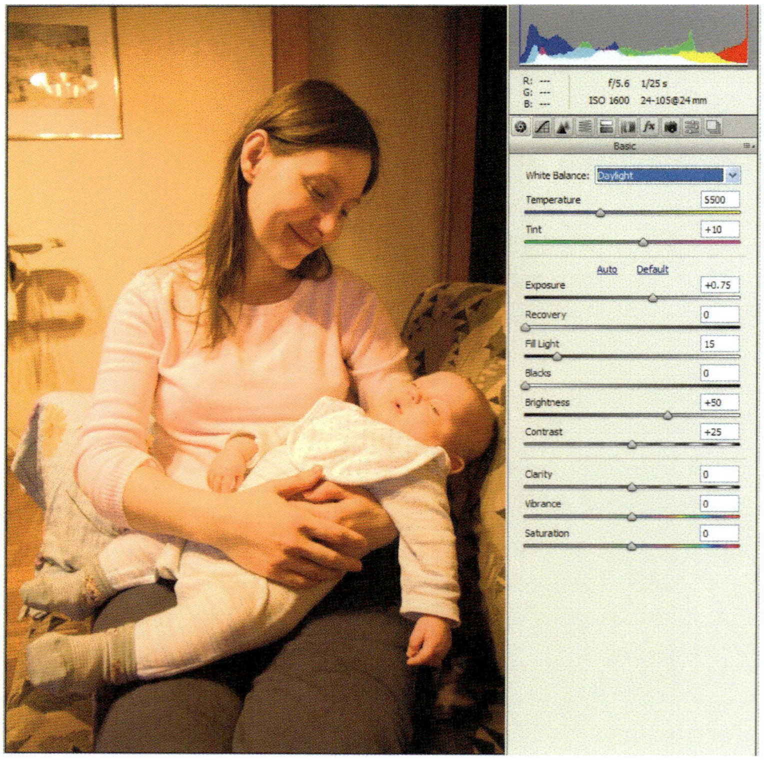

Setting the correct white balance

With film we would have had to buy a special tungsten balanced film to shoot indoors under artificial light and make your whites white, so to speak. But like ISO, we have the advantage of being able to change the white balance per image. For these conditions we need to set it to the tungsten setting. Hence the colour cast is gone, we see more natural looking skin tones, and the whites are white.

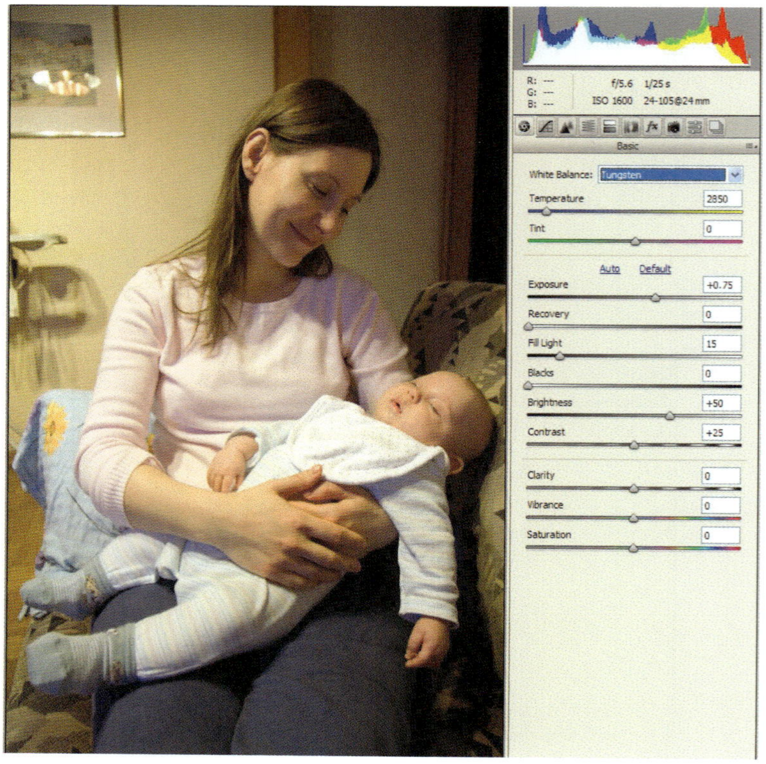

But why is it red, when we can see it as white with our own eyes?

Because our eyes have their own internal auto white balance. We have the ability to adapt and see most whites as white no matter what the colour temperature. The camera cannot.

The idea of white balance is to match the colour temperature setting of the camera with the temperature of the light source, therefore rendering whites and other colours correctly. Although you can set the actual colour temperature in kelvins using the "K" setting, there are also a bunch of presets that are much easier to use and understand.

The image with the white balance set to daylight has a red cast because the camera's colour temperature has been set higher than the temperature of the light source.
Camera = 5500k Light source = 2500 – 3500k

When the camera's setting is higher than the light source you will get a red colour cast. When it is lower, you will get a blue colour cast.

Here is a chart that shows the preset against the colour temperature. Refer to your camera's manual for the symbols associated with them.

Mode	Colour temperature (approx. K)
Auto	3000 - 7000
Daylight	5200
Shade	7000
Cloudy, Sunset	6000
Tungsten	3200
White fluorescent	4000
Flash	6000
Custom	2000-10000

Outdoors on a clear day we can see the tungsten setting has rendered the image with a blue cast because it's a lower temperature than the light source.

Camera = 2850k Light = 5500k

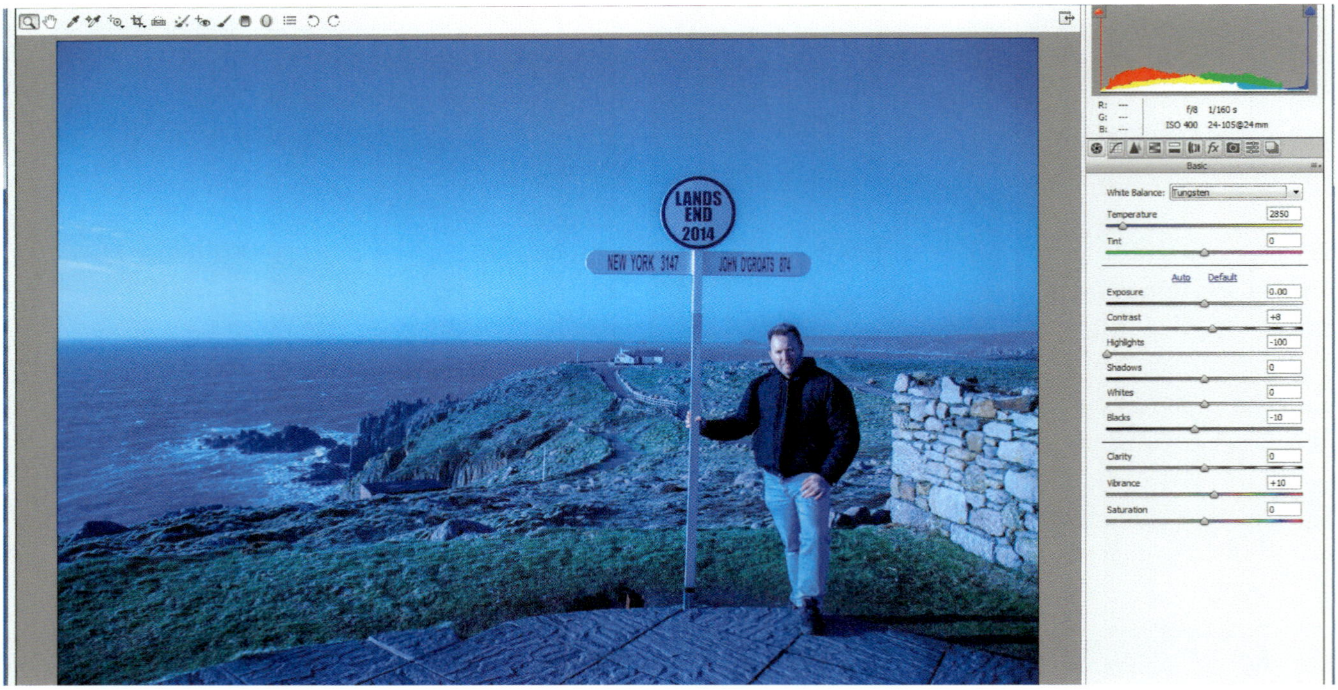

Daylight setting for outdoors on clear days with sun up high

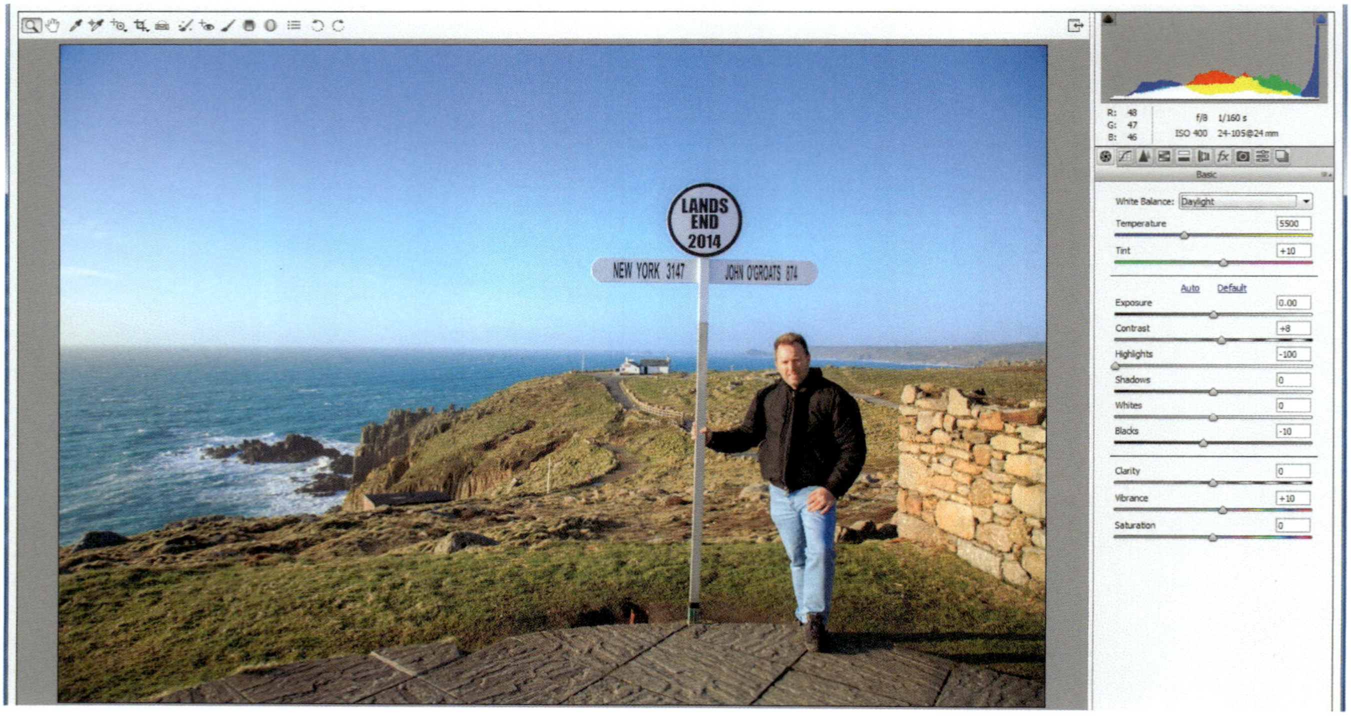

Here on a clear day the shade setting has rendered the image with a reddish brown tone, making the blue sky and the white clouds look dirty brown because the camera setting was higher than the light source.

Camera = 7500k   Light source = 5500k

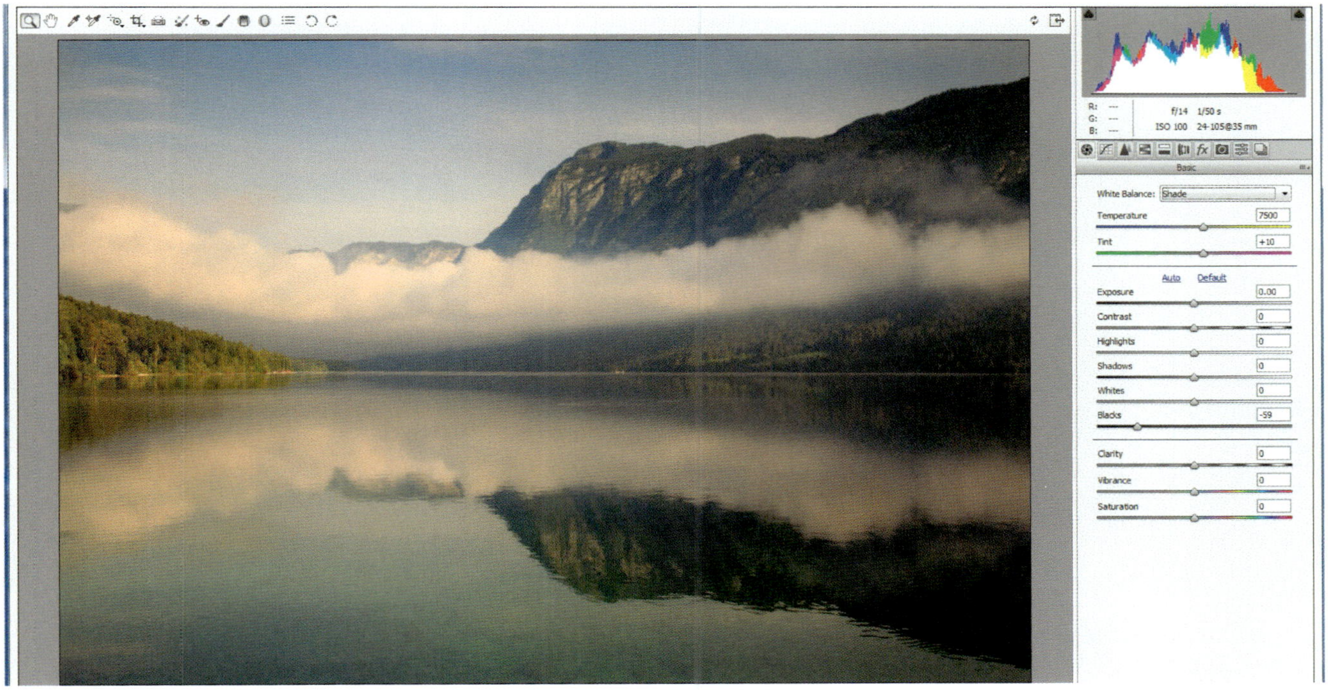

Camera set to daylight

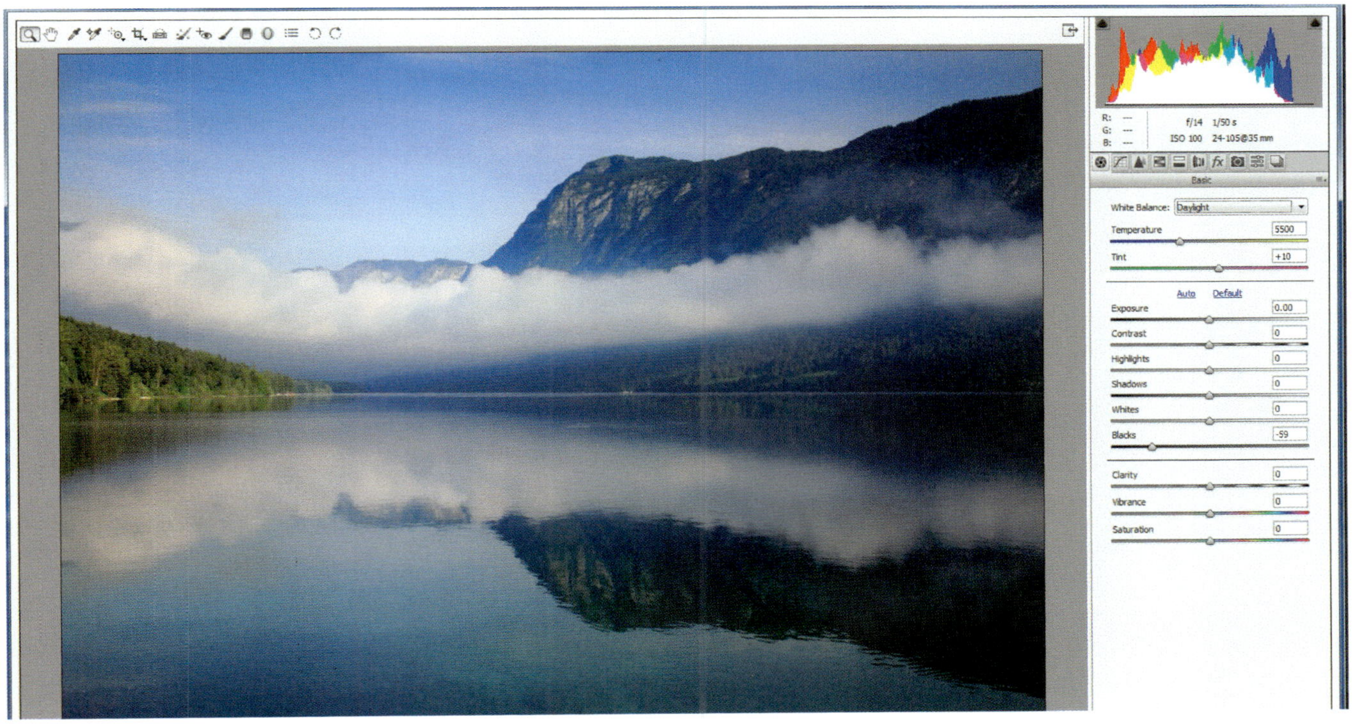

Moonlit nights

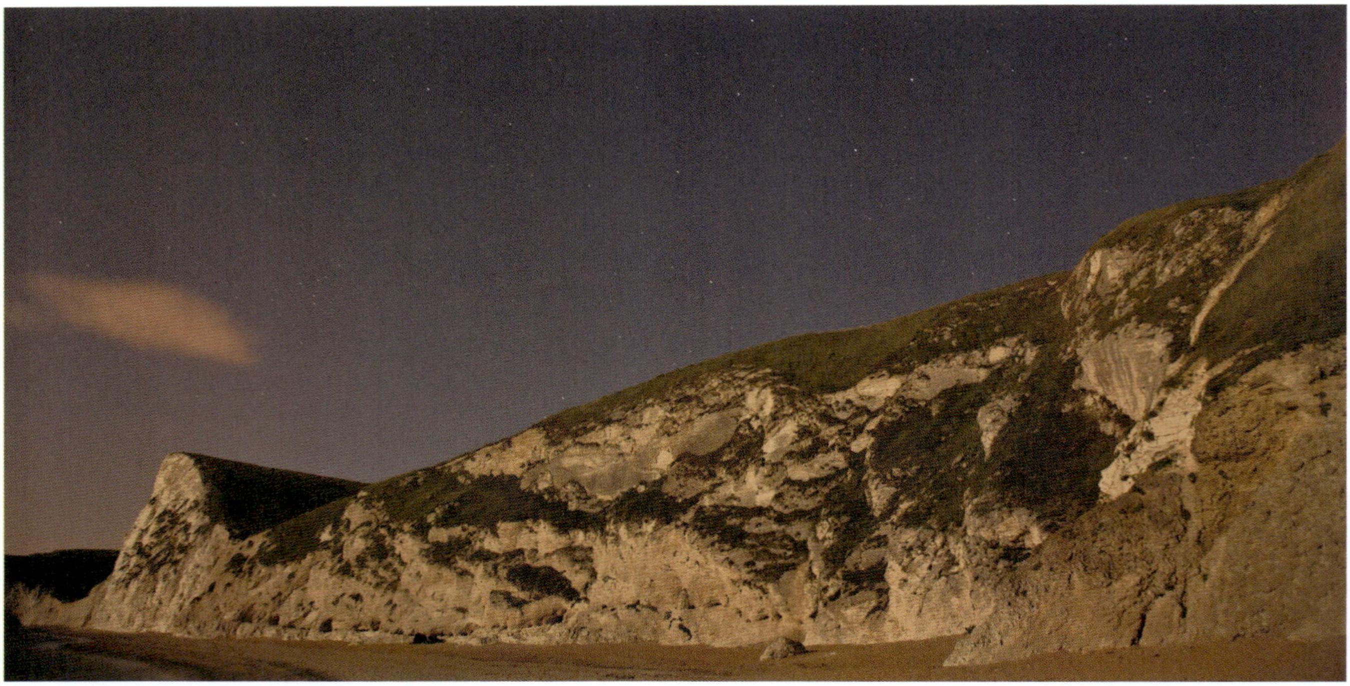

Moonlight has a lower colour temperature and as this was set to daylight it's too warm.

White balance to fluorescent (3800k)

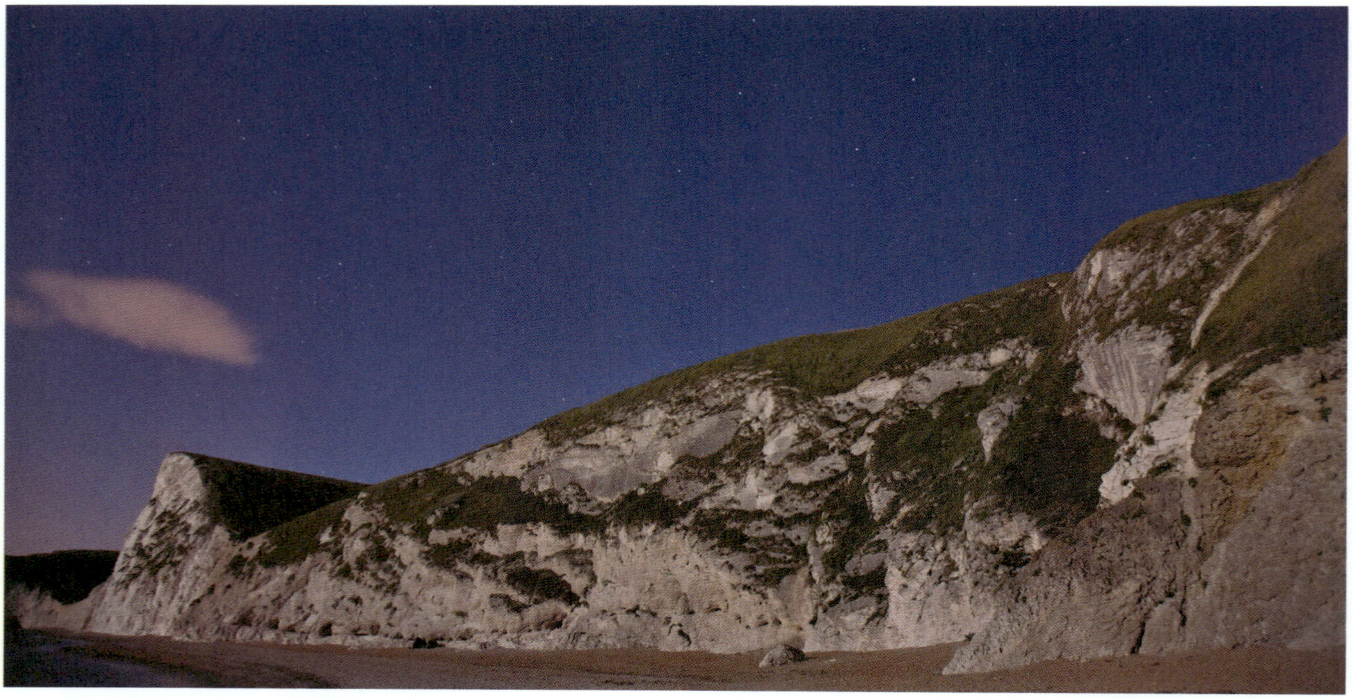

Durdle Door beach, Dorset, UK

Creative use of white balance

We don't always want to get the white balance correct. Get creative sometimes:

As a warm up filter

Film landscape photographers often have a warm up filter on their lenses when shooting at sundown or sunup. This filter is red and is used to enhance the warmth of the scene by adding more red overall. With digital this is no longer necessary because we can do the same with the white balance by increasing the colour temperature setting on the camera.

By setting the white balance to shade (7500k) I have enhanced the colours of this misty sunrise. Be careful though, as this technique doesn't suit all images. If there is blue sky in your image, it will be rendered dirty brown like in the photo we saw earlier. Remember that this will put a reddish-brown colour cast over the entire image, so it's only suitable when the scene already contains mostly red or brown, such as sunrises, sunsets and autumn scenes.

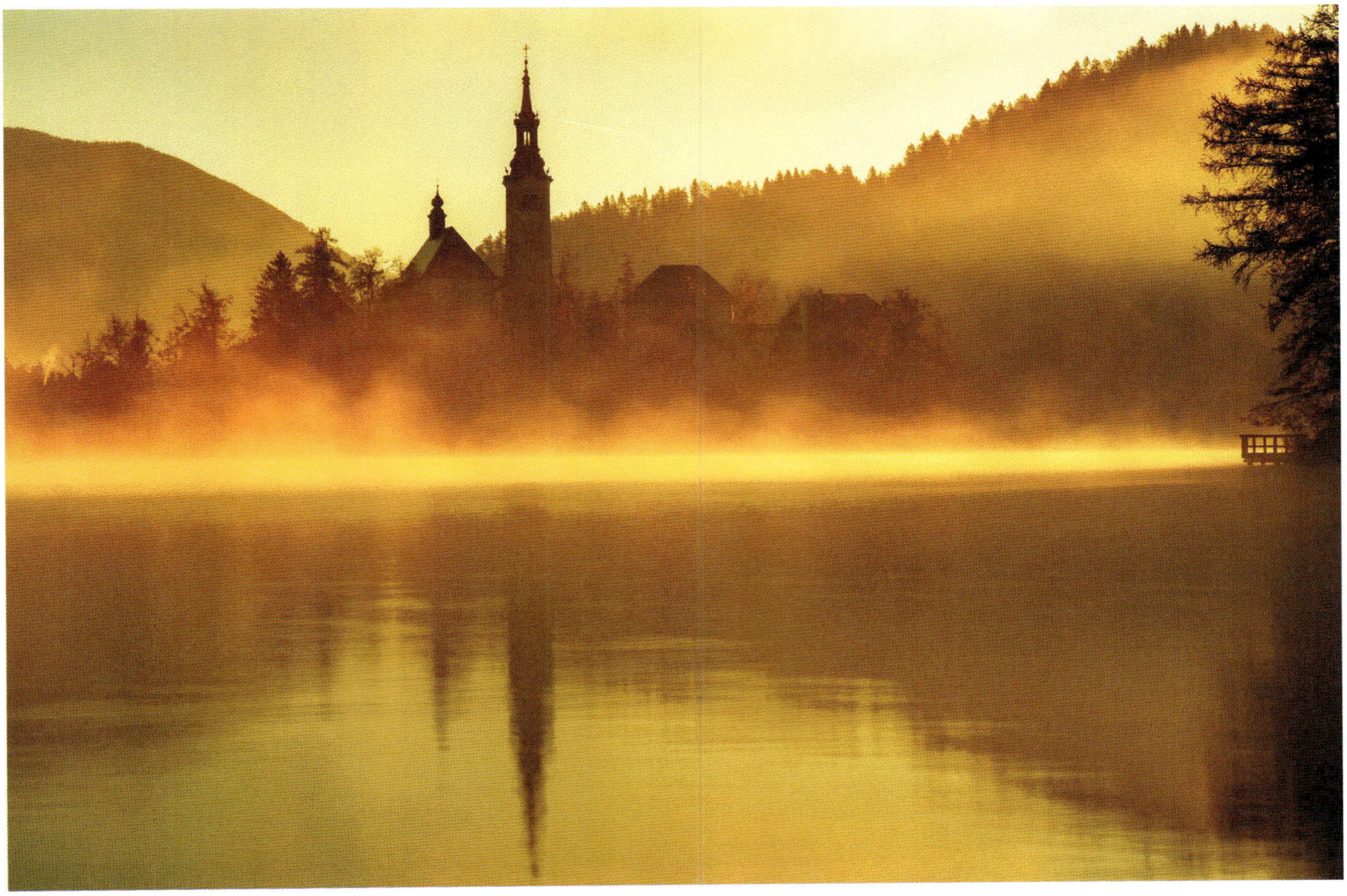

Misty sunrise at Lake Bled, Slovenia

As a cooling filter

Another filter is the cooling filter, which is blue. This is used at dusk or dawn to enhance the blue tones seen at twilight (also known as the blue hour).

Although your manual may tell you to set your white balance to cloudy for twilight periods, it's actually better to set it to daylight to retain the lovely blue tones you get during the twilight period at dawn or dusk.

Twilight has a high colour temperature, so setting at daylight adds more blue (cooling).

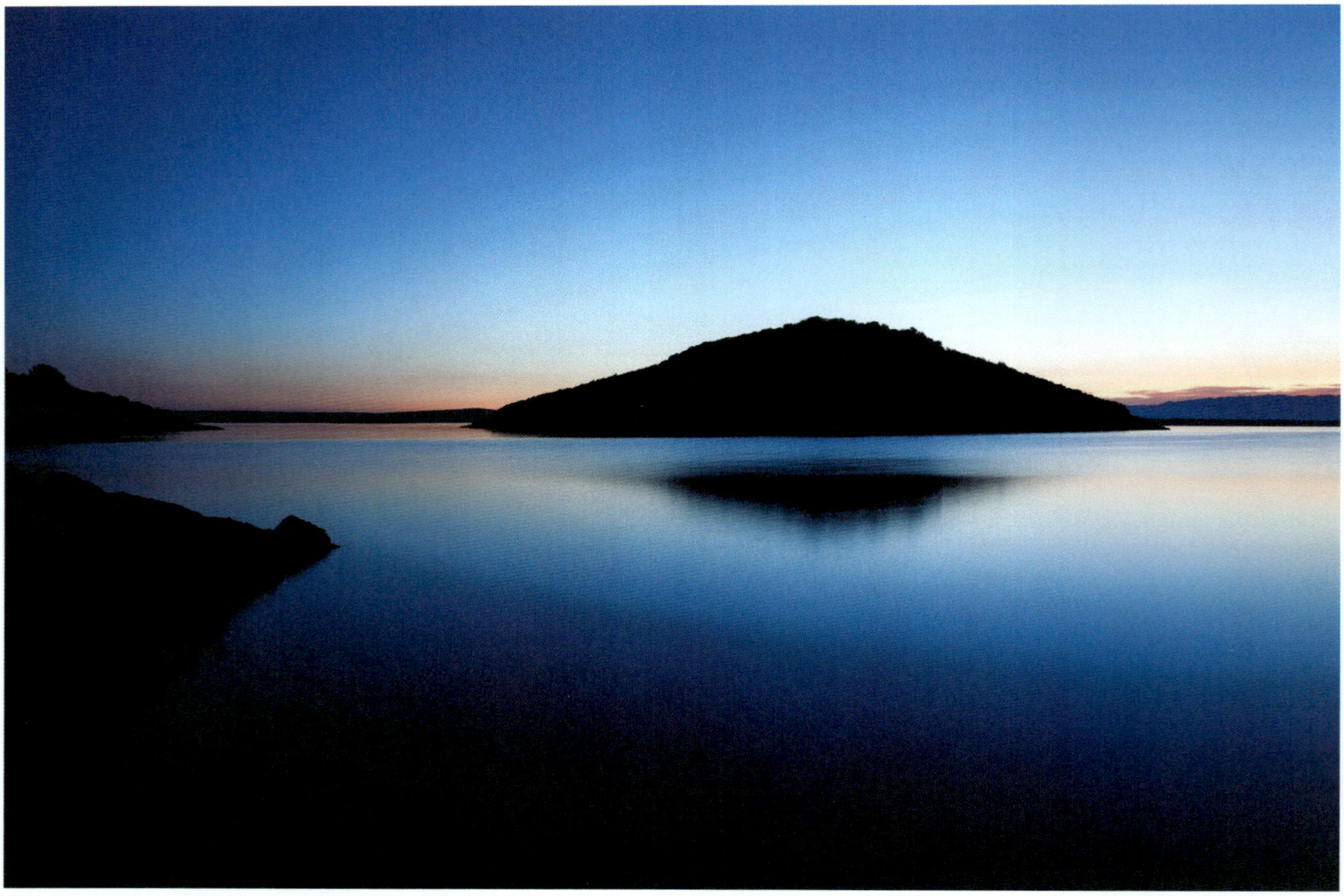

Dawn at Losinj Island, Croatia

Creating other effects using the white balance

For this photo of Lake Bohinj in Slovenia I set the white balance to daylight (5500k)

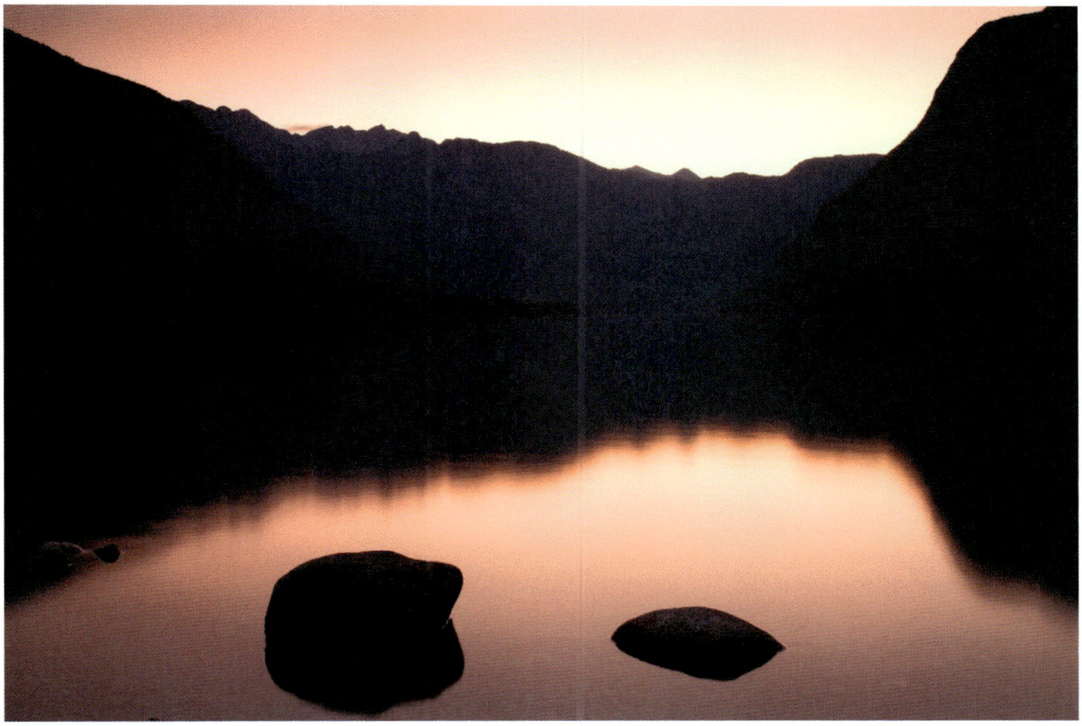

For this version I set the white balance to fluorescent (3800k)

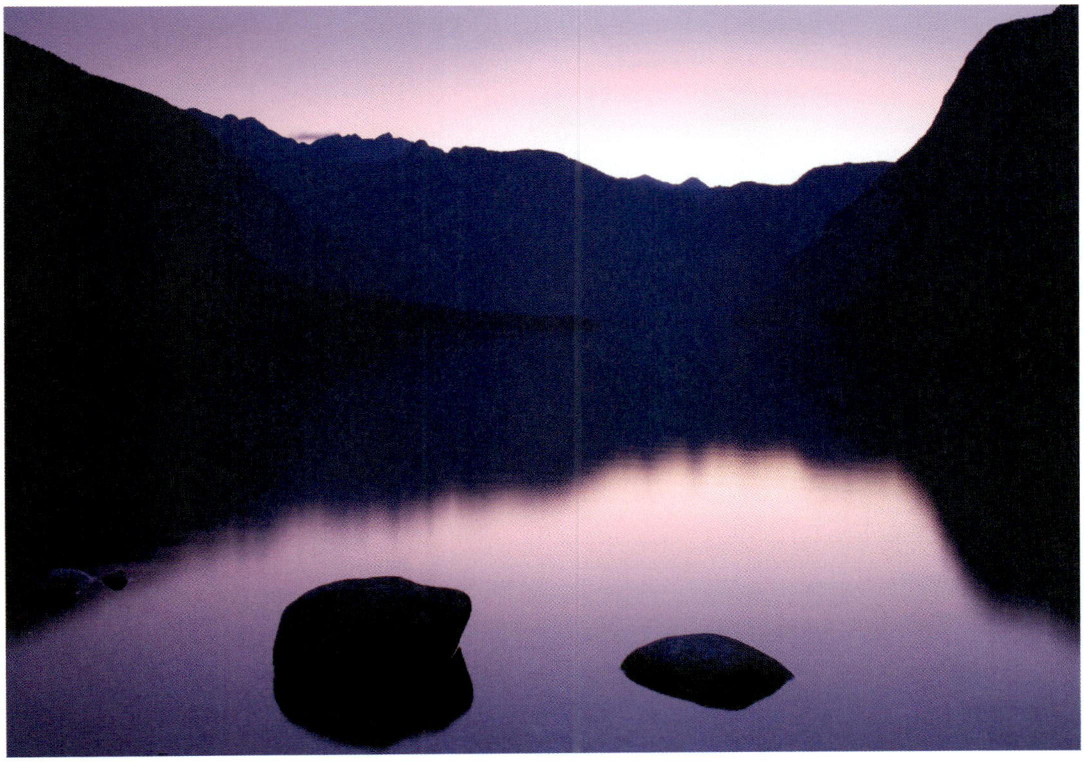

Part 7
Measuring the light

Unfortunately it's not simply a case of choosing the settings and away we go. We have to correctly expose the photograph. To do this we need to let the right amount of light fall on the film or sensor. If there is too much light, the photo will be overexposed (too bright). If there is not enough light, the photo will be underexposed (too dark)

In order to get the exposure right we have to measure the amount of light in the scene. Once this is done, we or the camera can calculate the appropriate settings.

In the case of using shutter priority, we choose the shutter we want (having already set our ISO), then measure the light to calculate the aperture needed to get the scene exposed the way you want.

When aperture priority is set, we choose the aperture we want, then the camera measures the light to calculate the shutter speed needed.

Test:

Manually set your camera to 1/125, F16 & ISO 200 in a room and take a photo. You will see that the picture will be underexposed (dark).

Now go outside to somewhere bright and set the camera to 1/30, f5.6 & ISO 800. You will see that the picture will be overexposed (too bright)

How it works

When you half press down the shutter button, not only does the autofocus run, but the camera's built in light meter is also measuring the light. There are four different metering modes (depending on which camera you use):

1. Evaluative Metering
2. Partial Metering
3. Spot Metering
4. Centre Weighted Average Metering

Evaluative Mode

The evaluative meter setting reads the light from a wide range of the scene and then calculates the average of that scene. This is suitable for landscape shots with a wide range of bright and dark areas.

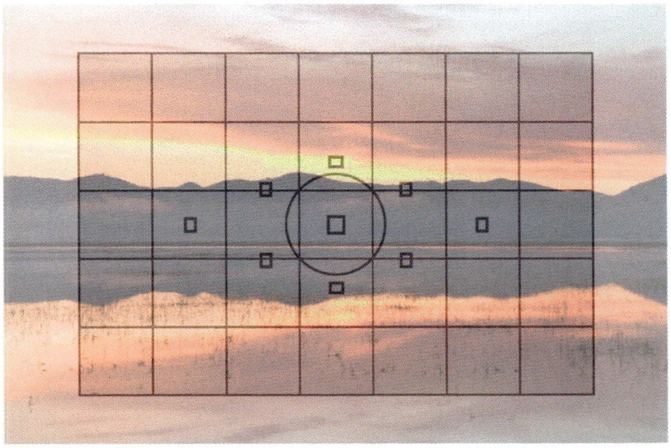

Partial Mode

The partial meter setting reads the light from the circle indicated here and again takes an average from within that circle.

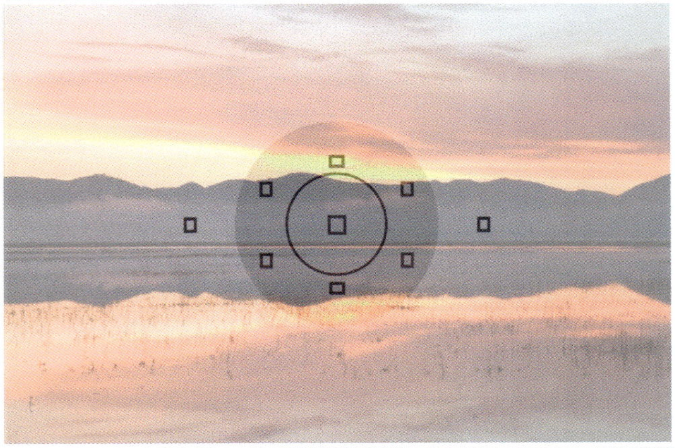

Spot mode

The spot meter setting takes its reading from the centre focal point. This is best for measuring the light at an exact point of the scene, and also for portraits to take a light reading from the subject's face.

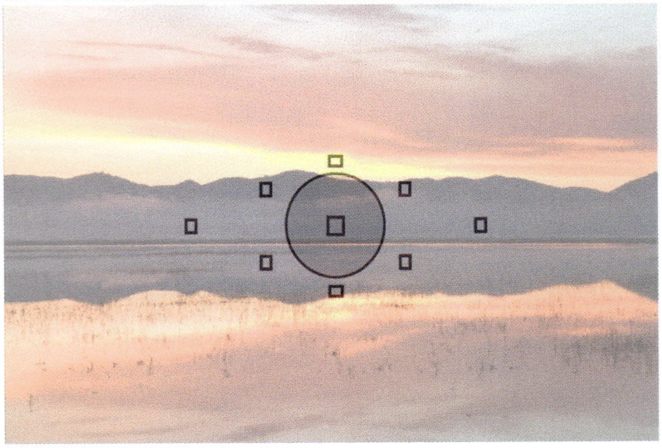

Centre Weighted Mode

Centre weighted average meter setting is weighted for the centre and then averaged out for the entire scene.

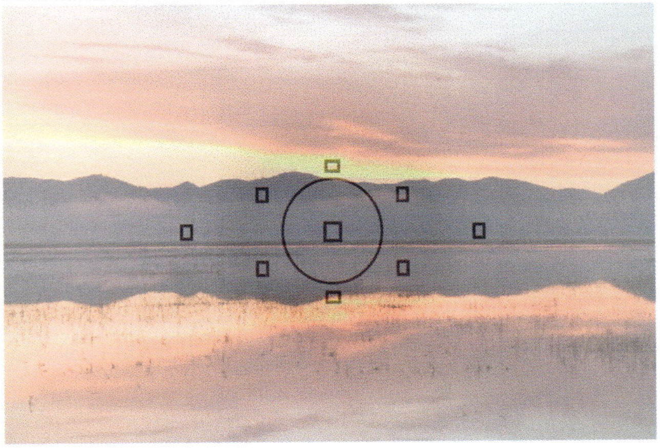

The Histogram:

The histogram shows us the tonal range within an image. It's shown in graphical form and is a great indicator of whether or not we have exposed our image well. Each point along the graph represents a tonal value starting at 0 and going through to 255.

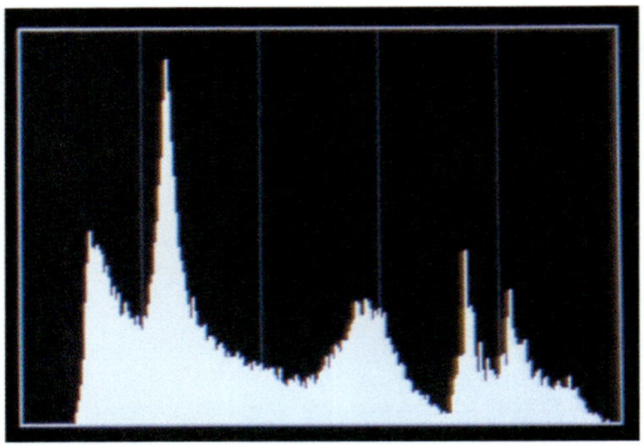

Shadows, Midtones, Highlights

0 far left indicates how much shadow detail is present
255 far right indicates how much highlight detail is present
The midway point indicates how much midtone detail is present

Anything beyond 255 is completely white with no detail present.
Anything below 0 is completely black with no detail present.
You can also think of these as colours:

- Shadows = Black or dark colours
- Midtones = Grey or muted colours
- Highlights = White or bright colours

The height of each line represents the amount of pixels in your image that contain that tone. So for example, the big peak shows there are a lot of pixels containing that particular tonal value. Notice also that on the far left there is an area with no lines. This means that there are no pixels with those tonal values. So there are no dark shadows from 0 to about 10.

Histogram on your camera

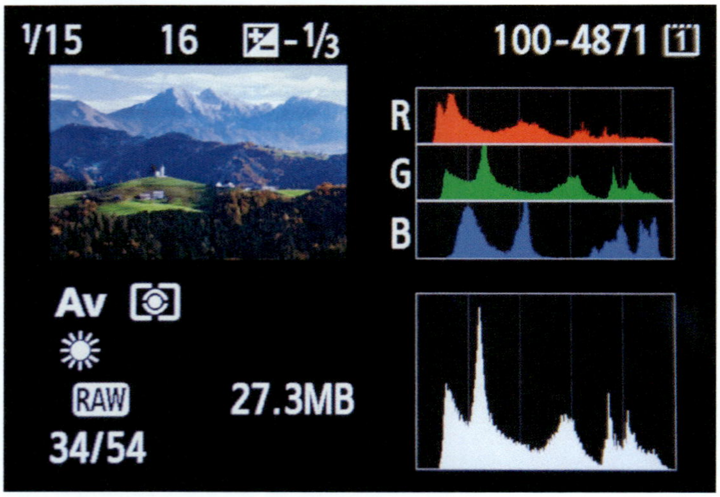

On your camera, not only are you able to view the histogram when reviewing a photo you have taken, but also on the liveview function when taking the photo. Check your camera's manual for exact details, but it usually involves pressing the info button to bring it up. This is an essential tool for checking that your exposure is good, both while taking the photo (if using liveview) and afterwards.

There are two options when using the histogram. As you can see on the image here, you can view a breakdown of the three colour channels, red, green, blue (RGB) or the histogram as a whole. Or both, like here.

The histogram for this photo has a fairly even spread of tones across the range. There is a fair amount of shadow detail, representing the dark areas of the trees and the hills. The highlights on the right represent the sky and clouds. And in the midtone area there is also some detail.

This histogram is also an indication that the photo has been well-exposed. Everything falls within the range of the graph, 0-255, and nothing is pushed too far to the left or the right. When this does happen, we have problems, as we are going to see on the following pages.

Clipping:

Notice that on the far right of the histogram for the photo below there is a spike. This means that the image has some areas which are completely white with no details. This is known as clipping. Clipping has occurred because the sky is overexposed and the detail is blown out. The histogram has been pushed too far to the right and is off the scale.

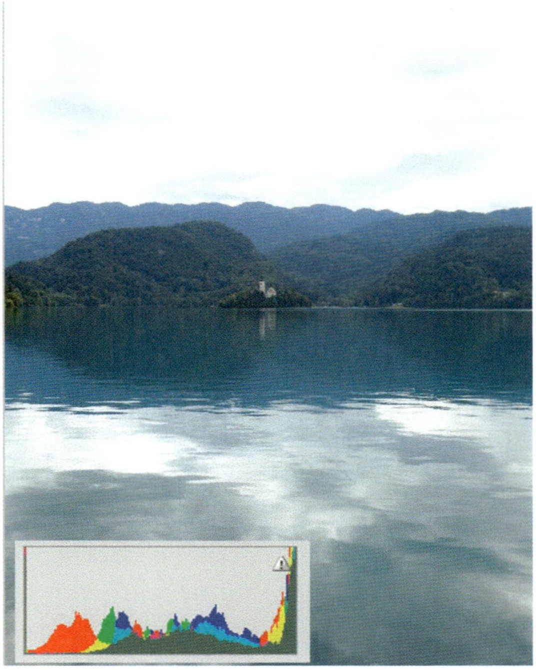

What you see is what you get?......... NO

The tonal range (or range of luminosity) of a photo is much lower than our eyes. We can see more detail in a wider tonal range than this histogram. So in a high contrast scene, where the difference between the darkest point and brightest point is very big, we will be able to see the detail in the darkest part and the brightest part, but the camera will not. This photo is a good example of this. While the sky and the water were very bright, the mountains were quite dark in comparison.

This photo was metered for the church and the mountains. These are nicely exposed, showing lots of detail. But because of the extreme difference in brightness, the sky is now too bright and overexposed.

With my eyes I could see more detail in the sky.

The histogram has clearly shown us that the pure white parts are off the scale and contain no detail. So that is why it is good to check this during or after taking the photo by looking at the histogram. Then you will be able to adjust your exposure to compensate.

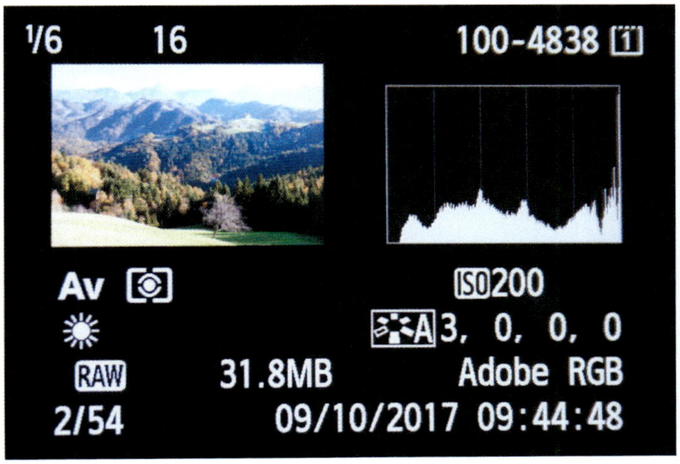

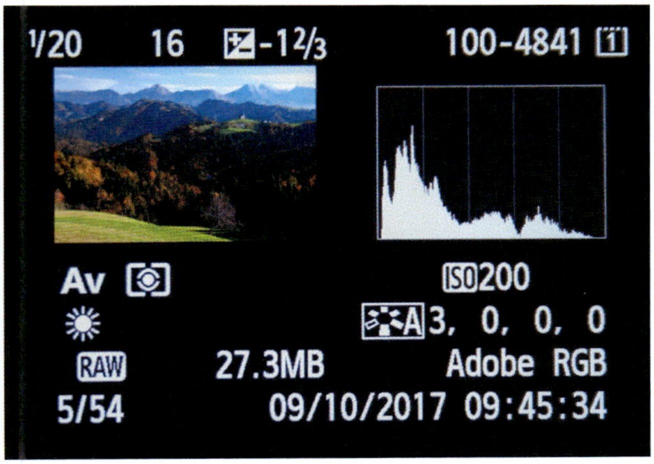

As illustrated by the images above, the first histogram is pushed off to the right and is clipped; indicating that the scene is too bright (overexposed) and much of it has fallen outside the tonal range of the camera. In the second I increased the shutter speed to reduce the amount of light falling upon the sensor. Now the histogram is pushed more to the left and has fallen within the tonal range of the camera. Now the image is well exposed.

Overexposure (too bright):

When an image is too bright it is considered to be overexposed. This means that the film or sensor received too much light, a result of the exposure time being too long. Notice how on the histogram that everything is pushed too far to the right. This is usually an indication of overexposure.

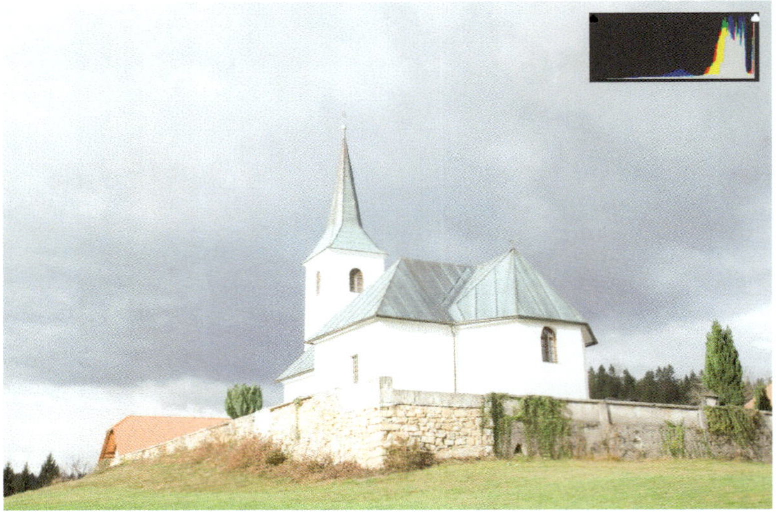

Underexposure (too dark)

When an image is too dark it is considered to be underexposed. This means that the film or sensor didn't receive enough light, a result of the exposure time being too short. Notice how on the histogram that everything is pushed too far to the left. This is usually an indication of underexposure.

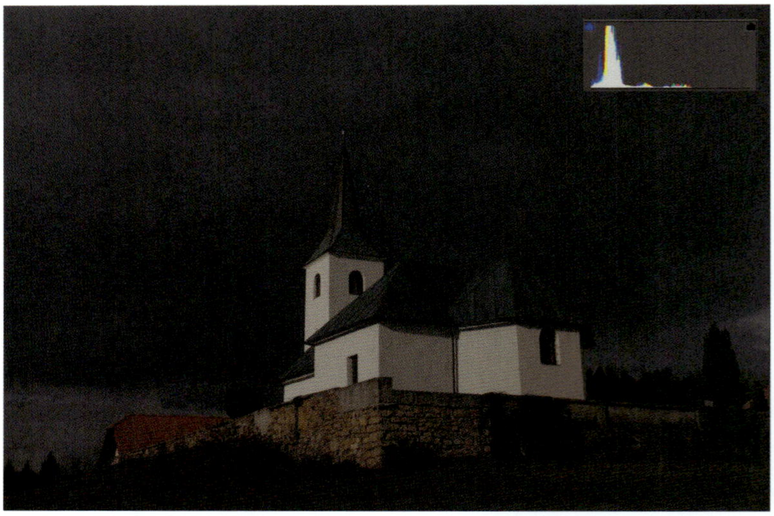

Well exposed

A well exposed photograph, like the one below, will usually have a good spread of details across the histogram and not be too bright or too dark.

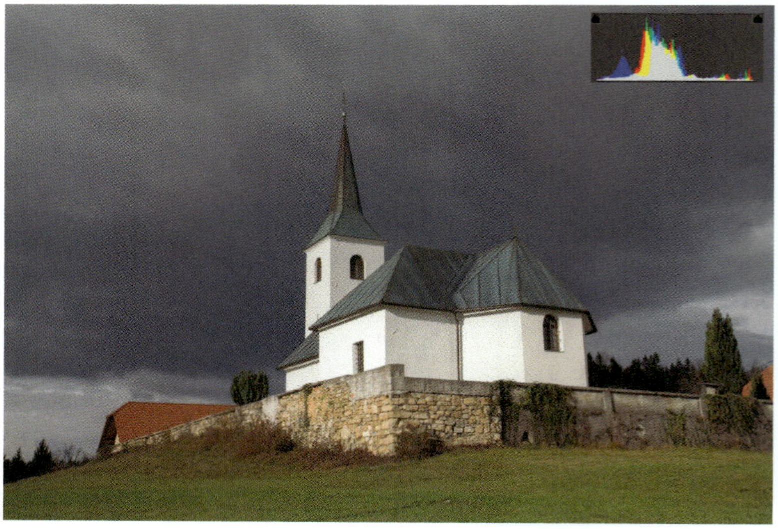

Highlight burnout warnings

In the photo to the right a shaft of sunlight was shining over the top of the waterfall, while the rest of it was in the shade.

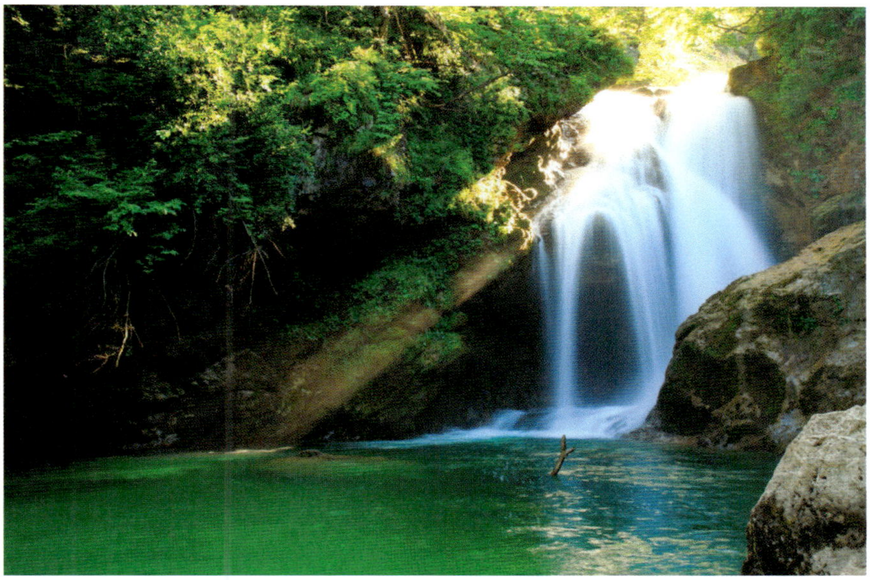

You can clearly see that the very top parts of the water are overexposed.

However, there is also a highlight warning tool which is available in most cameras.

If you turn on this feature then you get what is commonly known as "the blinkies"

The blinkies will flash over areas which are burned out.

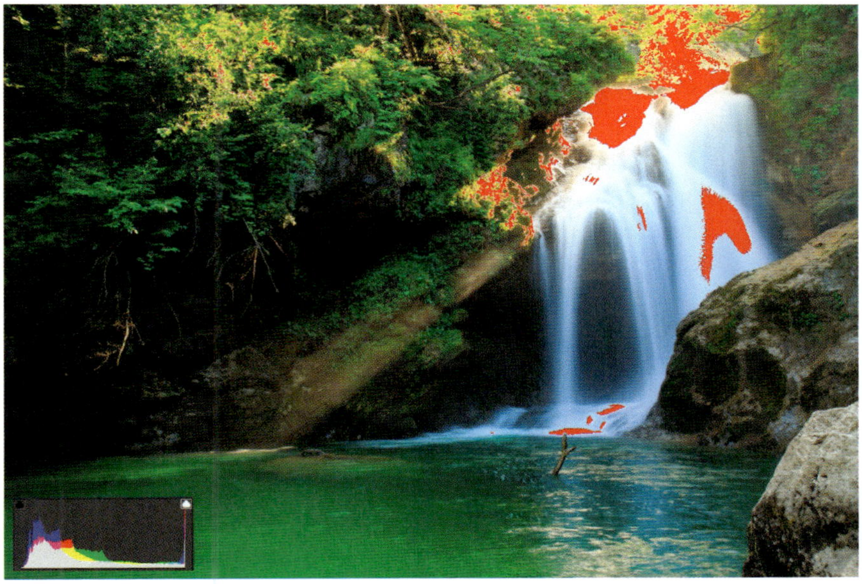

This feature is also available in Adobe Camera Raw (ACR) and other photo editing programs.

As you can see by the photo here, in the histogram there is a spike at the right end.

Notice also the small triangle at the top of the spike. When you click this triangle in ACR, you get the blown out areas highlighted in red.

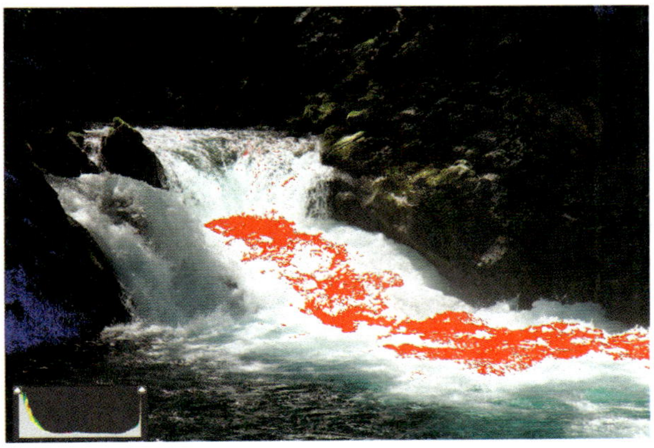

Shadow warnings

In Adobe Camera Raw you can also click the triangle on the left side to bring up the shadows warning. Just like with the highlights, it marks the areas where there is zero shadow detail in purple.

Correct exposure, is there such a thing?

Not really. While there are many cases where the exposure is incorrect, there isn't a definitive correct exposure because it is all down to what the photographer wants to achieve.

A photographer doesn't photograph a scene, a photographer makes a photo of a scene. How you choose to make that photo depends on many things, not least of all how you choose to expose for the scene.

In the photo above I measured the light more towards the highlights. It was shot at 30 secs, F16 ISO 50. The intention here was to make it slightly darker to capture the depth of colour in the sunset, the mood of the sea and create an overall darker image with deeper, bolder colours and more contrast.

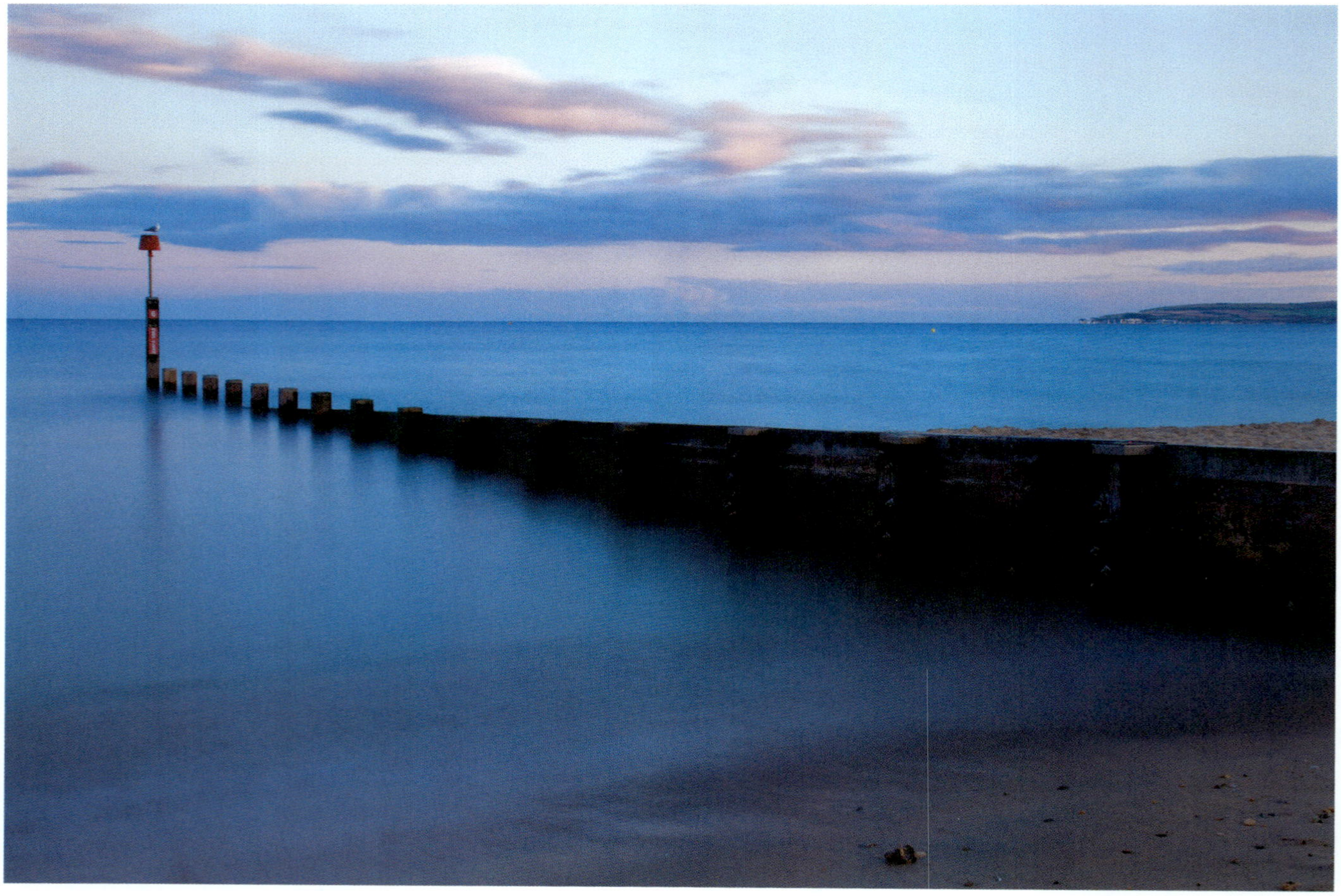

A Brighter Exposure

In this photo I measured the light more towards the midtones. It was shot seconds after at 77secs, F16 ISO 50. Here I've created a lighter, high key version with softer, more subtle colours.

So, your exposure will very much depend on how you want your picture to look. Expose for the highlights to create a slightly darker image with more colour depth, contrast and details. Expose more towards the midtones or shadows to create a lighter image with softer colours and a more milky, etheral feel.

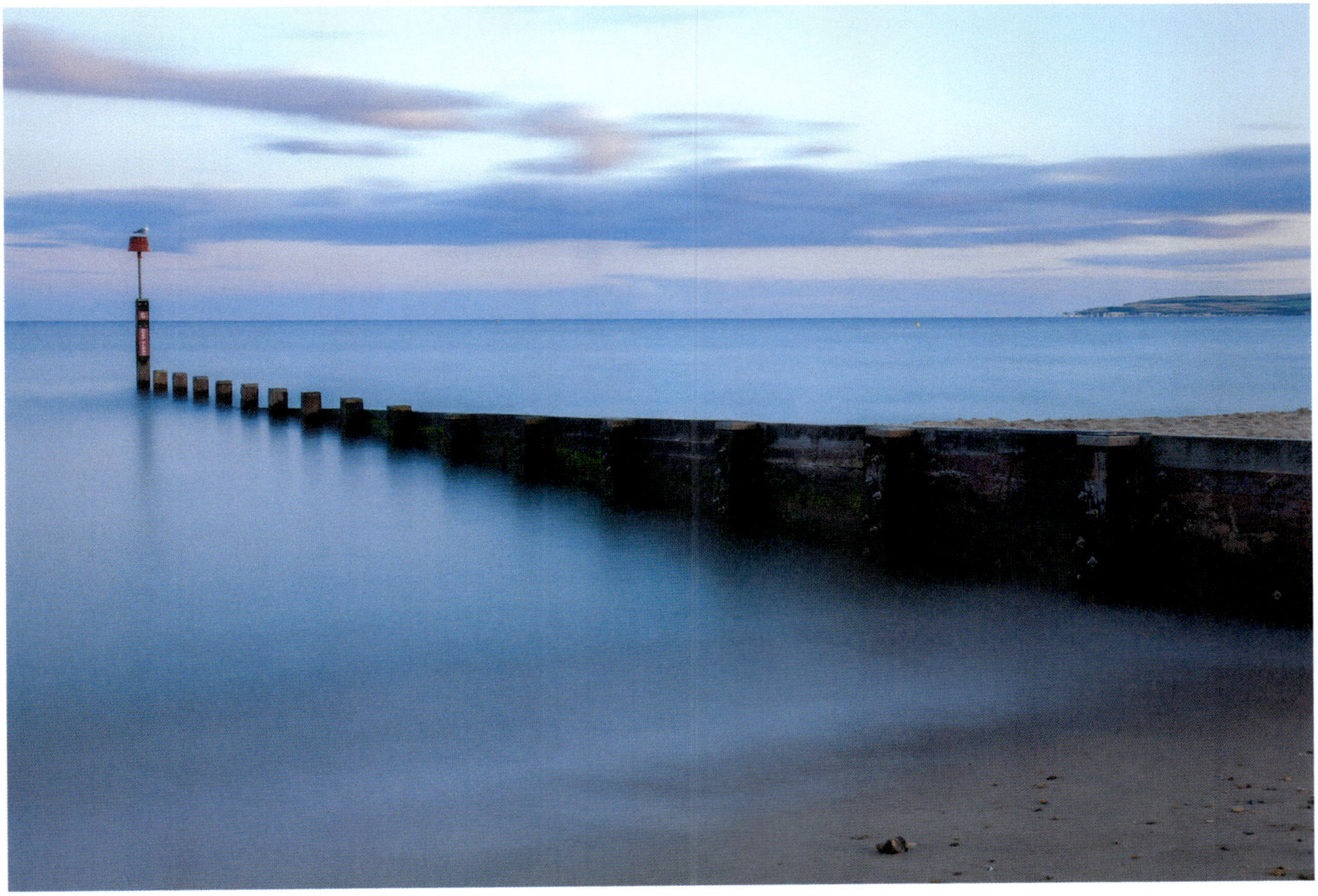

High key scenes:

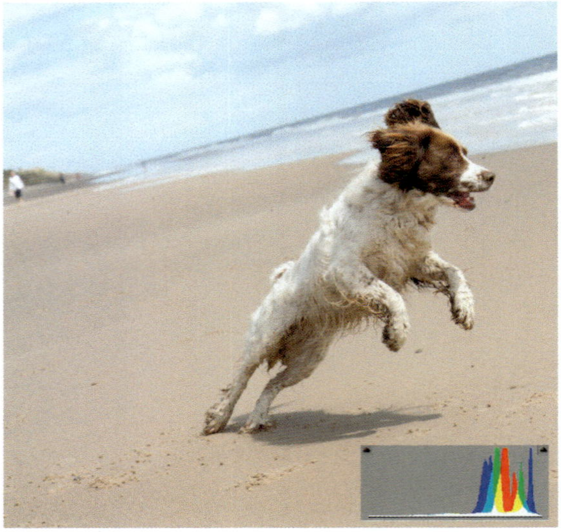

Some scenes are predominantly bright (known as high key scenes)

Here, on a good exposure, the histogram is pushed more towards the right to indicate the predominantly bright scene. The histogram shows how much of the detail is between the midtone and the highlight area.

Notice how there is nothing in the shadow area to the right, and also that there are no dark colours or shadows in the scene. There is also very little midtone colours, except for the brown on the dog.

Underexposed

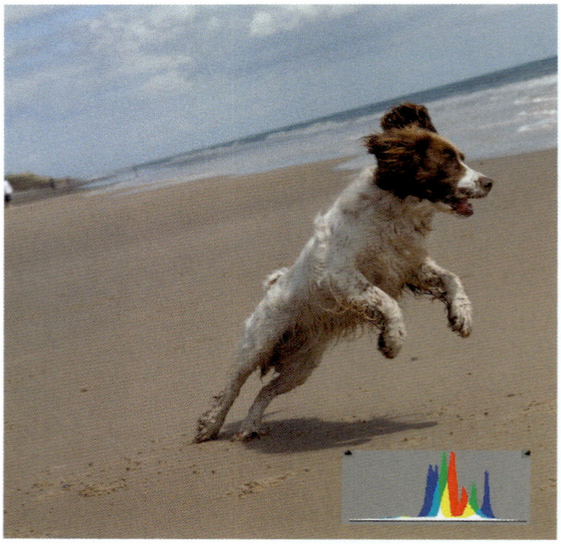

Although the histogram is more centralised in this exposure, and the detail more evenly spread across the range, this image is underexposed (too dark). As we know this is a high key scene we also know it's too far to the left.

A high key scene should be exposed so that all the detail is pushed more to the right.

Overexposed

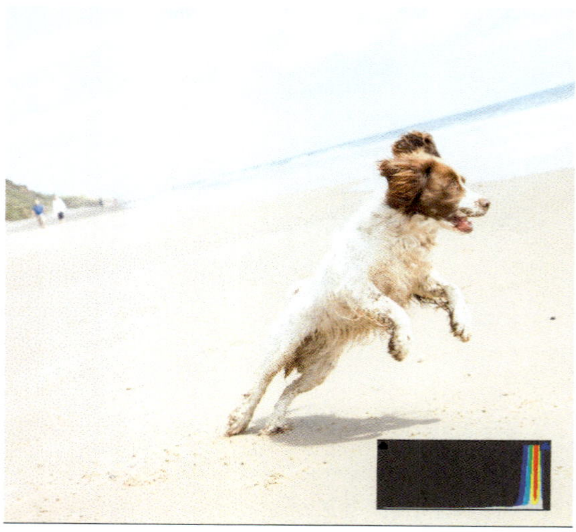

This image is overexposed (too bright). The histogram here is pushed too far to the right. So the trick is to expose to the right just enough, but not too much.

Low key scenes:

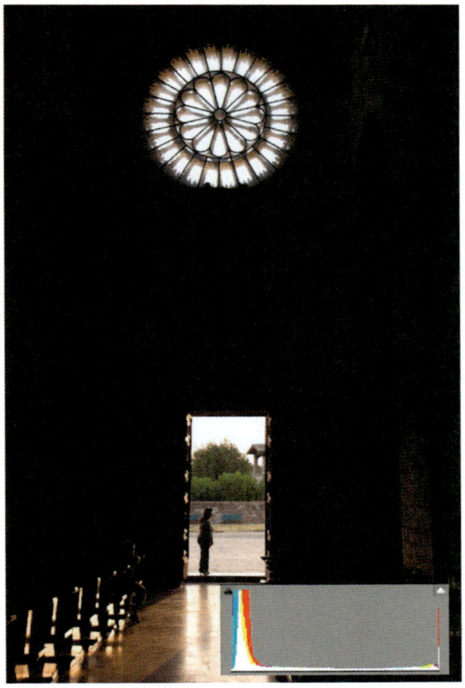

Some scenes are predominantly dark (known as low key scenes)

Here the histogram is pushed more towards the left to indicate the predominantly dark scene with lots of shadows and dark colours.

The histogram here shows how much of the detail is on the left side

.

Notice how there is very little detail in the midtone and highlight area.

The spike on the far right is a blown area which is from the bright sky coming through the window.

Underexposed

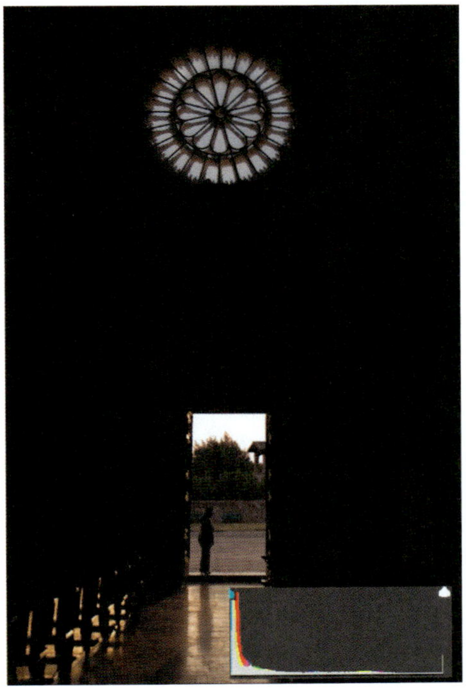

In the exposure to the right the scene is too dark and the histogram pushed too far to the left.

Overexposed

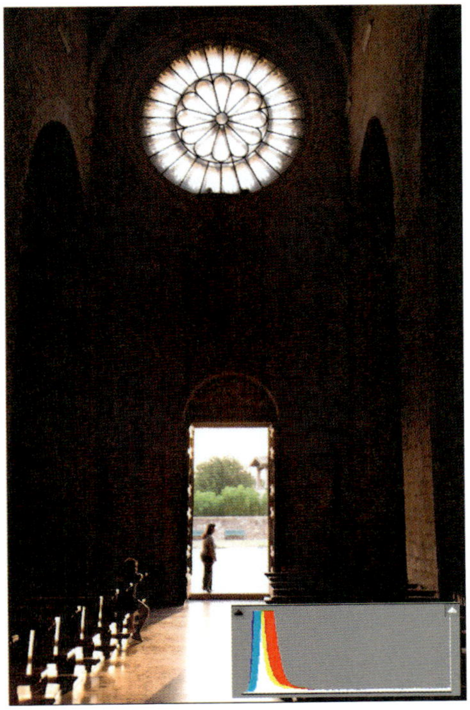

In this exposure to the left the scene is too bright and the histogram pushed too far to the right. As a result the scene lacks the deep shadows it requires to make it a low key image.

Low Contrast Scenes

Many scenes are naturally low in contrast, like the misty lake scene here.

As you can see by the histogram, much of the detail sits around the middle of the graph.

Notice also the gaps either side. This is because there are no areas of deep shadow or bright highlights, so there is no detail recorded.

This scene is predominantly made up of midtones.

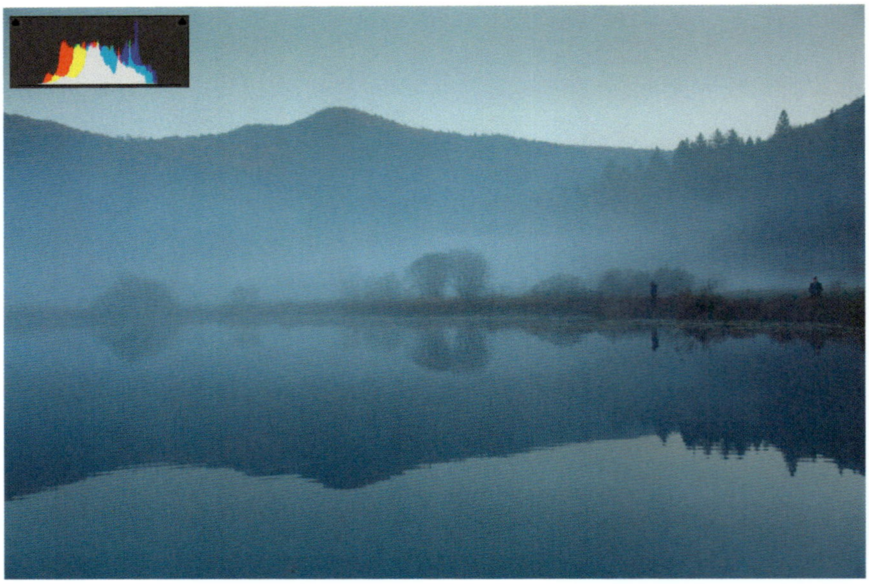

Using levels to boost the contrast

With scenes like this, one thing you can do is use the levels adjustment in Adobe Photoshop or Lightroom, and your camera's photo editing software. You can also do it in Adobe Camera RAW.

Simply move the left and right sliders up to the start of the graph. You can see the result here. This effectively spreads the histogram out across the full range of tones and as a result boosts the contrast.

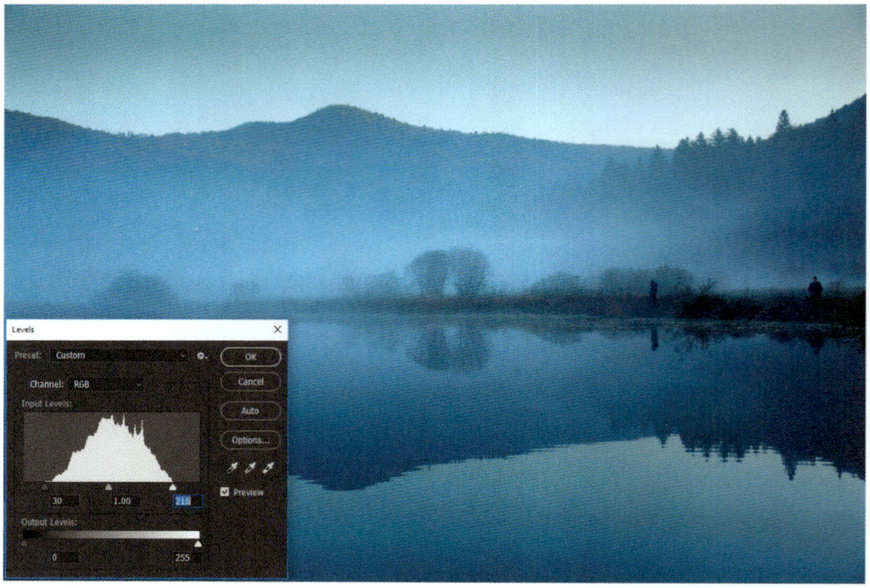

Part 8
Exposure compensation

Flaws with Camera light meters:

Unfortunately the camera's built in light meter is not perfect, and it sees colours as being bright or dark. Camera manufacturers have designed their meters to measure midtone colours, therefore:

Bright colours such as white and red can make the camera think the scene is brighter than it is, and will therefore **underexpose.**

Dark colours such as blacks can make the camera think the scene is darker than it is, and will therefore **overexpose.**

High contrast scenes, like we saw before with the lake and much brighter sky, are difficult for the camera's internal meter. Therefore it may not calculate the exact exposure you want.

You can override the camera's reading and settings by using a feature called exposure compensation. Essentially what you are doing is forcing the camera to take a brighter or darker exposure than the internal meter wants.

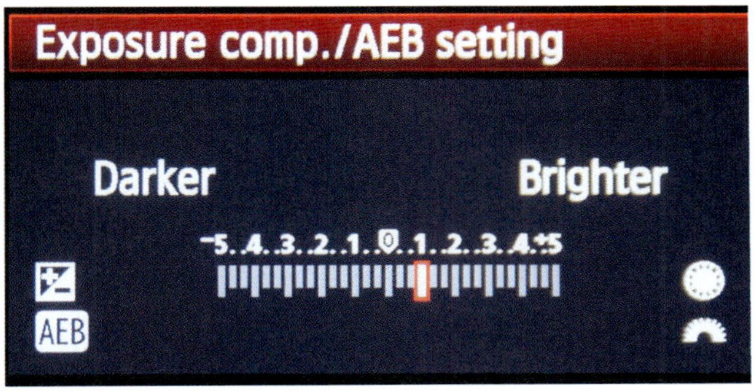

Increased exposure (+) (Brighter)
Here you choose to increase the exposure. You can add in increments of 1/3 stops up to 2 or more stops to make the photo brighter.

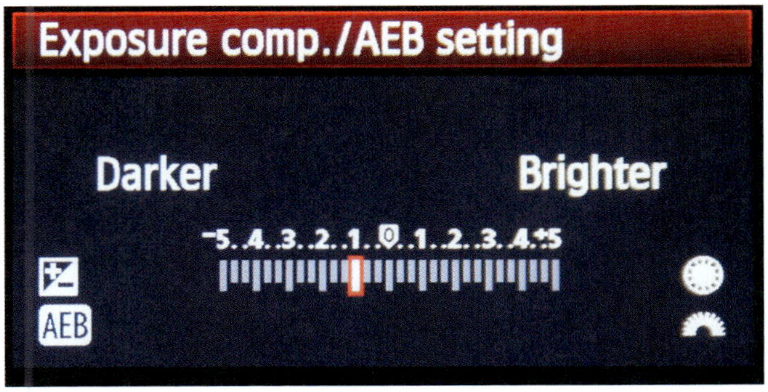

Decreased exposure (-) (Darker)
Here you choose to decrease the exposure. Again you can reduce by 1/3 stops up to 2 or more stops to make the photo darker.

At a glance
+1 = brighter image -1 = darker image
For bright colours -whites, reds etc. = increase exposure For dark colours - blacks = decrease exposure

Underexposed

Camera meter's exposure 1/125 F16 ISO200

Snow is classic example of how the camera's meter will underexpose. The brighter the light falling on the snow, the more the meter will read the white colour as brighter than it is. The photo below is underexposed.

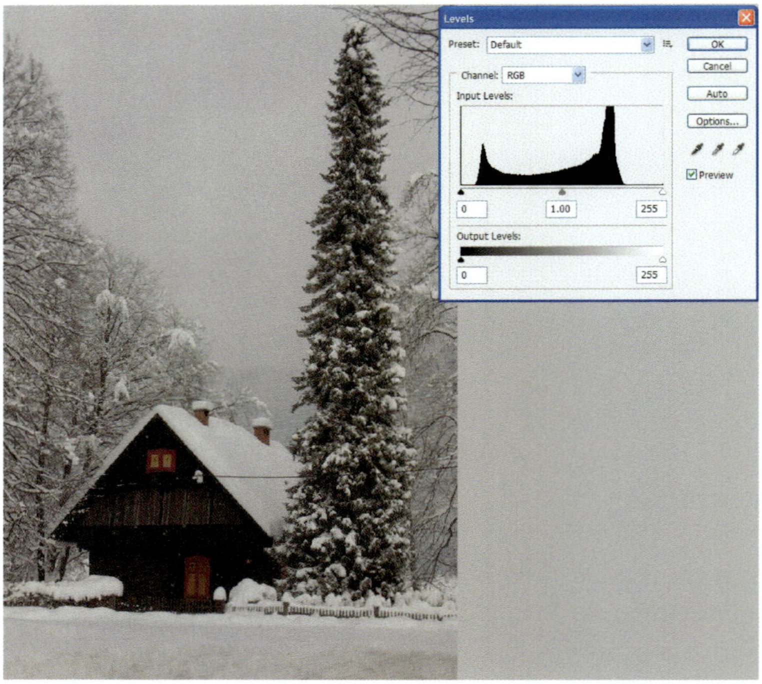

Exposure compensation used

Correct exposure with exposure compensation set to +1

1/60 F16 ISO200

By dialing up +1 I have increased the exposure time and corrected the photo.

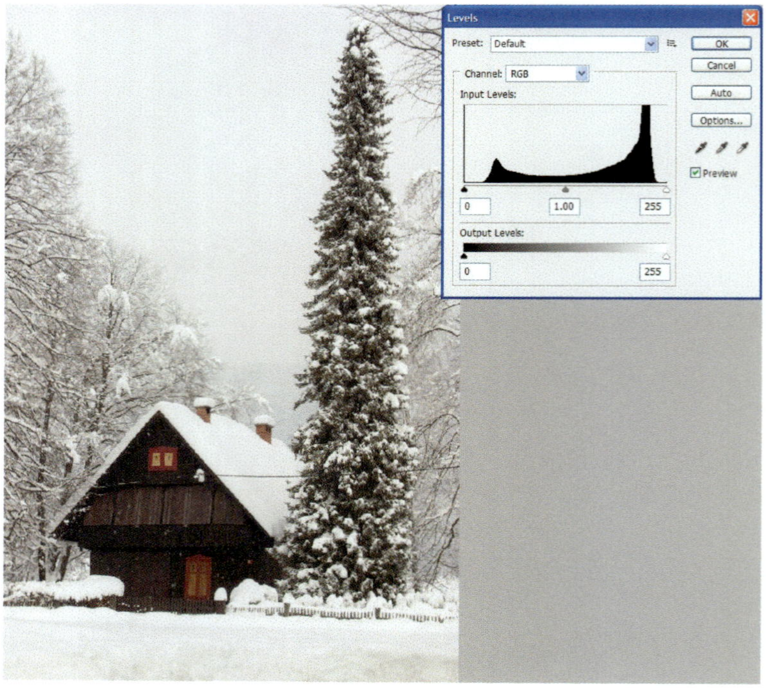

Overexposed

This photo is overexposed because I took the meter reading off the cat. The black colour of the cat has fooled the meter into thinking there is less light than there actually is so it has set a longer exposure in error.

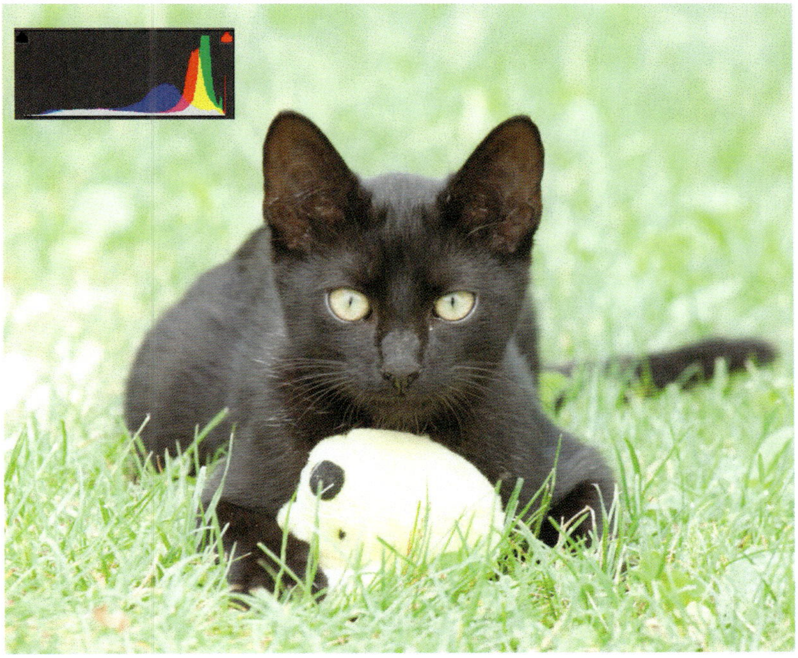

Camera meter's exposure
1/60, F11, ISO800

Exposure compensation used

Correct exposure with exposure compensation set to -1

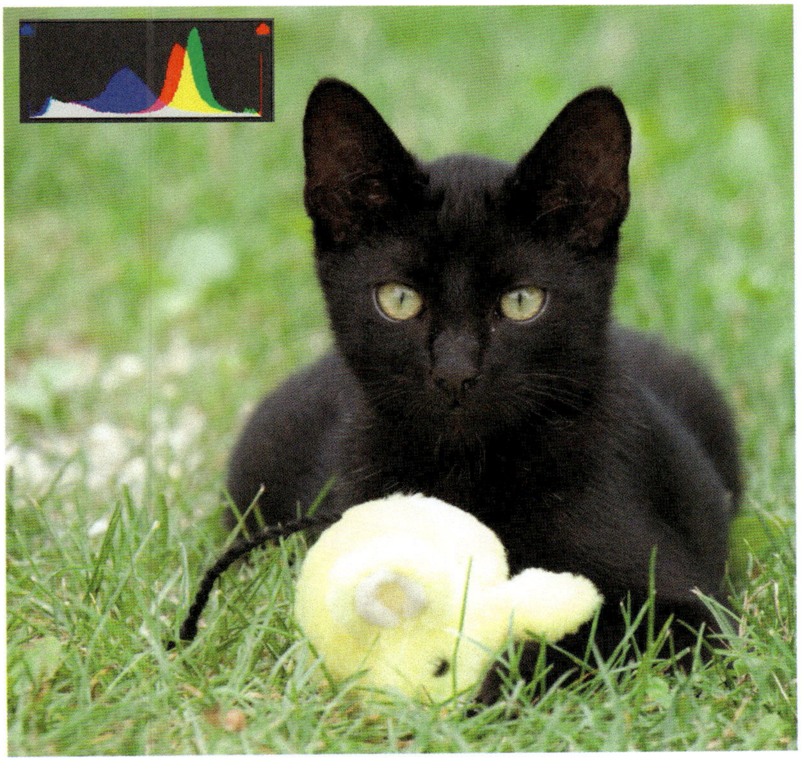

1/125, F11, ISO800

By dialing down one stop (-1) I have decreased the exposure time and improved the exposure.

Part 9
Image file formats – RAW, TIFF & JPEG

With traditional film the image is captured on the frame and held there, as long as it isn't exposed to any more light, until it is processed. Chemicals are used to alter the properties of the silver halide pieces to make them permanent. With your image on film, a print is then produced. Even with film the final look of the picture very much depends on the processing technique, and professional photographers can spend hours in the darkroom perfecting an image. Different types and makes of film are designed to give different results, so photographers choose their film accordingly.

Digital photography is different to film in the way that it captures an image. Essentially, the electronic sensor is designed to capture as much data from the scene as possible. Once it does this, the camera's computer processes the data and produces a photo from it, which it then saves to the memory card. The final image very much depends on the camera setting or profile used. If you have set the camera to shoot landscapes, then the computer will work to produce a final image with bright colours and sharp detail. Should you set the camera to shoot portraits, then it will work to produce natural looking skin tones, and soften facial features.

So whatever you are shooting, any digital image requires some or more post processing to produce the desired effect the photographer is looking for.

JPEG: is the most popular file format due to the small file size taking up less space on your hard drive or memory card. JPEG is a compressed format, so once your image is produced by the camera then all other data is deleted and only the data for the image is saved. While this is an advantage for people wanting to get as many photos on a card as possible, if you want to do any extra post processing or editing of the image, then this will result in a loss of quality. Also, each time you re-save a JPEG you will lose data. For this reason it's known as a lossy format.

RAW: If your camera has it, then you should always shoot in this format. When you shoot in RAW then every single byte of data the sensor captures is saved, and therefore the file contains a wider dynamic range with much more detail, tonal range, contrast and colour. Saving in RAW not only allows you complete control over how the image is processed (rather than letting the camera do it), but it gives you more flexibility when it comes to processing and editing without losing quality. A RAW file editor program will allow you to adjust white balance, exposure and retrieve lost detail in overexposed areas (within reason). This can be essential when applying effects such as blending different exposures, or compensating for the extremes of light and contrast that the camera cannot otherwise handle. RAW is also a great format when learning, because it allows you correct minor mistakes you make in exposure. If an image is over or underexposed, you can adjust it either way.

TIFF: is a lossless file and therefore there is no data loss or compression. You can also save images in 16-bit format, which will contain more colour detail. Like the RAW, the TIFF file is very tolerant to editing, so you can do much more to it to it without losing quality. This is also the best format to save in if you want to make your images bigger by upsizing.

What I do is shoot in RAW then process and save as TIFF, add final touches such as cleaning away dust spots, then save a JPEG version. If I need to make changes, I edit the TIFF file and then re-save the JPEG.

TIP: While learning, set your camera to save both RAW and JPEG, if possible. That way you have the best of both worlds.

Part 10
When to go full manual

You may hear others telling you things like, "You're not a true photographer unless you use manual mode" or patronising social media posts saying things like, "Everyone is a photographer until full manual mode." But, quite frankly, this is a load of rubbish. There is absolutely no reason why a photographer, pro or not, is any less of a real photographer whether they use aperture priority, shutter priority or full manual. A good photographer knows when to use which setting.

For example, the aperture or shutter priority modes will at the same time measure the light and set the non priority settings accordingly. This can be essential when working in rapidly changing lighting conditions, or fast moving subjects where the light isn't constant. In situations like this you need to work fast and don't want to start shooting away in manual only to find that the light has changed because of a cloud moving in, or because the change in composition has meant your scene is now darker or much brighter. In each case your photo will likely not be properly exposed. By the time you realise this and make adjustments, the light and moment will have gone. Also, why complicate your life any more than you have to? If controlling depth of field is your priority, then aperture priority is the best choice because you can easily and quickly alter this setting without having to worry about the rest. If you want to control how much you freeze or blur your subject and are less concerned about depth of field, then shutter priority is the one to choose. The reality is that even in full manual mode you are not going to be able to set each one independently the way you want it, because the light will dictate that and in most cases you are going to have to make some compromise. You can't say that you want an exposure of 1/500 at F16 if the light is too low, unless you dramatically increase your ISO. Yes in full manual you can fine tune your exposure but, as you've just learned, you can also use the exposure compensation adjustment to do that in the priority modes.

However, if you have the time and you want to take full control, there's no reason why you shouldn't. Also, when the light is constant, but there are other factors at play which could cause your camera to under or overexpose, then you may need to consider using full manual mode.

When to use it

When I was photographing these snowboarders there was a variety of dark and light colours set against a bright blue background. As you can see here, some were wearing bright colours and using bright snowboards, some were wearing black. Although the light was constant, the camera would be fooled each time by the mix of colours. So in a situation like this, as I did, it is best to take some test shots to determine the best settings, then go full manual to fix shutter speed and aperture. Then you can concentrate on focusing and framing.

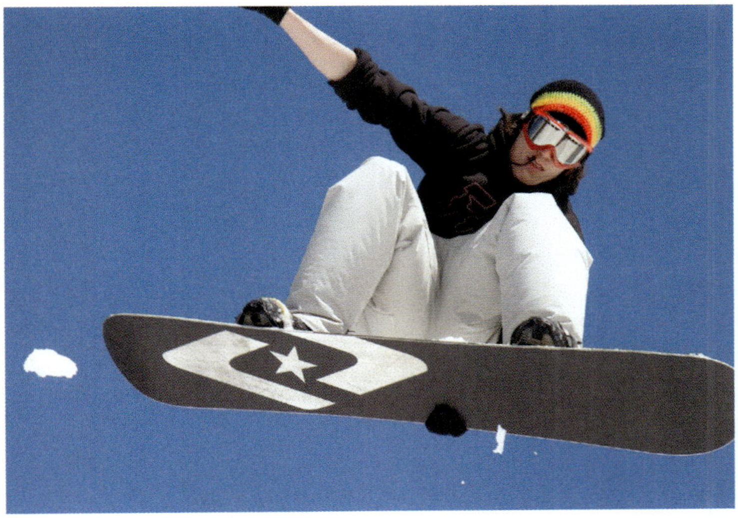

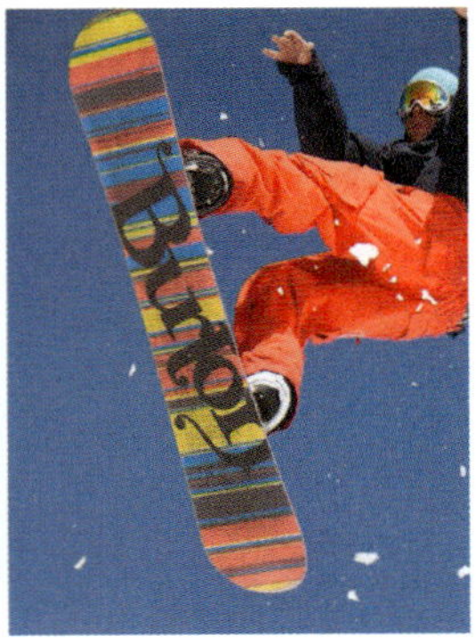

High contrast scenes

In a high contrast scene like the one below, it can sometimes pose a problem when shooting handheld and altering your composition each time. Although the light here was consistent, depending on where I measured the light would make a huge difference to my exposure. Expose for the extreme highlights and everything would be too dark, expose for the extreme shadows and I would burn out my highlights too much. Correct exposure was here critical.

Even though the light was fairly constant, I knew it would be fleeting and I had to work fast to get as many shots as I could before the moment vanished. The last thing I needed was to be constantly having to choose the best place to measure the light, along with focusing and composing.

So I took a few moments to take some test shots to determine the best settings, and then set it all up in full manual. This way everything was fixed and I could then concentrate on my focusing and composition. Each time I checked my histogram and when necessary made a slight adjustment to the shutter speed to correct exposure

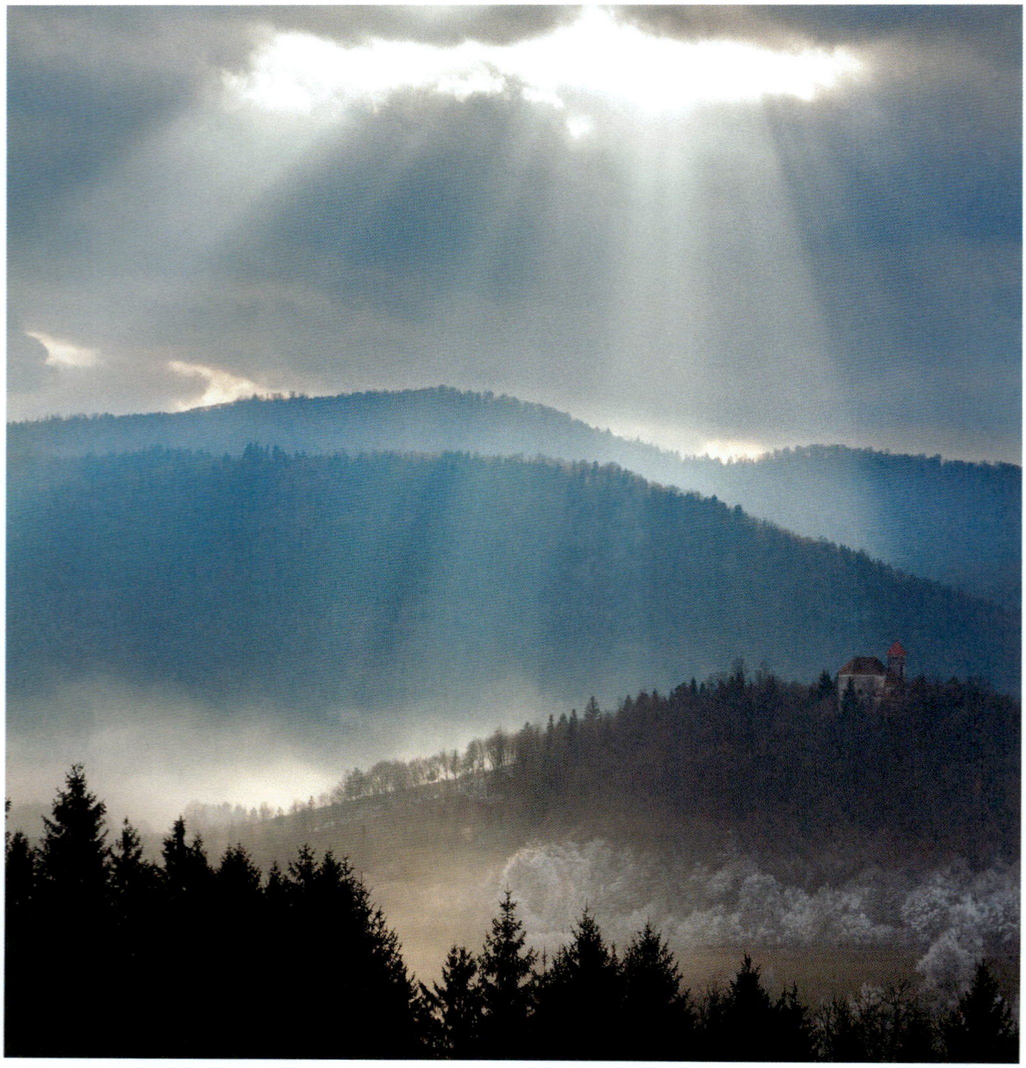

Part 11
Some of my favourite photos

Lake Bled, Slovenia on a misty autumn morning

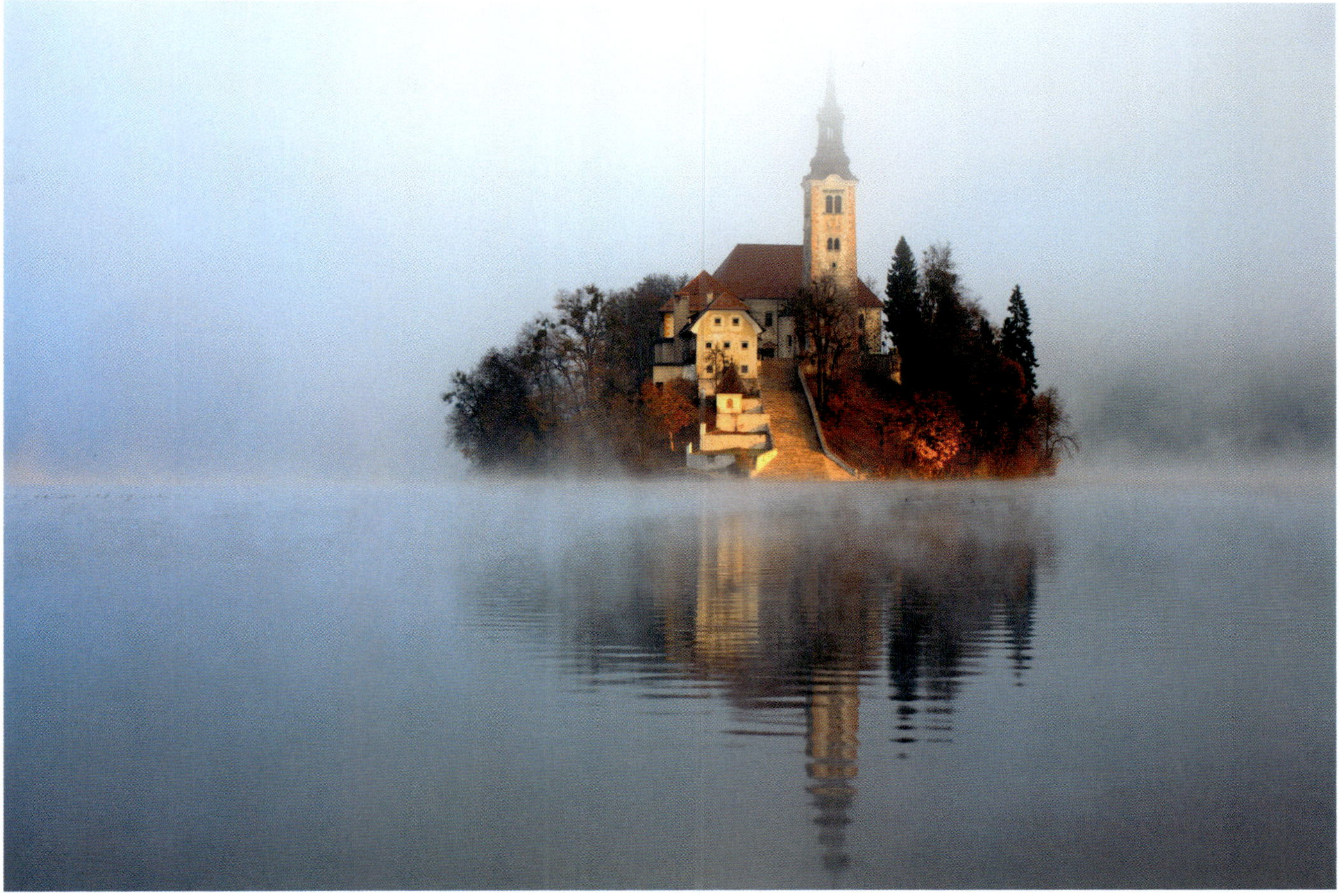

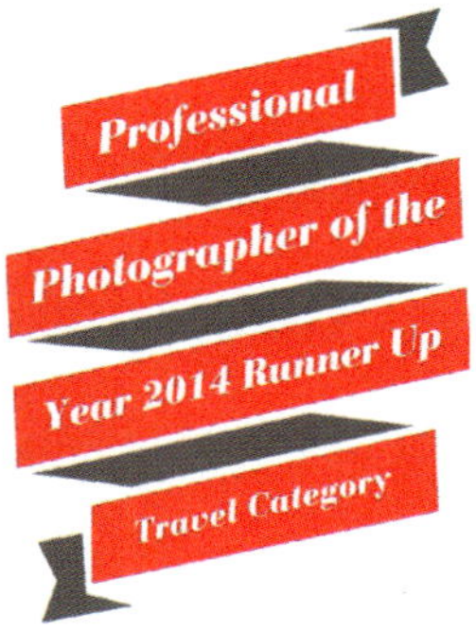

I was extremely pleased with this photo when I took it and even happier when it came third in the travel category of the Professional Photographer of the Year 2014 competition.

Many people in Slovenia have commented that they've never seen a photo of Bled like this before. This for me is a huge compliment, because Lake Bled is probably Slovenia's most photographed location and there are thousands of great photos of this iconic view. So it just goes to show you how even a location that has been photographed to death can always reveal a truly unique moment. I have visited Bled on numerous occasions and have photographed and viewed it from all angles, so knowledge of the place played a key part here. I had been photographing since dawn, having captured many other great images. At sunrise, I ventured to this spot, knowing that the sun would rise to the right and hopefully light the front like it has. I just prayed that it would penetrate the mist enough. It did, for a very brief moment, and I captured this image; one of my favourites.

Durdle Door, Jurassic Coast, Dorset, UK

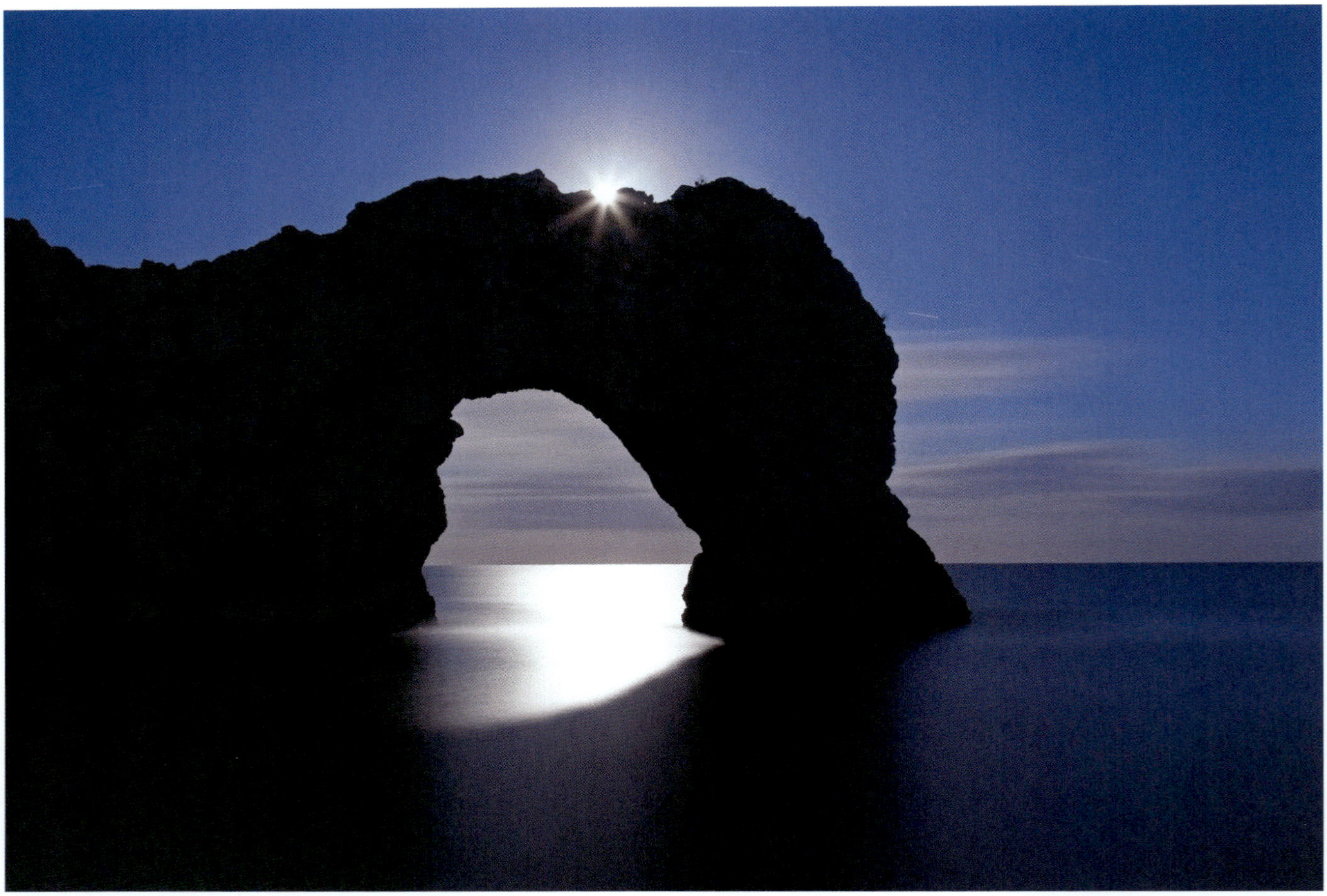

Again, this is an iconic location in the UK and has been photographed by hundreds of photographers since the dawn of photography. For me this is one of many examples of how you never know what Mother Nature will throw your way.

It was July, high summer and not the best time to photograph this view. The sun rises and sets too far north over the hills, so by the time it's low enough to cast the warm soft light that you need, the arch has fallen into the shade.

I came down here to capture the sun going over the cliff, and once it had I decided to stick around for a bit and take a walk along the beach. I was about to leave, because the sky was too clear to produce any nice clouds at sunset, when I suddenly spotted the moon rising out at sea.

I set everything up and began shooting and watching its movement, until it became clear that it would rise over the arch like this. I got myself into position, anticipating this shot and walked away at midnight with my best and most unique photo of Durdle Door.

Saint Mary's Lighthouse at Whitley Bay, UK

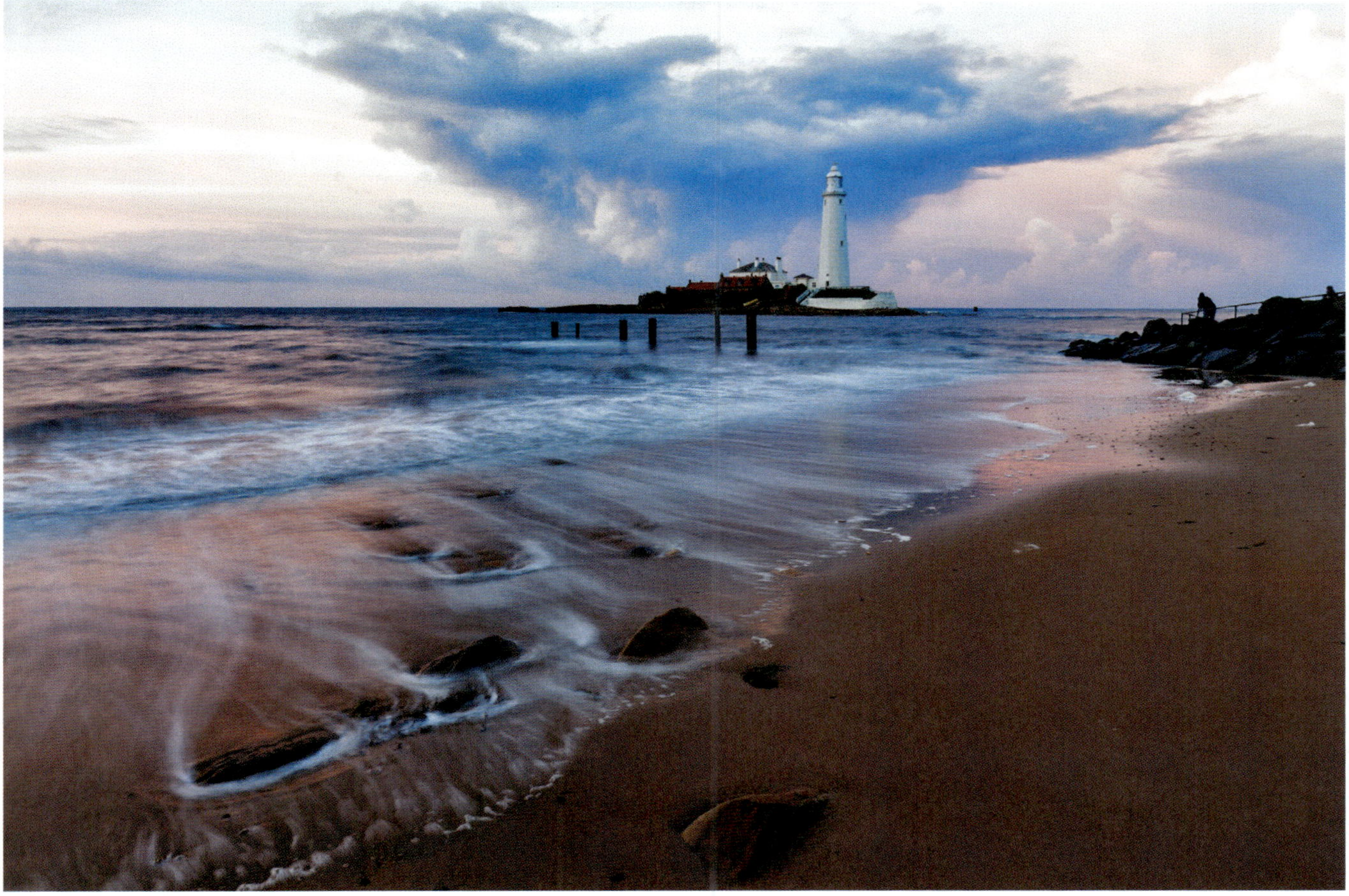

There was a photography workshop group here when I arrived photographing from the classic viewpoint of this location, the edge of the causeway, so I looked across and decided to head over to this beach instead. I was glad because as the sun set this great bit of cloud started moving across the scene and I had room to move around and find this composition, which was my favourite of the evening.

Yet another well-photographed location but I feel I've captured a more unique moment than this group did!

Loch Ness, Scotland

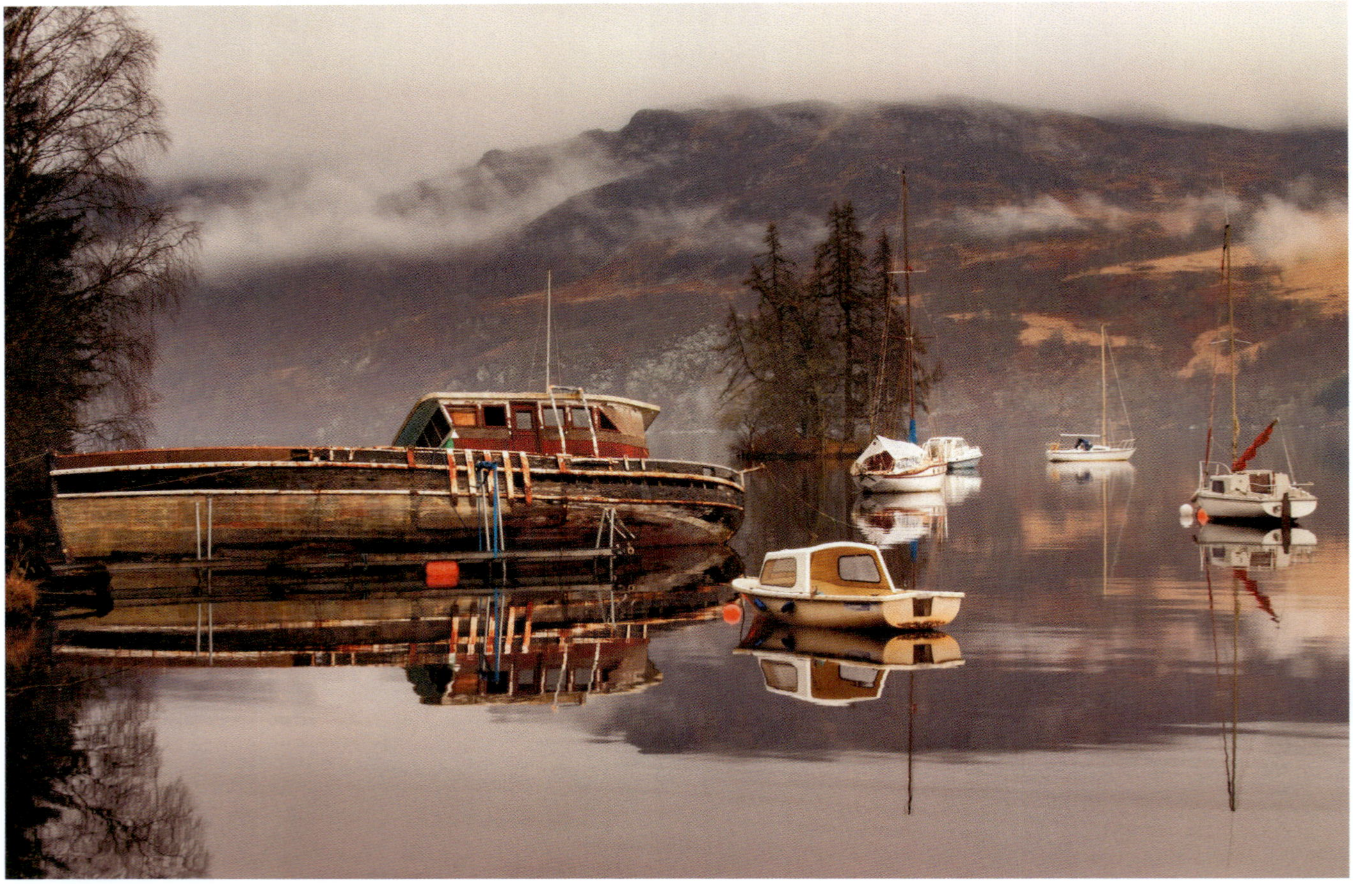

This photo is an example of how much I have learned over the years about composition and processing. I originally took this back in 2006 and recently reprocessed it. Taken on a misty Sunday morning, I had spent the weekend at Loch Ness and was heading over to Aberdeen when I spotted this scene on my way out. When I first processed these, I chose another to go on my website and up for sale. It was a popular image. But when I went through them all again 11 years later, I saw that this one was a better image. In the first, as you can see below, the boat was actually obscuring the reflection of the wreck. Over the years I've learned to look at the little details. So it just goes to show how much you learn over time, and how it's always good to review your old images to see if they can be improved. This was also taken on a low end 6mp SLR, so you can see that it's not only how great your camera is that counts.

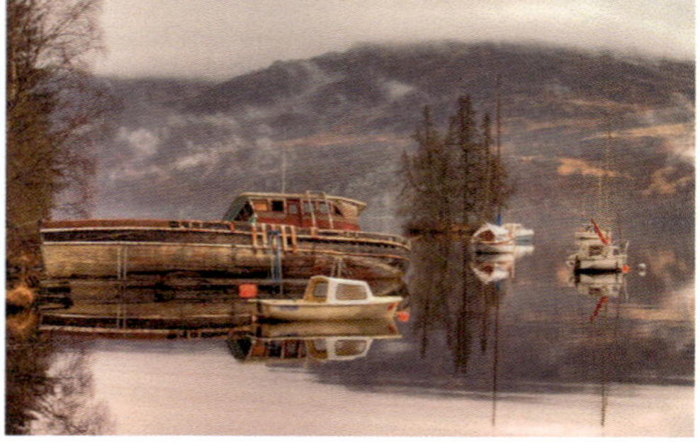

The photo to the left was also an example of my HDR phase. There was a short period when I discovered software that would boost an image's dynamic range, giving you more detail in the shadow. It's a craze that still goes on, but I am happy to say that I got over it and have since learned how to process my images manually and have more control. As I have shown you here in the book, shadows enhance and give dimension to an image, so the absence of them in HDR, makes many images look flat.

Zaosiri Beach, Lošinj Island, Croatia

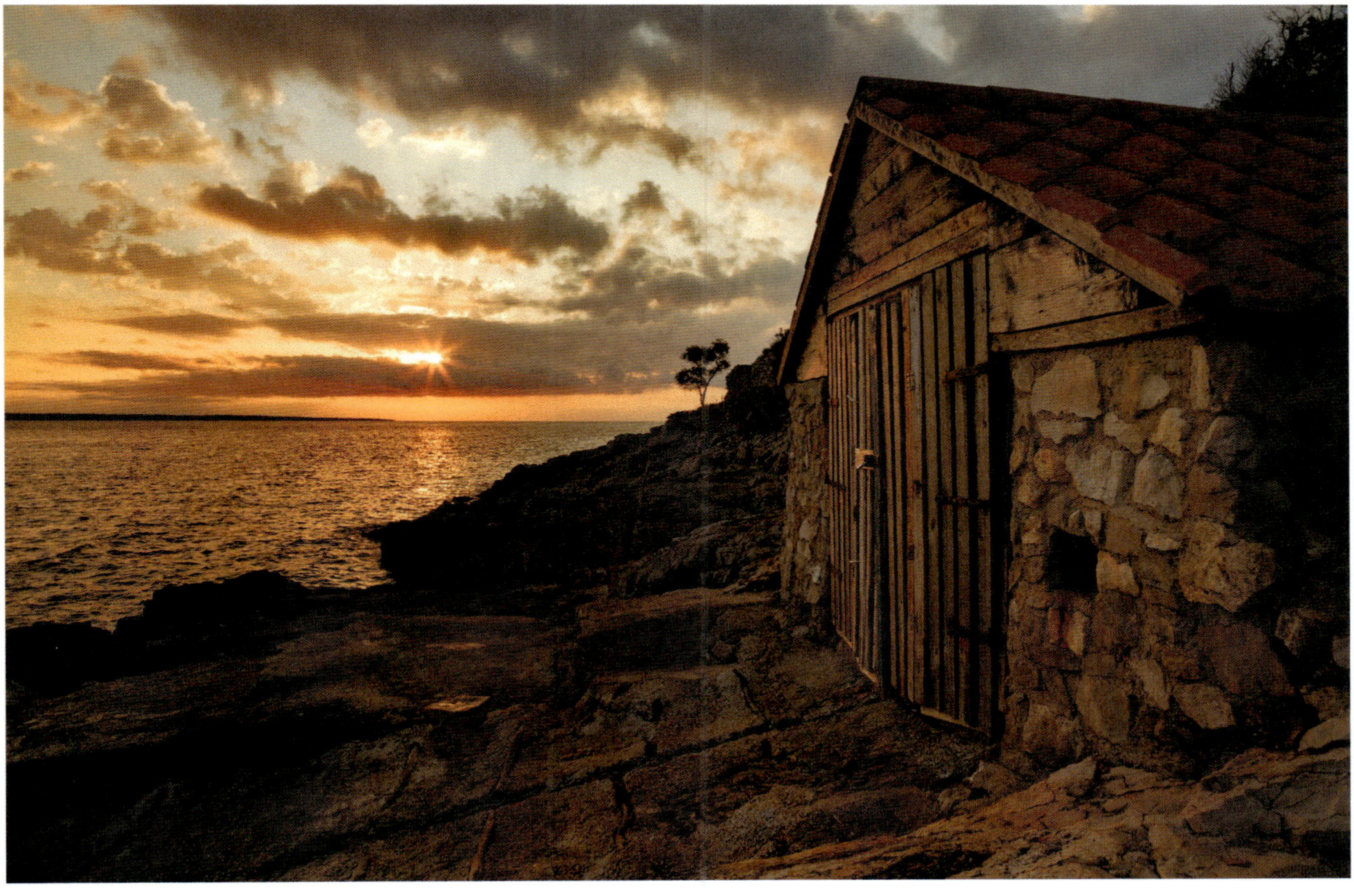

Patience and perseverance

I had originally chanced upon this scene and this composition in 2013 while on my first visit to the island in August. The first evening I took a walk down a small trail that led to this little beach and cove. Upon spotting this boathouse and realising its orientation, I had immediately visualised this image. A quick check on the photographer's ephemeris confirmed that in high summer the sun would rise just where I wanted it. But I wanted clouds, and it was summer after all. So every morning I dutifully got up before dawn and trudged down to the beach with camera and tripod. The first morning I was rewarded with some cloud, but the shot still wasn't quite how I wanted it. This was followed by a week of blue skies! My wife was happy, but I was not.

We returned again in 2014, a bad year for weather all across Croatia. That week I was rewarded with a full week of cloudy mornings and days! I got everything from dramatic sunrises, storm clouds and even lightning. I was happy, my wife was not! However, despite this wonderful week, I still wasn't getting the right clouds for this shot. Finally on the last morning, which started off with virtually zero clouds at dawn, but then as sunrise approached cloud started to build. I watched like an expectant child as the cloud built on the horizon, the sun rose above the mountains, the cloud edged ever closer, split apart and pinched that rising sun in just the right place. Mother Nature had rewarded my patience and perseverance at getting up at 5am every morning!

Jamnik Church, Slovenia

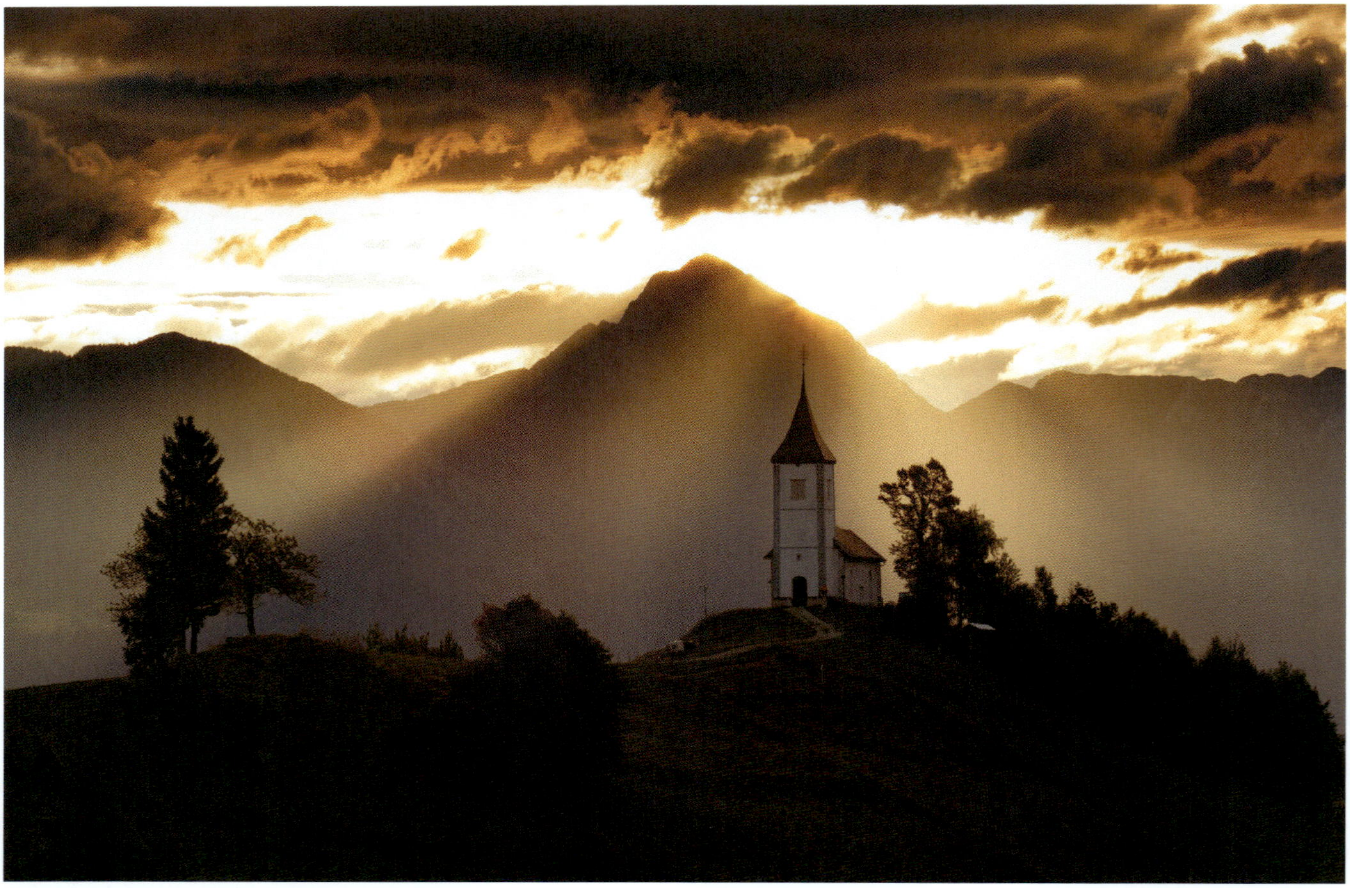

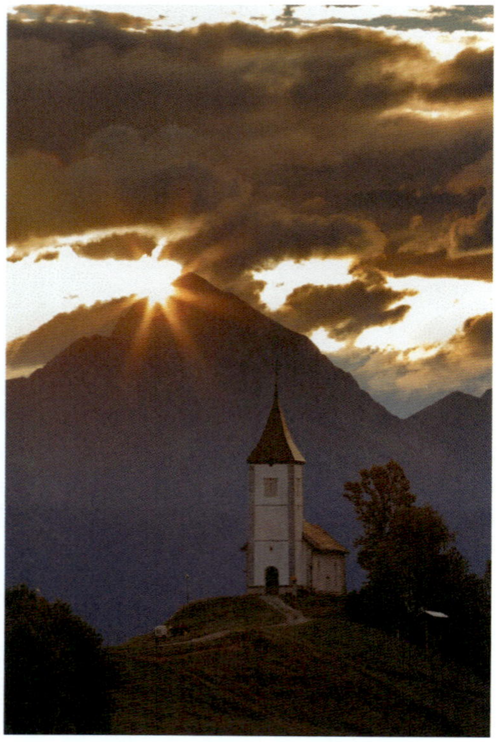

This little church is a popular location for photography all year round. Autumn, winter and spring mornings usually see it surrounded by mist and fog. It can be photographed at both sunrise and sunset. But in late spring and summer when the sun moves northwards, it rises right behind this mountain peak. I was here one morning, having already photographed it a few weeks before with a workshop group. Because of that, and with help from the photographer's ephemeris, I knew where it would rise and was waiting.

You never know how things will go. The previous session has been great also, but on this morning the thick cloud above and the gap between them produced these beautiful rays of light over the church with stunning intensity.

I took the photo to the left a few moments later as the sun burst over the mountaintop.

About the author:

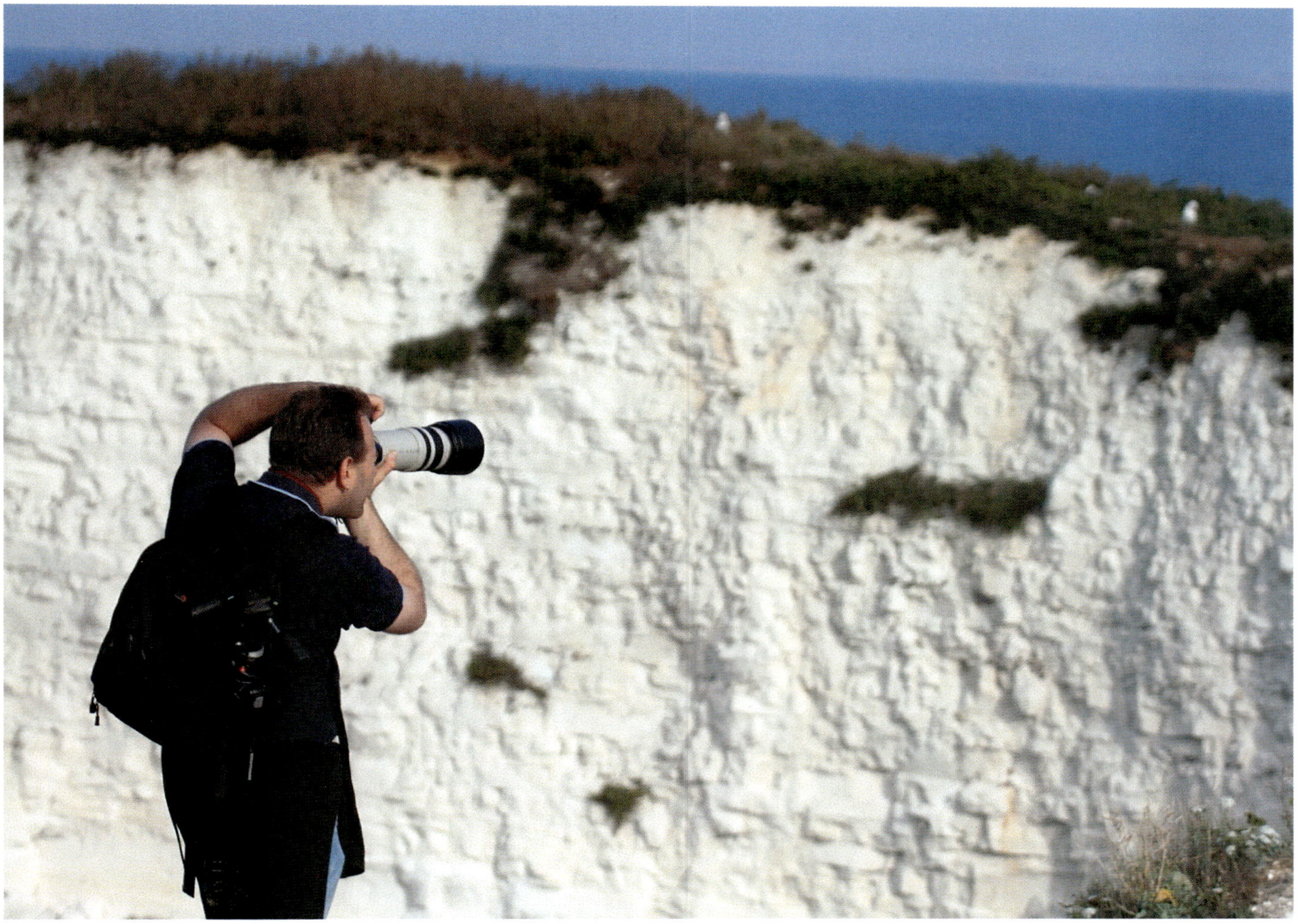

Ian Middleton is a professional writer, photographer and teacher. He is the author of several travel and photography books. He divides his time between his homes in the UK and Slovenia, where he runs regular workshops and tours. He started out in both writing and photography back in 1997 when backpacking around the world. Ian's photos, articles and stories have been published in a number of books and magazines, including Landscape Photography Magazine, Lonely Planet, Bradt Travel Guides, Eyewitness Guides, the Guardian Newspaper and more. He is the author of several books, and the co-author of a unique travel guide to Ireland and its ancient history and legends: *Mysterious World: Ireland.* One of his photos of Lake Bled in Slovenia came 3rd in the travel category of Professional Photographer of the Year 2014, and several others have been in the top ten or highly commended.

Check out his websites and blog for more tips and information:
www.ianmiddleton.co.uk
www.ianmiddletonphotography.com
blog.ianmiddletonphotography.com

Ian runs regular workshops and photography field tours.
More details here: www.ianmiddletonphotography.com/tours/

Other useful websites

www.ianmiddletonphotography.com/free-photography-ebook/ (A free digital version of this book is available on my website)

www.photoephemeris.com (A great piece of software for showing you where the sun and moon rise and set at any place and any time of the year.)

www.dofmaster.com (Contains tables and software for calculating the hyperfocal distance.)

www.sat24.com (A great website that can also be downloaded as a phone app. This gives you a satellite picture of any given area in the last two hours. It's great for seeing cloud coverage and movement.)

www.clearoutside.com (This is an international weather forecast website for astronomers, but is also a great forecast to help see how much cloud coverage or fog there will be in a given location when planning a photoshoot.)

www.landscapephotographymagazine.com (A digital monthly magazine.)

www.dpreview.com (Digital Photography Review website, dedicated to reviewing all photography equipment.)

www.photo4me.com (a print on demand website for anyone wishing to sell their photos.)

Ian's other books

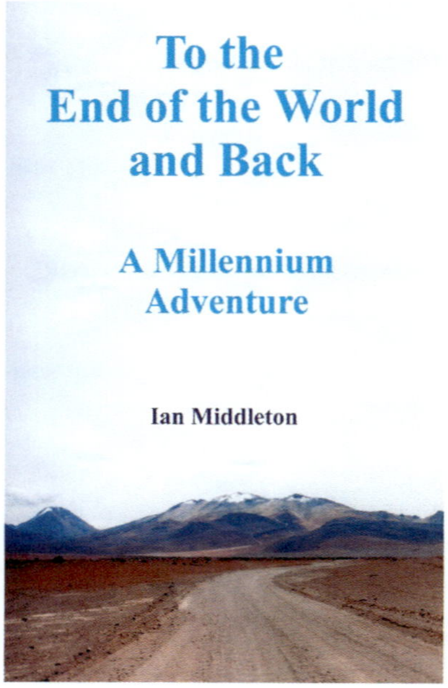

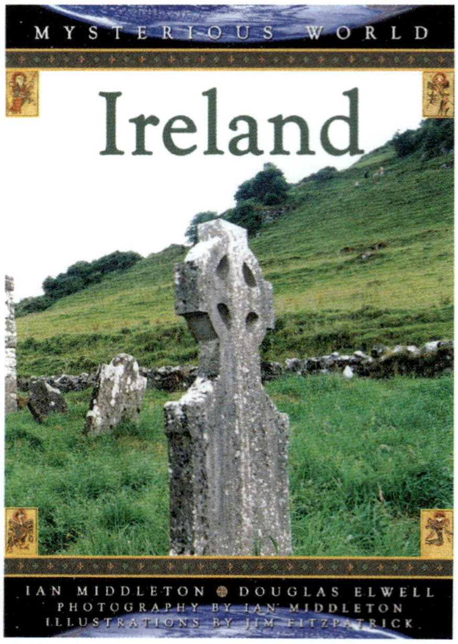

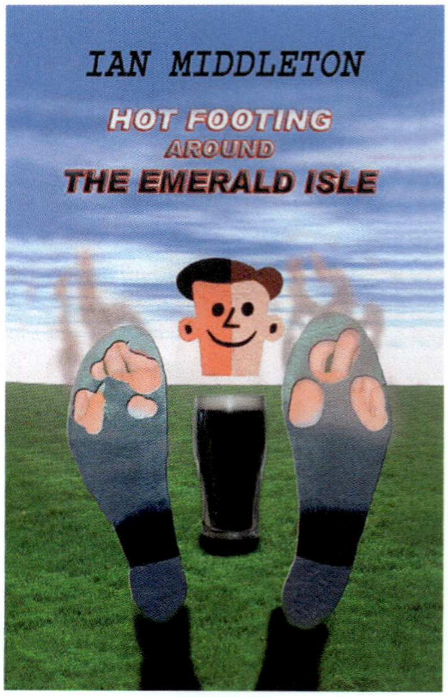

Printed in Great Britain
by Amazon

72179389R00067